As Per New Revised Syllabus of Shivaji University, Kolhapur and Solapur University, Solapur

A Text Book of...

ECOLOGY, ETHOLOGY, EVOLUTION & APPLIED ZOOLOGY

∞ For ∞

B.Sc. Part I : ZOOLOGY (Paper - IV)

Semester – II

∞ By ∞

PRIN. DR. KISHORE PAWAR
(M.Sc. Ph.D.)
Karmveer Abasaheb Alias N.M.
Sonawane Arts, Science and
Commerce College,
Satana, Nashik

DR. ASHOK E. DESAI
(M.Sc. Ph.D.)
Associate Professor in Zoology,
Department of Zoology,
KTHM College
Nashik - 422 002

DR. DAMA L. B.
D.B.F. Dayanand College of
Arts & Science, Solapur.
Dist. Solapur,

DR. PATIL R. N.
Head, P.G. Department of Zoology and
Chairman BOS, Shivaji University,
SGM College Karad, Dist. Satara

NIRALI PRAKASHAN
ADVANCEMENT OF KNOWLEDGE

B.Sc. Part I ZOOLOGY ISBN 978-93-5164-929-8

First Edition : **February 2016**
© : **Authors**

The text of this publication, or any part thereof, should not be reproduced or transmitted in any form or stored in any computer storage system or device for distribution including photocopy, recording, taping or information retrieval system or reproduced on any disc, tape, perforated media or other information storage device etc., without the written permission of Authors with whom the rights are reserved. Breach of this condition is liable for legal action.

Every effort has been made to avoid errors or omissions in this publication. In spite of this, errors may have crept in. Any mistake, error or discrepancy so noted and shall be brought to our notice shall be taken care of in the next edition. It is notified that neither the publisher nor the authors or seller shall be responsible for any damage or loss of action to any one, of any kind, in any manner, therefrom.

Published By : **Printed By :**
NIRALI PRAKASHAN Repro Knowledgecast Limited
Abhyudaya Pragati, 1312, Shivaji Nagar,
Off J.M. Road, PUNE – 411005
Tel - (020) 25512336/37/39, Fax - (020) 25511379
Email : niralipune@pragationline.com

☞ **DISTRIBUTION CENTRES**
PUNE
Nirali Prakashan : 119, Budhwar Peth, Jogeshwari Mandir Lane, Pune 411002, Maharashtra
Tel : (020) 2445 2044, 66022708, Fax : (020) 2445 1538
Email : bookorder@pragationline.com, niralilocal@pragationline.com
Nirali Prakashan : S. No. 28/27, Dhyari, Near Pari Company, Pune 411041
Tel : (020) 24690204 Fax : (020) 24690316
Email : dhyari@pragationline.com, bookorder@pragationline.com
MUMBAI
Nirali Prakashan : 385, S.V.P. Road, Rasdhara Co-op. Hsg. Society Ltd.,
Girgaum, Mumbai 400004, Maharashtra
Tel : (022) 2385 6339 / 2386 9976, Fax : (022) 2386 9976
Email : niralimumbai@pragationline.com

☞ **DISTRIBUTION BRANCHES**
JALGAON
Nirali Prakashan : 34, V. V. Golani Market, Navi Peth, Jalgaon 425001,
Maharashtra, Tel : (0257) 222 0395, Mob : 94234 91860
KOLHAPUR
Nirali Prakashan : New Mahadvar Road, Kedar Plaza, 1st Floor Opp. IDBI Bank
Kolhapur 416 012, Maharashtra. Mob : 9850046155
NAGPUR
Pratibha Book Distributors : Above Maratha Mandir, Shop No. 3, First Floor,
Rani Jhanshi Square, Sitabuldi, Nagpur 440012, Maharashtra
Tel : (0712) 254 7129
DELHI
Nirali Prakashan : 4593/21, Basement, Aggarwal Lane 15, Ansari Road, Daryaganj
Near Times of India Building, New Delhi 110002
Mob : 08505972553
BENGALURU
Pragati Book House : House No. 1, Sanjeevappa Lane, Avenue Road Cross,
Opp. Rice Church, Bengaluru – 560002.
Tel : (080) 64513344, 64513355,Mob : 9880582331, 9845021552
Email:bharatsavla@yahoo.com
CHENNAI
Pragati Books : 9/1, Montieth Road, Behind Taas Mahal, Egmore,
Chennai 600008 Tamil Nadu, Tel : (044) 6518 3535,
Mob : 94440 01782 / 98450 21552 / 98805 82331,
Email : bharatsavla@yahoo.com

niralipune@pragationline.com | www.pragationline.com
Also find us on www.facebook.com/niralibooks

PREFACE

The authors are indeed very happy to present this book **'A Text Book of Ecology, Ethology, Evolution and Applied Zoology'** for the students of B.Sc. Zoology Paper IV, Semester II of Shivaji and Solapur University.

The book has been written according to the new revised syllabus, Board of Studies of Zoology has thoroughly revised the syllabus which has been designed with the topic of Ecology, Ethology, Evolution and Applied Zoology.

There was a long felt need of the students as well as teachers community for a text book which covers the entire syllabus prescribed by Board of studies. The present book is an outcome of our sincere efforts. We tried our level best to present the subject matter in easy style and in a comprehensive manner. The text book is profusely illustrated with number of clear line drawings.

No doubt, there are several textbooks written by Indian and foreign authors on the subject, but they are costly and number of copies are very limited in the college libraries. The students can not get the matter on prescribed syllabus in one book and they also cannot afford the costly books. Therefore we have presented all the topics in one book in a low price. We sincerely feel that this book will fulfill the requirements of students and teachers.

We are thankful to Shri. Dineshbhai Furia, Shri. Jignesh Furia, Shri. M.P. Munde and the entire staff of Nirali Prakashan for taking keen interest in publishing this book and bringing out in time.

Constructive suggestions for improvement of the book are most welcome.

Authors

This book is
Dedicated to the
Cherished Memories of our friend
Late Prin. Dr. M. M. Phadtare
Shri Shivaji College, Barshi, Dist. Solapur

SYLLABUS

SHIVAJI UNIVERSITY, KOLHAPUR

ZOOLOGY : B.Sc. PART-I, SEMESTER-II,
PAPER – IV : ECOLOGY, ETHOLOGY, EVOLUTION AND APPLIED ZOOLOGY

UNIT – I (16)

1) **Ecology**
    - (a) Abiotic factors – Temperature, Light, Water and Soil
    - (b) Biotic factors –
        - i) Intraspecific associations
        - ii) Interspecific associations
    - (c) Brief idea of species, community, Niche and Ecosystem
    - (d) Food chain, Ecological pyramids and energy flow with reference to pond and grass land ecosystem

UNIT – II (8)

1) **Ethology**
    - (a) Mimicry in monarch butterfly and in stick insect. Camouflage in chameleon
    - (b) Courtship behavior in Scorpion and weaver bird
    - (c) Social behavior in Honey bees

UNIT – III (8)

1) **Evolution**
    - (a) Formation and dating of fossils
    - (b) Connecting link- Peripatus and Archaeopteryx
    - (c) Living fossil – King crab (limulus) and Sphenodon

UNIT – IV (8)

1) Applied Zoology – Sericulture
    - (a) Types of silk moth
    - (b) Morphology of mulberry silk moth
    - (c) Life Cycle
    - (d) Rearing of silk moth
    - (e) Economic importance

❖❖❖

SOLAPUR UNIVERSITY, SOLAPUR

ZOOLOGY : B.Sc. PART-I, SEMESTER-II
PAPER – IV : ECOLOGY, ETHOLOGY, EVOLUTION AND APPLIED ZOOLOGY

UNIT – I (16)

1) Ecology
1. Introduction, definition, aim and scope of Ecology [2]
2. Biotic factors : Brief idea of following animal associations with suitable examples
    A) Intraspecific associations:
        i) Beneficial: Mate and reproduction, Parental care, Groupism, and Social behaviour.
        ii) Harmful: Cannibalism and Competition
    B) Interspecific associations: Neutralism, Symbiosis (Commensalism and Mutualism), Antagonism (Predation and Parasitism), Types of Parasite and Host. [5]
3. Abiotic factors: Introduction and Effects on Plants and Animals:
    I) Temperature ii) Light iii) Water iv) Humidity v) Soil vi) Wind vii) Fire [3]
4. Brief idea (definition) of Species, Community, Niche, Ecosystem, Biome and Biosphere. [3]
5. Grass land and Pond ecosystems with reference to Food chain, Ecological pyramids and Energy flow. [2]
6. Ecological successions : Introduction and Types, Primary and secondary succession. [2]

UNIT – II (8)

II) Ethology [4]
1. Mimicry — Stick insect and Camouflage — chameleon
    (b) Courtship behavior in birds, weaver (baya) birds.
    (c) Social behavior in Honey bees: Casts, swarming, absconding, Nauptial flight and communication (waggle and round dance).

UNIT – III (8)

III) Evolution [6]
(a) Organic evolution concepts
(b) Paleontological evidences
(c) Anatomical evidences

IV) Applied Zoology [8]
1. Brief idea (definition and scope) of Sericulture, Apiculture, Poultry science, Dairy science, Fishery science, Pearl culture, Lac culture, Goat farming and Piggary.
2. Vermitechnology : Techniques and importance of Vermiculture, Vermicompost and Vermiwash

❖❖❖

CONTENTS

UNIT 1... Ecology — 1.1 – 1.74

UNIT 2... Ethology — 2.1 – 2.30

UNIT 3... Evolution — 3.1 – 3.40

UNIT 4... Applied Zoology — 4.1 – 4.125
Sericulture (For Shivaji University only)
Brief Idea of Some Branches (For Solapur University only)
Vermitechnology (For Solapur University only)

UNIT 1...
Ecology

Contents ...

1.1 Aim and Scope of Ecology
    1.1.1 Introduction
1.2 Biotic and Abiotic Factors
    1.2.1 Biotic Factors Intraspecific and interspecific associations
    1.2.2 Abiotic Factors
1.3 Brief Idea of Some Ecological Terms
1.4 Energy, Flow food Chain and Ecological Pyramids with Reference to Pond and Land Ecosystem
    1.4.1 Functions of Ecosystem
    1.4.2 Food Chain
    1.4.3 Food Web
    1.4.4 Ecological Pyramids
1.5 Ecological Succession (Solapur University)
*   Points to Remember
*   Exercise

1.1 Aim and Scope of Ecology

1.1.1 Introduction

Ecology is one of the important branches of science which is also called as Environmental Biology. This is one of the young branches which is connected with the organisms and their environment. The name ECOLOGY is derived from two Greek words i.e. *Oikos* = House and *Logos* = Study. Therefore, the studies of inter-relationships of organisms with their physical and biotic environment can be called as Ecology.

E. P. Odum (1963) defined Ecology as structure and function of nature.

Earnst Haeckel (1866) defined Ecology as a branch of science which deals with the total relationships of organisms to both their organic and inorganic environment.

All organisms live in environment. The structure, growth, reproduction etc. of an organism are controlled by the environmental factors like Soil, Temperature, Water, Nutrients in the soil etc. Along with these factors the organisms themselves interact with each other. Structure and numbers of organic community of a given area depends upon environmental and biotic factors which are present in that area.

In the early days, ecologists used to separate study of ecology into plant ecology and animal ecology just like biology. However, modern ecologists feel that as the environments which govern the life of plants and the animals is the same. Both the branches of ecology i.e. animal ecology and plant ecology must be unified and studied as a whole.

Broadly ecology can be divided into : (i) *Autecology* and (ii) *Synecology*. Autecology is a branch of ecology in which we study an individual species or its population in relation to its biotic (living) and abiotic (non-living) environment. In this branch, one will study a species of organism or its population throughout its life, its interactions with the environment and among themselves. For example : In a forest, if we study the population of a rat or rat species, its increase in number, food taken by it, its relation to plants and other animals living in that locality, its birth rate, death rate and their interactions within their own population it is autecological study.

Synecology is a branch of ecology which deals with the structure, number, development, distribution and interactions of organic community of a locality with the environment and amongst themselves as a whole. For the synecological study, the autecological knowledge of individual species is necessary. Thus, autecological studies are necessary to understand the synecology of a given community. If we study the different plants and animals living in a forest and their interrelationships with the environment and among themselves called a synecology of forest.

Based on level of organisation, kinds of environment and taxonomic position, ecology can be subdivided into many branches. Some of the important divisions are as given below :

(1) Habitat Ecology : Study of different habitats of biosphere (life supporting zone) is called as habitat ecology e.g. Marine ecology, Freshwater ecology, Forest ecology, Cropland ecology, Grassland ecology, Desert ecology etc.

(2) Population Ecology or Demecology : Study of populations of different species of a ecosystem concerning their birth rate, death rate and the different factors affecting their growth in size and number called as population ecology.

(3) Ecosystem Ecology : Deals with analysis of ecosystem in relation to structure and function, the interrelationships of components of ecosystem. The reciprocal relationships of living and non-living components of ecosystem are studied in detail in this branch.

(4) Conservation Ecology : On the planet earth, the different raw material like coal, water, oil, minerals etc. which are required for the welfare of man are limited. They must be properly used, if they are misused future or man's life will be in danger. To avoid the difficulties for the future generations we have to plan the utilization of the resources properly. In this branch of ecology, we study the proper management methods of natural resources like land, water, forest, sea, oil, minerals etc. for the benefit of the human beings.

(5) Production Ecology : This branch deals with the gross or net production of different ecosystems, like freshwater ecosystem, marine (sea) ecosystem, agriculture, horticulture and proper methods of management of these ecosystems so that maximum production can be achieved by human-being.

(6) Radiation Ecology : In this branch, we study the effects of radiation and radioactive substances on organisms and environment. In recent years man is establishing a number of nuclear reactors to get more and more energy for his factories etc. This is leading to side effects and accumulation of dangerous radioacitve waste in large proportions. If this is not properly managed the existence of human race will be in danger. Radiation ecology studies help us to understand the problems and possible remedies for the same.

(7) Paleoecology : With the help of fossil studies (Palaentological) we can have idea about the nature and structure of the organisms living in the geological past. In this branch of ecology, we study about the different forms living in different times in the past and the environment prevailing at that time. We also study how these life forms and the environment changed from time to time due to some specific factors. This knowledge help us as a guide to the future changes which we may try to bring in nature to suit the betterment of human life.

(8) Gene Ecology or Ecological Genetics : In nature, we find that particular species of a genera are having capacity to survive and other fail to live and become extinct. This has been found to be due to the presence of particular genes present in these surviving species. At the same time we find that some species have a sort of genetic plasticity more than the other species. This helps them in struggle for existence. In gene ecology, we study the relationship of genes and their adaptability in nature.

(9) Space Ecology : This is one of the most modern and latest branches of ecology. Man is trying to reach to other planets which are located far away from earth. For this he has to travel millions of kilometres for a number of days. In this branch of ecology construction and usage of partial or complete regenerating systems in space ships and effects of space travel on the organisms are studied.

(10) Taxonomic Ecology : This branch of ecology is connected with different taxonomic groups. This branch can be subdivided into many branches viz. Plant ecology, Animal ecology, Microbial ecology, Vertebrate ecology etc.

(11) Human Ecology : This branch deals with mainly the relationship between man and his environment.

Scope and Significance of Ecology :

Ecology is a complex branch of biology which is related to almost all branches of science. Ecologist uses the knowledge of Chemistry,

Physics, Botany, Zoology, Microbiology, Mathematics, Statistics, Morphology, Anatomy, Taxonomy, Cytology, Genetics, Physiology, Biochemistry etc. He also requires the knowledge of usage of Radioactive isotopes, spectrometer, calorimeters, pH-meters, computers etc. to understand the ecological problems.

An Ecologist must have a knowledge of use of pesticides, detergents, sewage disposal, powerdams, urban development, atomic radiations etc. to understand the ecological problems.

In recent days, man for his own needs started changing the natural communities thinking that it will result in giving better life for human beings. Expecting major benefits man changed the environment, but this many times created more problems than it solve. Thus unplanned (with half knowledge) changes brought about by man resulted in Ecological Boomrangs or Ecological Backlashes. Few examples will make it clear that how the ecological boomerangs resulted due to the unplanned interference of man in nature.

(1) In our own country the thick forest were cut down to meet the needs of agriculture, timber, fuel, food for cattle etc. Thus, the clearing of forests increase the agricultural land to increase the food needed for our ever increasing population. But this deforestation resulted in constant floods of major rivers and soil erosion in the low areas. Thus every year country is losing property worth of some crores and human lives due to the floods.

(2) Industrial expansion in almost all countries with a view to benefit the population has resulted in many problems like air and water pollution, increase in the urban population formation of slum areas causing social unrest and health problems.

If we study closely the civilized man's actions which are aimed for benefit of man have resulted in creating problems which he can not solve. So it is essential for every country and man to think and study closely the ecological aspects of the natural communities before trying to change the natural systems. Unless we are sure about the after effects and results we must not play with the natural ecosystems if not the existence of man itself may be in danger.

1.2 Biotic and Abiotic Factors

1.2.1 Biotic Factors and Animal Associations

Biotic factors of environment are plants, animals including human beings and microbes.

Plants : The green plants, certain bacteria and algae which can synthesize their own food with the help of chlorophyll in presence of sunlight. They are called autotrophs or producers.

Animals : These animals cannot produce their food material but depend on plants and other organisms to obtain their energy for survival. These are called heterotrophs or consumers. There are primary consumers which eat green plants. They are called herbivores. Organisms which eat a herbivore are called secondary consumers. The organisms which eat secondary consumers are called tertiary consumers.

Microbes : They are also called decomposers, because they are responsible for decomposition of dead organic matter. Certain fungi and bacteria play this role.

The animals live in the environment which is made up of abiotic factors and biotic factors. Abiotic factors include physical factors such as light and temperature where as the chemical factors consisting of various elements and their compounds. The biotic or biological components or factors include other animals, plants and micro-organisms. In nature living organisms cannot live in isolation. They always form variety of associations or communities and each of which consists of individuals belonging to one or more species. Therefore, the individuals of such associations are all dependent on each other for survival, to a greater or lesser extent.

Animal Associations

Animal associations may occur between the individuals of the same or different species, ages, sizes or sexes. They live together for variety of purposes such as reproduction, feeding, protection, transportation etc. Animal associations are sometimes very intimate or very casual and mutually beneficial or may not be beneficial or extremely one sided i.e. only one member gets benefits.

The animals of a particular community live in a particular geographical area characterized by specific environmental factors. The place where the animal normally live is known as their habitat. For example: freshwater habitat, desert habitat, or parasitic habitat are the different types of habitats of animals. However, an animal does not only occupy a given physical space. The survival of the animal depends on how it can respond to the different components of its environment by developing habits.

Each animal which occupies a particular physical space called ecological niche. It is the place where animal plays its functional role in the community, how it is influenced by (and affects) the environmental factors and how it interacts with other animals and plants. In short, animals habitat is its address, its habits are its life style and the niche is its profession.

Generally, the animal associations of animals are classified into tow broad categories namely, intraspecific associations and interspecific associations.

(1) Intraspecific Association

In this type of animal association, the animal living together are of the same speces, thus they are call *conspecific*. When two or more individuals of a same species collectively share a habitat and occupy a common niche, and form the population. For example: mating partners, a family, a troop of monkeys, a herd of cattle, a school of fish, and a colony of bees. Another unique example of extremely intimate association of this type is found in the deep sea fish, the angler fish *Photocorynus spiniceps*. These fish wander over a very large area of the deep seas and therefore chances of contact between

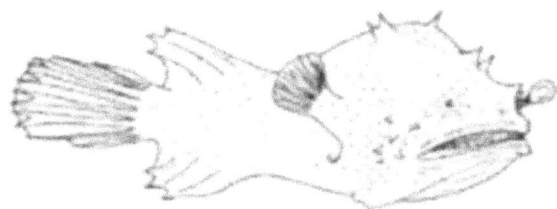

Fig. 1.1: Sexual parasitism in the deep sea angler fish-*Photocorynus spiniceps*

males and females are limited. Therefore males are permanently adher to the head of the large female (Fig. 1.1). It is believed that the female angler 'picks-up' a male they are young and fairly large in number. The significance of this type of association is reproduction.

(2) Interspecific Association

The association between the animals of two species is called interspecific association. The animals are known as heterospecific. This type of association exhibits many different kinds (Fig. 1.2). They are classified into following types:

1. Parasitism
2. Mutualism
3. Commensalism
4. Phoresy
5. Proto-cooperation
6. Neutralism
7. Amensalism
8. Competition (Direct/Indirect)
9. Predatism.

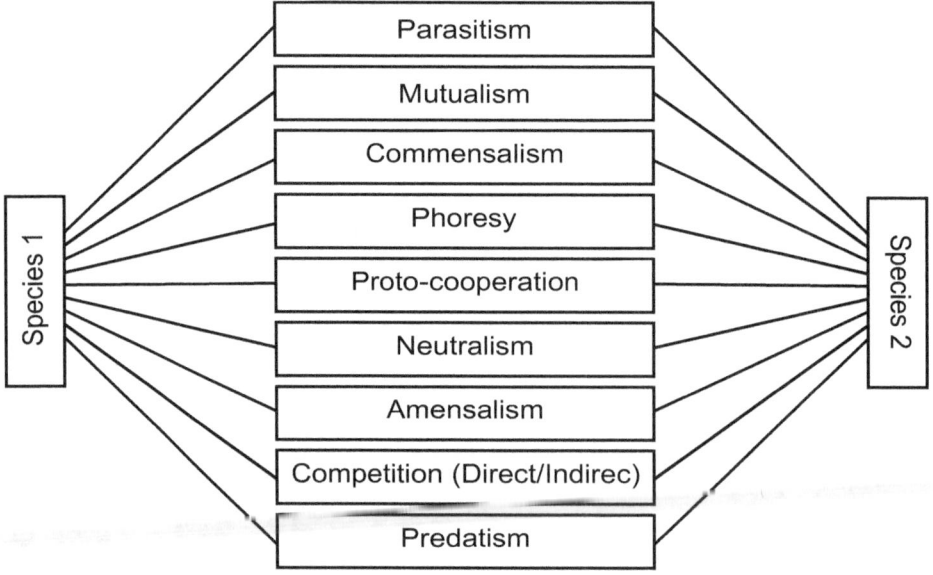

Fig. 1.2: Types of interspecific associations

The first four (1 to 4) associations exhibits varying degrees of physical contact among the animals and they are together known as symbiosis which is described in detail.

Symbiosis

The term symbiosis (Greek *sym* = together, *bios* = life) was proposed first by **de Bary** in 1879 to mean "living together" of two species of organisms. This association is generally of a friendly nature and not harmful to each other. In symbiosis, one oraganism is called symbiont which is generally smaller than its associate called host.

Although a symbiont lives in close physical contact with its host, the partnership exhibits different degrees of intimacy, wide variation in permancy of the association, and degree of pathogenicity. Thus, such partnership received special names such as *Phoresis commensalism, mutualism* and *parasitism*. The generally accepted criteia for distinguishing these associations are the degree of dependence and the relative benefit or loss resulting from it. Thus, relationships are board units in a spectrum of associations and there is no sharp demarcation between them. Depending on the type of association the symbiont is variously known as a phorent, a commensal, a mutualist or a parasite. Let us see the characterstics and the distinguishing features of these different associations are :

Phoresis: It is a non-obligatory and usually accidental type of association in which one organism merely provides support, shelter or transport for another organism of different species. The common example, we observe barnacles living on the shell of oysters. The oyster acts here as host which simply serves as a substratum for its phorant, the barnacle. Both the animals are completely independent of each other so far as their life activities are concerned. If the association is merely a passive transportation of the symbiont (commensal) by the host it is called *phoresy*.

Commensalism: It means eating at the same table. (Latin **cum** = together, **mensa** = table). This occurs when one member of the associating pair, usually the smaller, receives all the benefit and the other member is neither benefited nor harmed. The commensal eats the food of its host, not vice versa. The basis for a commensalistic relationship between two organisms may be space, substrate, defense, shelter, transportation or food. Best example of this association is that of the sucker fish or remora (*Echeneis nawoates*) and its large, powerful and fast moving host such as a Shark. (Fig. 1.3) or a Whale.

Fig. 1.3 : Commensalism Shark with remora fish

Remora is carnivorous fish growing to about 50 cm in length. It can swim independently but is more often carried about by the unwitting host to the underside of which is attached. For this purpose the first dorsal fin of the remora is modified into a flat, multilaminated, adhesive disc or sucker. The food of Remora consists of other fish and probably scrap of food that become available as the host tears apart its prey.

There are four major types commensalism. Depending on the biological nature of the bond between the partners, they are classified. In all the cases the food of the commensal is in the close vicinity of the host. They are as below:

(i) Phoretic or transport commensalims: There are many examples in animals in which they depend on the larger partners for the purpose of transportation. A variety of organisms live in fresh, moist lung. Dung is the partly digested organic substances with abundant microorganisms and it acts as a temporary habitat for these organisms. Variety of nematod worms, beetles, insect larvae live in it. In this temporary habitat the insect larvae complete the life cycle rapidly and flying or walking adults disperse to fresh sites.

Pelodera coarctata is freeliving dung nemated which feeds on the bacteria. This namatod undergoes resting larval state called the 'dauer' which attach themselves to the different body parts of the dung beetle *Aphodius fementarius* (Fig. 1.4). When beetle moves to fresh dung heaps, it also carries the dense clusters of attached dauers where they leaves the beetle. The learvae feed and develop independently. Thus, the nematods and beetle exhibit the example of phoretic commensalism.

Fig. 1.4 : Phoretic commensalism of the larval nematodes (arrows) with dung beetle

Synoecious commensalism: (Greek *syn* = with, *oikos* = house). This is a type of association in which one animal which is usually smaller and more active occupied the dwelling of another, but neither assoicate suffers any apparent damage. The tiny pea crab *Pinnixa faba* male (small) and female (large) sheltered by the shell of gaper clam *Schizothaerus nuttalle*.

Protection and camouflage Commensalism : This type of association is based on one animal is protecting or camouflaging its partner. The best known example of this kind is that of the sea anemone **Adamsia palliata** living on the shell of the hermit crab **Eupagurus bernhardus**. In this case, the sea anemone is transported and gets food which is scattered by the crab.

Fig. 1.5 : Hermit crab and sea anemone is situated on the shell of mollusc

The crab is covered by its commensal anemone, and gets protection from predators like octopuses. The tentacles of the anemone possess hematocysts or stinging cells.

Another example of camouflage: Commensalism is 2 and 3 toed sloth found in American Jungles. The body of these animals is covered with blue and green algae which enable these forest creatures to disappear in their surroundings.

Cleaning commensalism : There are many examples in which small marine fish and shrimps regularly clean bodies of large fisher and turtles. They remove the scraps of food, damaged and decaying tissues and copepods, isopods, fungi etc. which are harmful and irritating to the host. Some cleaner fish do their cleaning job in the juvenile stages. The example of the large fish the grouper fish and its tiny commensal, the neon goby.

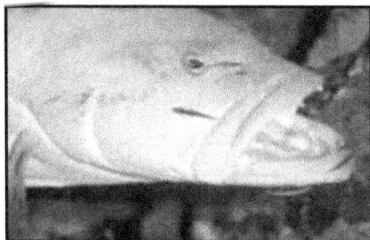 

Fig. 1.6 : Grouper fish and cleaning fish neon goby

Like cleaner fish, there are also cleaner shrimps such as ***Hippolysmata californica***. They remove the ectoparasites of the fish. Some times shrimps enter in the mouth as the host often opens its mouth and pick its teeth or gills. Sometime shrips are allowed to make minor incisions in order to remove subcutaneous parasites.

Some terrestrial animals also show the cleaning commensalism. For example: the Indian cattle egret **Bubulcus ibis** removes ectoparasites from cattle, deer and rhinoceros. These gregarious birds seen with grazing cattle running in and out between their legs and lunging out to seize insects disturbed from grass by the grazing movements of the cattle or sometimes they ride upon the backs of the cattles and picking up the ectoparasites from their hide. Another interesting example of the Egyptian plover, (Pulvianus aegyptus) which cleans the teeth of the Nile crocodile.

Mutualism : In this association both the partners are beneficial to each other by exchanging the metabolites. (Latin ***mutuus*** = exchanged). Without this association the individuals usually cannot survive independently. In this association each of the interacting species functions as both host and parasite.

The well known example of mutualism is the termite and flagellate protozoan ***Trichonypha campanula***. (Fig. 1.7). Termite ***Zootermopsis angusticollis*** is wood eating insect which lives in moist decaying trunks of wood. Its mutualist the flagellate protozoan lives in the intestine of termite which produces the enzymes celluloses useful for digestion of cellulose. Cellulose is the major food of the termite but it is unable to digest it. Protozoan gets shelter and it hydrolyses the cellulose. Due to enzymes the cellulose is finally converted into glucose and it is utilised by both the partners. If the flagellates are removed (defaunation) from the hind gut of the host termite suffer from starvation or even death occurs. Likewise, the flagellates can not exist anywhere else except in the termite's intestine.

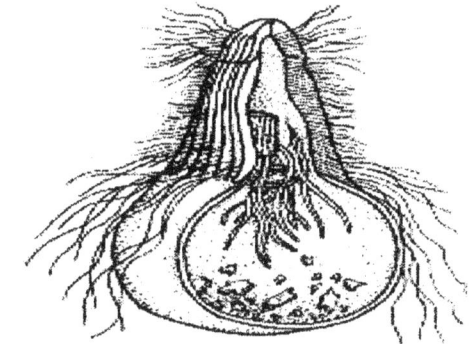

Fig. 1.7 : Trychonympha lives in the intestine of the host

Moreover, sexual reproduction of *Trychonymphs* is stimulated by the insect moulting **hormone ecdysone** and it is secreted in the termite when it moults. The protozoan forms resistant cysts on the gut lining of the termite. It is lost at the time of moulting and cysts are also pass out to be available transmission to fresh termites. In this way, the termite host flagellate mutualist association is thus ensured.

In the rumen of herbivorous animals many bacteria and ciliate exhibit mutualism. This types of association is also seen in plants and animals. The best example of unicellular algae such as zoochlorellae are harboured by coelenterates such as chlorohydra and planarian like convoluta. Lichens i.e. association of fungus and algae is also the best example of mutualism. The leguminous plants (pea, bean etc.) also keep the nitrogen fixing bacteria called **Rhizobium** in the root nodules.

Parasitism: The original meaning of the word 'parasite' (Greek. **para** = beside, **sitos** = food) was "one who eats at another's table" or "one who lives at another's expense" and had no reference to pathogenicity. Parasitism is a unique kind of symbiotic relationships in which the parasite remains very close to its food or host. It is defined as an animal or plant which lives partially or wholly at the cost of another living organism called host. Some other older and recent authod defined as "the parasite usually produce some degree of injury or damage on the host". Some investigators include the killing of the host by the parasite in their definition of parasitism. Crofton started that the ability of the parasite to kill the host differentiates parasitism from commensalism. Anderson believes that the inducement of host mortalities and/or a reduction in host reproductive potential is a necessary, but not sufficient, condition for the classification of an organism as parasitic. These investigations and others generally are considering populations of parasites and hosts, certainly not individual parasites. Majority of the parasites live in harmonious equilibrium with their hosts. Numerous parasites apparently are commensales most of the time, but are pathogenic (produce a disease) when their numbers become unusually high. *Entamoeba histolytica*, a well known parasite of man can cause dysentery, but most of the time it lives in the small intestine as a non-pathogen, harmless symbiont. It becomes pathogenic only when certain physiological changes occur in the host and probably also in the parasite. On the other hand there are many instances in which parasite also has a beneficial effect on the host.

The concept of parasitism that clearly separates if from other categories of symbiosis is based on biochemical relationships between host and parasites. If a species of parasite has lived with its host species for millions of years, each partner must have had to adapt itself to the other in many ways. Among the morphological and functional changes that a free living organism must undergo to become a parasite are metabolic changes that require the presence of host tissues or fluids. Parasites, therefore, are metabolically dependent upon their hosts.

Cameron stated that a parasite is "an organism which is dependent for some essential metabilic factor on another organism which is always larger than itself. Smyth also described parasitism as an intimate association between two organisms in which the dependence of the parasite is metabolic. In his definition the important addition that in parasitism some metabolic by-products of the parasite are of value to the host.

Thus, the modern definition of parasitism is an obligatory association between two distinct species in which the dependence of the parasite upon its host is a metabolic one involving mutual exchange of chemical substances. This dependence is the result of a loss by the parasite of genetic information.

Thus, the term parasitism consists of both host and parasite. If parasite is able to live independent of its host then it no longer can be called a parasite. The host serves as functional habitat or niche of the parasite.

Parasites are generally smaller than their hosts and depend upon hosts for nutrition, habitat, developmental stimuli, enzymes, vitamins, control of maturation, reproduction and transportation. Thus in parasitism food is not the basis.

If the parasite wants to survive happily then it should not harm the host. If host dies ultimately parasite must also perish. But in practice the parasite always produce adverse effect on its host and host always tries to neutralize the effect. Thus, both the partners in parasitism are adapted to each other and hence they continue the host parasite system.

There is fundamental difference between predator and parasitism. British ecologist Elton commented that predators live on capital and parasites on income. The table 1.1 gives comparison between predatism and parasitism.

Table 1.1: Predators compared with Parasites

		Predator	Parasite
1.	Victim known as	Prey	Host
2.	Manner of feeding on individual feeding	Destructive consumption	Cropping or sampling
3.	Food provided by victim	Whole of the body or fragments.	Selected tissues, bodyfluids, excretion etc.
4.	Lethal to victim	Yes, usually	Exceptional
5.	Habitat	Coexists with prey	Usually lives in or on the host. (host as habitat) in parasitic stage.
6.	Size compared with victim	Larger (or stronger)	Smaller or much smaller.
7.	Numbers compared with victim.	Less numerous	More or much more numerous.
8.	Encounter with prey or host	Momentary	Prolonged and/or repeated
9.	Effect of grouping or crowding of victims.	May protect prey	Encourage parasitism.
10.	Disease caused ?	Rare and indirect through stress	Common, direct may be great variety.
11.	Rate of multiplication compared with victim.	Slower	Much faster.

Contd...

12. Gene flow	Mostly in breeding	Out breeding.
13. Tolerance to environment.	Narrow	Broad
14. Changes in chromosome numbers.	None to many	Few or none.

(Source : Introduction to Parasitology Noble and Noble)

In case of predatism there is immediate killing of the prey. There is however, a modified form of internal predatism in which the victim is finally killed but only after a period of time.

This phenomenon is called parasitoidism typifies a law of Nature "live and let die" and this is found in many dipteran and hymenopteran insects. The wasp *Trichogramma minutum* is a parasitoiod of major insect pests such as the European corn borer (Pyrausta nubilalis), the codling moth (*Caprocapsa pomonella*) and the sugarcane borer (*Diatraea saccharalis*) when female wasp ready for eviposition, finds a suitable host-victim, she stings the host to render it immobile, and deposits one or more eggs by means of the ovipositor which is pierced in to the host body. The larvae (Parasitoids) that hatch within the host body, feed on the body fluids and tissues of the host, eventually killing it.

1.2.1.1 Types of Parasites

A parasite is a living organism (animal or plant) which receives nourishment and shelter partly or wholly from another organism, i.e., host, where it lives. Thus, parasite lives at the cost of its host. The host furnishes both the habitat and the food for the parasite which are physiologically dependent on it for life. Moreover, the parasite always does damage in some degree to its host. There is difference between parasite and predator. The parasite does not kill the host because death of the host is ultimately end of the parasite. Therefore, parasite lives in complete harmony with the host, since it gets necessary benefits from it. The predator kills its prey in order to feed upon its flesh. The parasites are true 'businessmen' in the animal kingdom because they live on income, whereas the predators live on the capital. Parasite is thus a black-mailer and predator is a burglar.

Several types of parasites are recognised, depending on their relationship to the host. The habit or location on or in the body of the host serves as one basis for classification of parasites.

1. Ectoparasite : The parasite lives on the external surface of the body of the host is called ectoparasite. e.g. Lice, Flea, Leech, Mosquito, Tick.

2. Endoparasite : The parasite lives inside the body of the host called endoparasite. The endoparasites may occur in different organs and tissues of the host, e.g. Tapeworm, *Ascaris* live in alimentary canal, *Trypanosome*, *Plasmodium*, are blood parasites; *Trichinella* lives in muscle; *Filaria* occurs in lymph vessels while itch mite *Sarcoptes* is a subcutanous parasite.

The amount of time spent on or in the host also serves as basis for classification of parasites.

3. Temporary parasite : Visits its host for a short period for food. Having satisfied hunger, it leaves the host, e.g. Mosquito, Leech, Bed-bug.

4. Permanent parasite : Leads a parasitic life throughout the whole period of its life, e.g. Tapeworm, Liverfluke, *Ascaris*, Intestinal protozoa.

5. Facultative parasite : Lives a parasitic life when opportunity arises. e.g. Free living nematodes *Rhabditis* and *Turbotrix*.

6. Obligatory parasite : Cannot exist without a parasitic life.

7. Occasional or Accidental parasite : Attacks an unusual host. e.g. common liver fluke of sheep occurs in dogs and cats. Tapeworm of dog found in-children.

8. Wandering or Aberrant parasite : Happens to reach a place where it cannot live, e.g. Ascarids of swine and man may wander from the intestine into the liver, body cavity or nostrils.

9. Stationary parasite : Parasite spends a definite period of development on or in the body of the host.

10. Periodic parasite : The parasite which remains with the host for only a part of its development and then leaves to complete it and continue a non-parasitic life known as periodic parasite.

e.g. Botflies and mermithid nematodes.

1.2.1.2 Types of Hosts

A host is an organism which harbours a parasite in or on its own body and it is always larger than the parasite. The parasites obtain shelter, and nourishment from the host. Hosts may be of various kinds and may play different roles in the life cycles of parasites. Different types of hosts can be recognised as follows :

1. Definitive Host

The host in which the parasite becomes adult, reaches maturity, and passes its sexual reproduction is called *definitive host*. For example, sheep is the definitive host of *Fasciola hepatica* and man is the definitive host of *Ascaris lumbricoides* and *Taenia solium*. In majority of cases, there is little or no doubt about the identity of definitive host in a life cycle (e.g. in human parasites, man is definitive host), but a few instances do create certain problems as in case of *Plasmodium*. The malarial parasite *P. vivax* produces male and female gametocytes in human blood, but actual fertilization occurs in the stomach of mosquito. Adhering closely to the definition, the mosquito is the definitive host because sexual reproduction occurs in it. Actually, sexual reproduction begins in human blood and fertilization occurs in the blood of the blood meal in the stomach of the mosquito. Hence, usually man is considered as definitive host and the mosquito the intermediate host.

Another difficulty arises in those animals which are parasitic in their larval stages and free living as adults. e.g. Ichneumon insects and Gordian worms, both of these mature in their hosts, but reproduce when free living. It is generally accepted that when only one host is there in the life cycle of parasite, it is the definitive host. Definitive host is also called primary or final host.

2. Intermediate Host :

The host other than definitive host in which a definite developmental phase, such as larval or asexual development is passed called as intermediate host. Mosquito is the intermediate or secondary host for malarial parasite and the snail, *Limnea truncatula* is the intermediate host of *Fasciola hepatica*. There may be just one intermediate host, as in the liver fluke, but in some cases, two or even three intermediate hosts may be involved in a single life cycle. e.g. ticks. A definite structural or metabolic change must occur in parasite within intermediate host and thus the host is essential to the parasite. Where there is more than one intermediate host, the parasite proceeds to a further stage of development in each successive host. In a few cases, larval parasites pass a stage in a host in which no development occurs, but it is essential for successful completion of the life cycle. This type of host serves only an ecological function of transmission and dispersal.

3. Paratenic or Carrier Host :

A host where the parasite remains viable without further development, is called *paratenic* (Greek *Paratenos* = to prolong) host. larval stage undergoes development in the paratenic host and it may or may not be an essential stage in reaching the definitive host.

Among the Acanthocephala (spiny-headed worms) a paratenic host is frequently included in the life cycle, where it provides the necessary ecological link between the intermediate host and the definitive host. Larval stages of spiny headed worms always pass through an arthropod intermediate host and the adults found in vertebrates. Unless the arthropod intermediate host and the vertebrate definitive host come into ecological contact, the life cycle cannot be completed without the inclusion of a paratenic host.

Centrohynchus is parasitic as an adult in a predator bird and its larval stages are found in insects, which serves as an intermediate host. Fully developed larval stages have also been reported from frogs, snakes, and small mammals. These small vertebrates feed largely on insects and are themselves fed on by predator birds. They therefore, provide the necessary ecological link between arthropods and predator birds, i.e. intermediate and definitive hosts. Small vertebrates in this case, are paratenic hosts.

4. Vectors :

The term vector has a great significance and has been used to describe almost all kinds of host, except definitive hosts. Vectors play a role of mechanical transmitter. In case of protozoan blood parasites, the parasite is transmitted from definitive host to definitive host by a blood sucking vector. No development occurs in the vector but the vector is essential for the life of parasite. Mechanical transmitters or vectors are therefore of great economic importance.

A number of important protozoa in the tropical countries e.g. *Trypanosoma evansi* which is transmitted mechanically by Tabanid flies in human beings. *Lankesterella* is blood parasitic protozoan of frogs, whose entire development occurs in the endothelial cells of the blood vessels. The sporozoites or infective stages are released into the blood and enter the blood cells and may be taken up in the blood meal of a leech. The leech can then infect another frog while sucking its blood or it may infect another frog on being eaten by it.

In some ways a vector is similar to paratenic host, but paratenic host is always found in addition to other intermediate host, while vector is not. A paratenic host is not necessarily essential in the life of the parasite, whereas vector is absolutely essential.

5. Reservoir Hosts :

Reservoir host is also described as a definitive host which acts as an outside source or reservoir of infection. *Trypanosoma brucei* is another blood parasitic protozoan in tropical Africa. This parasite infects cattle and causes nagana disease. The symptoms of the disease included intermittent fever, emaeiation and anaemia, sometimes resulting in death. This parasite is transmitted by vector tse tse fly *Glossina palpalis*. The fly sucks the blood of domesticated and wild ungulates and carries the parasite to all the wild game in tropical Africa. The disease nagana is found only in domesticated cattle and not in wild animals which naturally are resistant to the disease. Thus, all carriers provide a continuous source of infection and are called reservoir hosts.

Trypanosoma gambiense is parasite of man which causes sleeping sickness in Africa. The sleeping symptom is caused by the later stages of the parasite entering cerebro-spinal fluid of the spinal cord. The intermediate hosts are species of tse tse fly and many animals such as pigs, dogs, goats and antelopes in addition to man have a high rate of infection. Man's domesticated animals act as a source of infection for *Trypanosoma gambiense*, just as he himself acts as a source of their infection.

1.2.2 Abiotic Factors

Abiotic or non-living factors are essential for the survival of living factors of any ecosystem. They are : (1) Water, (2) Light, (3) Temperature, (4) Gases, (5) Humidity (6) Soil (7) Wind and (8) Fire.

(1) Water : Water is essential for the life and without water, life is impossible. The water available to plants and animals from soil comes as a result of rainfall. It occupies 71% of the earth surface in the form of fresh water, marine water and estuarine water. The water circulating between atmosphere and earth surface is called hydrologic cycle. The water is in the form of liquid, solid and vapour state. Water of the earth's surface reaches to atmosphere by two means namely evaporation and transpiration. Water plays an important role in an ecosystem which affects the distribution, growth and activities of organisms in it. The amount of rainfall and evaporation and their ratio determines the types of vegetation growing in an ecosystem. Depending on the availability of water, plants are called Hydrophytes, Xerophytes or Mesophytes. Xerophytes occur in the region of scarcity of water. The animals living in these conditions are called desert animals. Hydrophytic plants occur in water and the animals are called aquatic animals. According to the habitat, the plants and animals show certain morphological modifications. For example, xerophytes grow in conditions of very dry air, high temperature, strong winds, high transpiration rate and high evaporation. Hence, trees show very deep and long roots to absorb water. Plants may be succulents or with spines reduced leaves and heavy cuticle bearing leaves. The desert animal absorbs water by skin spines, e.g. Lizard. Certain animals like camel can store large quantity of water in the stomach.

The desert animals are, nocturnal and burrow deep into the soil, in the day time to avoid excessive heat and dryness. Desert animals moves more faster than other land animals.

(2) Humidity : The amount of water vapour or moisture in the air is called humidity. Humidity is of two types, namely, relative humidity and absolute humidity. The relative humidity is the ratio of the actual amount of water vapour in the air to the amount that can be held in the air, at a particular temperature and pressure. Absolute humidity is defined as the amount of water vapour or moisture present in the air.

Humidity plays an important role, as it affects the life of plants and animals indirectly. In warm and humid region, the birds and mammals tends to be darker in colour than those inhabiting the cold and dry regions. As the air warms up, the relative humidity drops because warm air can hold more moisture than cool air. Generally, relative humidity is low during day time and high at night.

Both excessive and deficient moisture can be harmful to the organism. Low relative humidity increases the loss of water through transpiration in plants. Hence, during winter, they shed leaves. Some plants as orchids, lichens, mosses etc. make direct use of atmospheric moisture. In fungi and other microbes it plays an important role in germination of spores and subsequent stages in life cycle.

Humidity is greatly influenced by intensity of solar radiation, temperature, altitude, wind, exposure, cover and water status of soil. Relative humidity is measured by the instrument called psychrometer or by paper strip hygrometer or thermo-hydrograph.

(3) Temperature : Temperature is a physicochemical, ecological abiotic factor. Temperature can be defined as the intensity aspect of heat. It is in the form of energy called thermal energy. Temperature is measured in Fahrenheit (°F) or Centigrade (°C). The biosphere obtains its thermal energy mainly from the sun in the form of solar radiation. Temperature affects all forms of life. It influences the various stages of life activities, such as growth, metabolism, reproduction, movement, distribution, behaviour, death etc. Temperature is variable factor. It varies from place to place and time to time. During day time, temperature is high and in the night, it is low. Temperature is high at sea-level and low at high altitudes. It is high at equator and low in the polar regions. Temperature is more in terrestrial habitat and low in the aquatic habitat.

Within a limited range of temperature, the rate of biochemical reactions double with every 10°C rise in temperature. This is known as **Van't Hoff's rule**. The temperature exerts profound influence on the physiological activities of organisms. Organisms differ in their tolerance limit to extreme temperatures. Most organisms perform their activities in a temperature range of 4 to 45°C.

Temperature affects plants and animals in various ways which are as follows:

(a) Effects on Metabolism : All metabolic activities are influenced by temperature. All chemical reactions, enzyme actions of organisms are controlled by temperature. It affects the rates of transpiration, photosynthesis in plants and respiration rates and other metabolic processes in plants as well as animals.

(b) Effects on Reproduction : Temperature also influence on the reproduction. Flowering in plants is affected by temperature. In animals maturation of gonads or sex cells and their liberation is influenced by the temperature.

(c) Effects on Growth and Development : Temperature influence on growth and development. Both extremely high and low temperature have adverse effects on the growth of plants. In animals also temperature affects growth as well as development. In blow fly, incubation period decreases with increase in temperature.

Temperature has effect on crossing over in *Drosophila*, and sex ratio in Rotifers and Daphnids.

Temperature also affects the coloration in some insects, birds and mammals. The warm and humid climate bear darker pigment than cool and dry climate. Temperature also affects morphology of the animals. Birds and mammals attain greater body size in cold regions than in warm areas. Cold blooded animals are smaller in cold regions. The tail, snout, ears and legs of mammals are relatively shorter in colder parts than in warmer areas. Desert and arctic fox show difference in the size of ears.

Temperature is also responsible for the distribution of animals.

(4) Light : Light is the most important and indispensible abiotic factor without which life can not exist. All plants depend on light for their energy and all animals depend on plants and hence, without light life is impossible. Sunlight is the ultimate source of energy for the biological world. Light is a narrow band of visible-radiant energy comprising wavelengths of 390 to 760 nm. If visible light is passed through a prism, it gives spectrum of seven different colours. Light is formed of energy called radiant energy. Ultra-violet radiation has damaging properties but most of it is absorbed by the ozone, which forms distinct layer in the stratosphere.

Chlorophyll is the dominant light absorbing pigment found in green plants. By the process of photosynthesis, it converts light or photon energy into chemical energy. Variation in the duration of light exposures also affects plant growth. Photo-period influences stem elongation, flowering, fruit growth and other physiological processes of plants and animals. Depending on the length of day required for the induction of flowering, plants are classified as short day plants, long day plant (more than 14 to 16 hours/day length) and day neutral plants which bloom regardless of the photo-period.

Light is not only responsible for photosynthesis, but it also plays an important role in transpiration and stomatal functioning. Photo-period also affects the structure of vegetative organs, growth, germination pigmentation, nutrition requirement and even susceptibility to parasites. Light affects chlorophyll production distribution of plants.

Light also has far-reaching effects on animals, by affecting their several types of activities like pigmentation, reproduction, development, growth, locomotion and migration. Light affects, particularly UV light induces gene mutations. Protective colourations, colour changes are also influenced by light. For vision, light is required, animals can do various activities through protective light. In dark, the animals do not show eyes. For example, in cave dwelling animals. Some animals like owls or loris can see even in dim light in night. Light affects the developmental process in many fish and in silk moth. A strong correlation exists between the reproductive cycles of some marine animals and the lunar cycle.

Light affects locomotion in animals and has an effect on the eye size of marine animals. Marine animals giving at a depth of 500 – 3,000 metres have much larger eyes than those inhabiting surface waters.

Biological production of light occurs in some bacteria, fungi and animals. Light production in animals is result of chemi-luminescent reactions.

(5) Atmospheric Gases : Upto the height of about 300 km, above the earth's surface, there is present some sort of a thick gaseous mantle. In gaseous mantle, there is found a mixture of different gases in different proportions. Of these various gases, such as nitrogen, oxygen and carbon dioxide are major components. Argon, neon, helium, crypton, xenon, hydrogen, methane, ozone are other gases in very minute proportion.

Table 1.2 : Relative proportions of various gases in atmosphere

Sr. No.	Gases	% (By volume)	Sr. No.	Gases	% (By volume)
1.	Nitrogen	78.08	7.	Crypton	0.00011
2.	Oxygen	20.94	8.	Xenon	0.00009
3.	Argon	0.9340	9.	Hydrogen	0.00006
4.	Carbon dioxide	0.0318	10.	Methane	0.0002
5.	Neon	0.0018	11.	Nitrous oxide	0.00005
6.	Helium	0.00052	12.	Ozone	0.000004

Oxygen : A supply of free O_2 is necessary for most forms of life. Aerobic organisms require it for getting energy through oxidative processes. Air contains about 21% oxygen and water usually contains about 4 to 10 ml oxygen per litre. In air, O_2 is abundantly available except at higher altitudes. Therefore, in high altitudes, (mountains) the respiratory activity of animals is increased significantly. Mammals react strongly to this change, when partial pressure of O_2 falls below 50% of its value at sea level. Because of their high O_2 requirement, they cannot remain at high altitudes for long time, if the partial pressure of O_2 is 45% below that at sea level O_2 acts like a stress factor at high altitudes. Water contains dissolved oxygen, which does not combine chemically with water itself. Animals living in water use this O_2 for aquatic respiration and metabolic activities. The aquatic animals develop different adaptation, such as skin, gills; for respiration. Some have special respiratory pigments which help the animals to get O_2 at very low partial pressure.

Carbon Dioxide : Air contains 0.03% of CO_2 which is essential for photosynthetic activity. CO_2 forms carbonic acid when mixed with water and therefore, amount of CO_2 present in water determines its pH. The pH of water determines the distribution of organisms. Sea water contains 3.5% salt and usually 47 ml CO_2 per litre. The concentration of CO_2 in water may also influence the orientation, movement and respiratory activity of organisms. At higher concentrations of CO_2, the rate of respiratory movement in some molluscs and arthropods increases. An increase in CO_2 content in the blood of animals usually causes decrease in O_2 carrying capacity of haemoglobin. Fishes are sensitive to CO_2 concentration in water. They usually choose streams containing a lower amount of CO_2, given an option.

(6) Soil : Soil is also called edaphic factor in which structure formation and characteristics of different soils are studied. It acts as a suitable substratum and medium for plants and animals. It is a bridge between inorganic and organic materials. The study of soil is called pedology or soil science.

Soil is a complex physical biological system providing support water, nutrient and O_2 for the plants. It is made up of mineral matter (40%), organic matter (humus) (10%), soil water (25%), soil air (25%) and biological system. The soil contains top soil, which may be of different colours depending upon the types of humus and mineral materials. The top soil is followed by subsoil, which contains the roots of most plants, humus and minerals.

Soil is formed from the parent rock material (bed rock) by the process of physical, chemical and biological weathering. Physical weathering caused by various climatic factors, such as light, temperature, water, wind etc. Chemical weathering involves the breaking down of complex compounds by the carbonic acid in water and by acidic substances derived from the decomposition process of organic matter in soil. Hydrolysis, hydration, oxidation and reduction are chemical processes which bring about the changes. These are irreversible changes occurring in rock constituents. Biological weathering involves the decomposition process by which organic materials are broken down and leads to humification and mineralisation. The organisms produce acid substances which help in the weathering of rock fragments. Humus is formed and it mixes with clay, sand and silt to form soil.

Soil Profile : Soil is formed of many horizontal layers arranged one below the other. This is called soil profile. The layers are called horizons. Soil is formed by 5 main horizons. They are O, A, B, C and D horizons.

'O' Horizon : It is the top soil, very rich in organic matter content, dark in colour and of light texture marked by intense biological activity. Life is abundant in this horizon. It is again divided into two parts. O_1 and O_2, O_1 horizon is the upper layer formed of fresh fallen dead leaves, twigs, barks, flowers, fruits and animal excreta. O_2 horizon contains humus.

'A' Horizon : It is the zone of alluviation or leaching. In this layer, humus mixes with mineral particles. It is divided into A_1, A_2 and A_3.

'B' Horizon : This horizon forms the subsoil and contains iron and aluminium compounds with clay and humus. It is again divided into three sub horizons, B_1, B_2, B_3. B_1 is transitional layer between A and B_1. The B_2 layer shows maximum accumulation of silicate, clay, mineral, iron and organic matter.

'C' Horizon : This is mineral horizon containing incompletely weathered large masses of rocks. It consists of $CaCO_3$ and $CaSO_4$. Long roots of big plants reach this horizon.

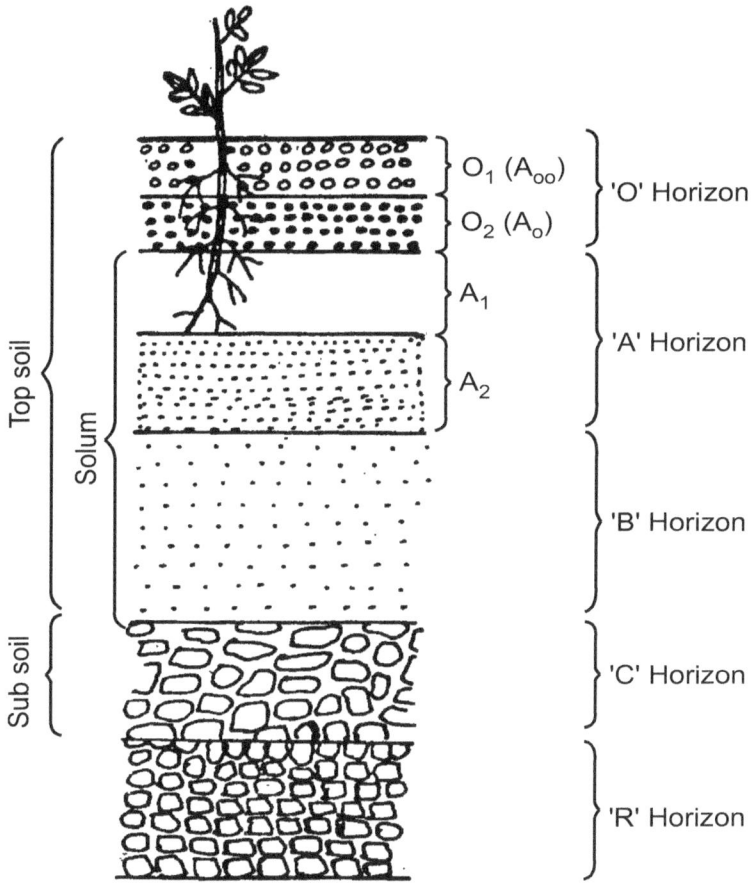

Fig. 1.8 : Hypothetical diagram of the soil profile to show principal horizons

'R' Horizon : This is parent, unweathered bedrock, upon which there is collected water.

Soil is classified on the basis of mode of formation. Residual and transported soil are two main types. Transported soil is classified as colluvial (by gravity), Alluvial (by running waters), Glacial (ice) and Eolian (by wind).

Soil contains various components which shows the physical properties of it, such as texture, mineral matter, soil porosity, soil air, soil water, soil organisms etc. Soil contains particles of different sizes which determine the water holding capacity of soil. Aeration and water holding capacity determines vegetation that can grow. Soil contains sand, clay and silt in definite proportions. It also contains mineral nutrients important for plant metabolism and growth. Soil also contains micro and macro elements which play an important role in development, metabolic functions and an enzymatic action.

Plants absorb water containing organic nutrients and minerals from the soil through their roots. The amount of soil water available to plants depend upon the type and properties of the soil. The source of soil water is rain.

Chemical Properties :

Soil solutes are partly organic and partly inorganic compounds, usually soluble in water. Sources of these solutes are organic matter, parent rocks and chemical reactions that occur around soil roots. The substances are usually in the form of bicarbonates, nitrates, nitrites, chlorides and sulphates of sodium, potassium, calcium, iron, aluminium and boron. Highly alkaline or saline soils are also devoid of vegetation and are highly unproductive.

Soil Organisms :

Soil organisms include microorganisms, such as bacteria, actinomycetes, fungi, algae, and soil animals, such as protozoa, helminth worms, nematodes, annelids, collembola, mites, insects and their larval forms, pupae, arachnids, and other arthropods, gastropods etc. Some mammals and birds use the soil for various purposes. They also play an important role in determining the physical and chemical properties of soil, soil fertility and so on. Earthworms and termites play a significant role in soil formation. Many animals shows burrowing or fossorial adaptations which shows certain modifications in their body and organs.

Soil is important factor for life, hence its conservation is also equally important for survival of animals and plants.

(7) Wind : Wind is nothing but the air in motion and it is important ecological factor of atmosphere. It has impact on plant's life mainly on flat plains, along sea coasts and at high altitudes in mountains. Wind is directly involved in transpiration, in causing several types of mechanical damage and in dissemination of pollen, seeds and fruits. It also modifies the water relations and light conditions of a particular area. The wind velocity is affected by various factors like geographic situation, topography and vegetation masses, and position with respect to shores. Wind effects are much pronounced in plants along sea coasts and high altitudes on mountains. The movement of air is from region of high to that of low pressure. The pressure differences are mainly due to differential heating of atmosphere. The equatorial regions receive more heat than north or south regions, thus low pressure occurs at lower latitudes. The air moves generally from the poles towards equator.

Wind brings about number of physical anatomical and physiological effects on plants which are as follows:

(i) Uprooting and breakage: The high velocity wind may break the living branches of trees and sometimes even their complete uprooting. Thus, vegetation in forests serve as natural windbreaks. Single or many trees which are uprooted in forest are called wind throws or windfalls.

(ii) Deformation: Strong winds from a constant direction some times cause permanent alteration in the form and position of the shoots. Deformation is very common in trees growing on ridges and along coasts.

(iii) Lodging : Lodging is a type of wind injury common in grasses, as wheat, maize, oat, sugarcane etc. where violent winds cause the flattening of these herbaceous plants against the ground.

(iv) Abrasion : Soil and ice particles which are carried by wind act as strong abrasive force. The buds and other parts of plants may be eroded away. Plants growing on sandy soil suffer more with such damage.

(v) Erosion and deposition : Due to soil erosion by wind roots of the plants are exposed. The soil deposited to the places due to wind is unsuitable for plant growth.

(vi) Salt spray : Along sea coasts, the salts of the water are carried along by strong winds in the vicinity of the ocean. Such salts are harmful to the plants growing there.

Anatomical and physiological effects :

(i) Compression wood : As result of wind deformation in trees develops a dense, reddish type of xylem called the compression wood, on the compression side.

(ii) Desiccation : Strong winds cause an increase in the rates of evaporation and transpiration. Plants loose the internal water balance and thus suffer from desiccation.

(iii) Dwarfing : Plants growing under the influence of drying winds generally suffer from dehydration and consequent loss of turgidity. Under these conditions, their organs become dwarfed. This is common in sea coast, arctic trees.

(8) Fire : Fires are sometimes caused naturally by lighting or volcanic activity which are rare and confined only to certain areas. Most of the fires are common in most of the regions are of biological origin. These are mostly man-caused and sometimes, chiefly in forest, develop due to mutual friction between (bamboos etc.) surfaces.

There are three types of fires namely:

1) Ground fires   2) Surface fires and   3) Crown fires

In case of **ground fires** organic matter accumulates richly as heaps and they catch fire which generally smoulder for longer periods. These fires are flameless and subterranean and kill almost all plants rooted in the burning material.

Surface fires sweep over the ground surface rapidly and their flames consume the litter, living herbaceous vegetation and shrubs and also scorching the tree bases if come in contact.

Crown fires are highly destructive, burning the forest canopy. Vegetation destruction is on large scale. These types of fires develop in dense woody vegetations.

Effects of Fire :

1) Fire has direct lethal effect on plants and animals.
2) Injured plants by fire develop large scars on their stems. Such scars may serve as suitable place for parasitic fungi and insects.

3) Fire brings marked alteration in litter and humus contents of soil, pH, and soil fauna. Sometimes thousands of years period required for such habitat to return of normal conditions.
4) Fire plays an important role in the removal of competition for surviving species. Abundance of surviving species is seen at the cost of those killed by fire. There is considerable reduction in competition.
5) Some plants, grasses are stimulated by fire to produce large quantities of seeds. In some grasses and legumes seeds would germinate only after these get fire treatment. They are fire tolerant species.
6) Some fungi grow in soils of burnt areas.
7) Some areas where fires are very common, the plants have developed some fire tolerant features or adaptations that favour. Their survival under such conditions.

1.3 Brief Idea of Some Ecological Terms

1. Species :

A species can be defined as an interbreeding group of natural population, which is reproductively isolated from other such group. Thus, the individuals of the group which can exchange the genes between themselves but they can not exchange the genes with others. In other words, each species is an isolated pool of genes flowing in a given environment.

Merrell (1962) defined the term species as a natural, biological unit, tied together by the bond of mating and sharing a common gene pool.

A species has the following general features or characteristics :
(1) Each species is an isolated, inter-communicating gene pool.
(2) The species fills an ecological niche which is not utilized by another species.
(3) Each species exhibits the process of constant adjustment with the environment.
(4) Each species has a constellation isolating mechanisms which directly or indirectly prevent exchange of genes with realted species.

(5) Closely related species have separate adjoining territories.
(6) There are no intermediate forms found in species.
(7) Each species has capacity to give rise to new species if geographical isolation is provided.
(8) Each species represents an ecological unit and it interacts with other species as a unit in a given environment.

Thus in another words, the species is population of group of individual with similar structural and functional characteristics. They have common ancestry and they show interbreeding only with each other and not with others.

The evolution or formation of new variety from pre-existing variety is called *speciation*.

2. Community :

A community is defined as an assemblage of different kinds of populations living in a particular area or habitat. Thus, community contains different types of organisms like microbes, plants and animals, which interact with each other. In other words, community is a natural, assemblage of microorganisms, plants and animals inhabiting a given area. In case of population a monospecific individuals are living whereas community comprises polyspecific individuals or many populations. The individuals are ecologically related and composed of two or more species. Forest community, pond community, marine community, grassland community etc. are the different examples of community.

In forest community there are different types of trees, herbs, shrubs, birds, lions, deer, foxes, monkeys and microorganisms. The pond community is formed by variety of aquatic plants, algae and animals like fishes, frogs, aquatic insects, crustaceans, snakes and micro-organisms. In the community, the organisms are important for the maintenance of the community.

Types of Communities : There are two types of communities distinguished as a *major community* and *minor community*.

   (a) Major Community : The community which is large, self sustaining, self regulating and complete independent unit called major community e.g. Forest, Pond community.

(b) Minor Community : The minor community is small and not self sustaining and independent unit. It forms secondary aggregations within the major communities and depends on other communities.

Characteristics of Community : A community is dynamic entity in an ecosystem, which includes many populations and they interact with each other. Community shows characteristic pattern called *community structure*. A community has number of characteristic features. They are as follows :

(a) Community Structure : Each community exhibits a definite structure which is also called trophic structure. It determines the patterns of movement of energy and nutrients through the community. *Producers* are the green plants which synthesize carbohydrate food by the process of photosynthesis in which they use CO_2, solar energy and chlorophyll, thus they are the main source of energy for community. The second component of the community are the *consumers* which can not produce food. They are herbivores (depend on plants) e.g. cow, deer or carnivores (depend on animals) e.g. Lion, Tiger, Fox. The *decomposers* includes micro-organisms like fungi, bacteria which decomposes the dead bodies of plants and animals of the community converting into nutrients useful for community.

(b) Diversity of Community : Each community is formed by heterogenous assemblage of plants and animals. They belong to different tax onomic groups. Thus in community individuals exhibit vast diversity because of many species.

3. Ecological Niche :

Since community includes large number of species. Each species has a specific position within the community called *ecological niche*. It is nothing but the functional status or total role of the species in the community. The term niche has been used in ecology with a variety of meaning. According to **Odum** niche is the profession of an organism in the community. He compared the habitat to the address. The role of individual in the community includes the feeding, behaviour, tolerance to the environment and interactions with other individuals. Thus in the community every population has an ecological niche which determines the structural, physical and behavioural adaptation of the population. Therefore, niche has been used in ecology with variety of meanings such as habitat niche, trophic niche, climatic niche etc.

The habitat refers to the totality of abiotic factors to which the species is exposed in the area e.g. forest habitat, freshwater habitat, marine habitat, costal habitat etc. There are organisms which are highly specialised regarding their habitat. For example, leaf miners of certain species live only in the upper photosynthetic layer of the leaves of certain species of plants, while other species live in the lower cell layer. Thus these layers or habitats are different for different species. On this basis the subdivisions of the environment are called microhabitats. Thus the leaf is the microhabitat for leaf miners within the total forest and different cell layers of the leaf constitute different microhabitats within the leaf for different species of leaf miners.

The Trophic Niche : In this case, two species live in the same habitat but they occupy different trophic niches because of different food habits. For example, two aquatic bugs *Notonecta* and *Corixa* live in the same pond but occupy different trophic niches. *Notonecta* is active predator which catch prey and feed on them, but the *Corixa* feeds mainly on decaying vegetation.

Multidimensional (Hyper volume) niche. In community, there is an aggregation of many environmental and functional variable which can be thought of as a point in a volume of space of infinite dimensions.

Ecological Equivalence : The organisms which occupy the similar ecological niches in different geographical areas is called ecological equivalence. For example, the kangaroos of Australia and Bison of North America. Both of them are grazing herbivores on grass lands of different geographical areas.

Advantages of Ecological Niche :
(1) The major advantage which organisms gain by occupying different niches is escape from continuous competition.
(2) Organisms occupied in niche get suitable substratum and microclimate.
(3) Segregation into niches also avoids confusion of activities between organism in the community and permits a more orderly and efficient life cycle for each species.

(4) The segregation of each species into different niches permits the full utilization of available resources.

(5) The individuals avoid the conflict with its neighbours and lead life orderly, productive and quite efficient

Community Dominants : There are variety of species in the community and some of the species play dominant role in it due to their number, size and activities. Therefore, such species are called *community dominants*. If these species are substracted from community there are drastic changes in it. For example, in a grassland community the grasses are dominant groups as well as in forest, trees are dominants.

Stratification : The arrangement of the organisms in different layers of the community is called stratification and it is of two types, namely vertical stratification and horizontal stratification.

Ecotone or Edge Effect : The zone or area lying in between two adjacent communities is called ecotone or edge effect. The estuary is the ecotone lying between river and sea. The border between forest and grassland is also called ecotone. The peculiarities or characteristics of ecotone are intermediate between two adjacent communities. Therefore, ecotone provides abundant food and shelter to the organisms of both communities. Ecotone exhibits more number of species and denser population than either of the neighbouring communities and this is referred as *edge effect*. There are certain species which are found only in this region called edge species.

4. Ecosystem :

The term ecosystem was first coined by **A. G. Tansley** in 1935. The term is derived from two words namely eco and system. Eco refers to environment and system refers an interacting, inter dependent complex. **Tansley** defined ecosystem as "the system resulting from the integration of all the living and non-living factors of the environment." An ecosystem is a basic functional ecological unit. It consists of living organisms called biotic factors and non-living substances or abiotic factors. Ecosystem is an interacting system where biotic and abiotic factors interact to produce an exchange of materials between the living and non-living factors. Thus, structural and functional system of communities and their environment is called ecosystem.

The central theme of ecosystem concept is that at any place where an organism lives, there is continuous interaction between the living and non-living components. i.e. between plants, animals and their environment. They continuously produce and exchange materials. This means, that these are mechanisms for continuous absorption of materials by organisms for the purpose of production of organic materials and their conversion back into inorganic form, much of which is then released back into the environment.

Structure of Ecosystem :

Any ecosystem is formed of two components namely abiotic and biotic components.

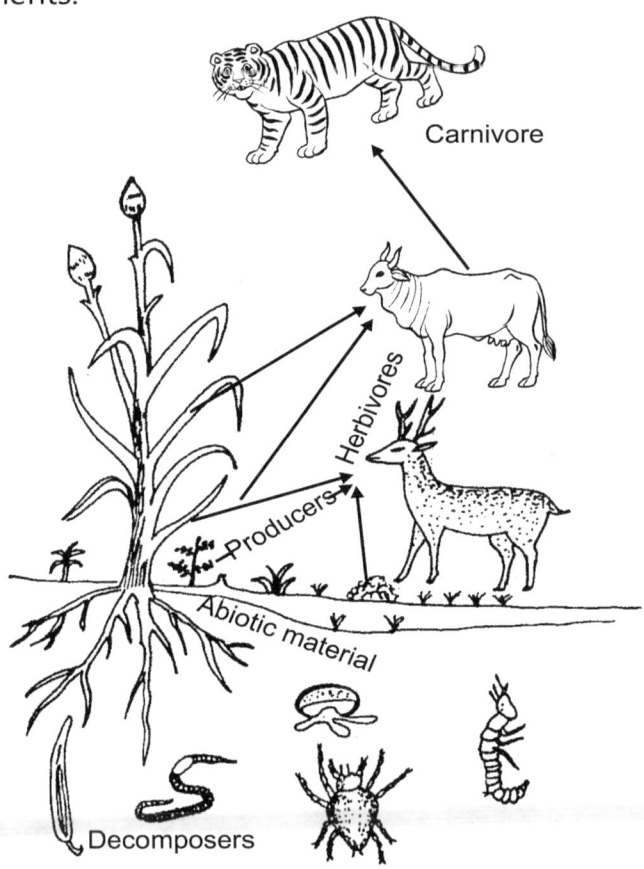

Fig. 1.9 : Grassland ecosystem showing component parts

(1) Abiotic or Non-living Components : These are non-living factors of the environment. Abiotic factors include inorganic substances such as P, S, C, N, H etc. Water, soil, air, light, temperature, minerals, climate, pressure etc. are important abiotic factors. For the survival of the biotic factors abiotic factors are essential.

(2) Biotic Factors or Living Components : The biotic factors include living organisms of the ecosystem. They are classified into two types.

(i) **Autotrophs :** Organisms, basically green plants, certain bacteria and algae that can synthesize their own food in the presence of sunlight. These are called autotrophs or producers. These organisms contain chlorophyll with which they can prepare their own food material. They do not depend on others for food.

(ii) **Heterotrophs :** All other organisms that do not make their own food but depend on other organisms to obtain their energy for survival. These are called heterotrophs or consumers.

Among consumers some animals such as insects, cow, rabbit, deer, goat etc. which can eat green plants are called primary consumers or herbivores. Organisms which eat a herbivore, like a frog that eats grasshopper are called secondary consumers. Organisms which eat these secondary consumers are called tertiary consumers. While the primary consumers are herbivores, the secondary and tertiary consumers are carnivores. Animals like lions and vultures which are not killed or eaten by other animals are top carnivores.

Heterotrophs are classified into two types i.e. macro consumers and micro consumers or decomposers.

Decomposers : Certain fungi and bacteria which are responsible for the decomposition are called decomposers or reducers. The role of the decomposers is very special and important. Certain decomposers are also called scavengers. They are saprotrophs and they break down complex compounds of dead or living protoplasm and release water, CO_2, phosphates and a number of organic compounds are largely the by-products and release in organic nutrients in environment, making them available again to autotrophs.

Consequently, an ecosystem is considered as a basic unit, where complex natural community obtain their food from plants through

one, two, three or four steps and accordingly, these steps are known as the first, second, third, and fourth trophic levels or food levels such as :
  (1) Green plants (producers), Trophic level – I
  (2) Herbivores (primary consumers), Trophic level – II
  (3) Carnivores (secondary consumers), Trophic level – III
  (4) Top carnivores (Tertiary consumers), Trophic level – IV

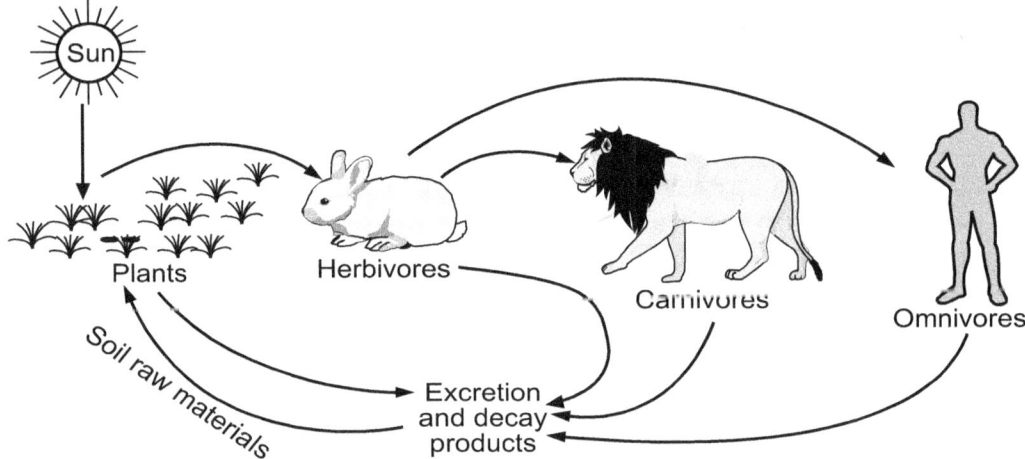

Fig. 1.10 : Generated scheme of nutritional relationships among different biotic components of an ecosystem

The amount of living material in different trophic levels or in a component population is known as standing crop. This term is applicable to both, plants as well as animals. The standing crop may be expressed in terms of :
  (i) Number of organisms per unit area or
  (ii) Biomass i.e. organism mass in unit area, which can be measured as living weight, dry weight, ash free dry weight or carbon weights or calories.

Different Types of Ecosystems : There are two major types of ecosystems; the aquatic and terrestrial.

Terrestrial ecosystems consists of :
  (i) Forest ecosystem
  (ii) Grassland ecosystem
  (iii) Desert ecosystem

Aquatic ecosystems are further distinguished as :
(i) Freshwater ecosystems which may be lotic (running water as spring, stream, or river) or lentic (standing water as lake, pond, pools, puddles, ditch, swamp etc.)
(ii) Marine ecosystem includes deep bodies as an ocean or shallow ones as a sea.
(iii) Estuarine ecosystem is transitional ecosystem between freshwater and marine ecosystem.

Sometimes ecosystems are broadly classified into two types namely,
(i) Natural ecosystems and
(ii) Artificial ecosystems (man engineered ecosystems).

Natural ecosystem includes terrestrial and aquatic ecosystems, and artificial ecosystem includes crop lands like maize, wheat, rice fields etc. where man tries to control the biotic community as well as physicochemical environment. Another type is a space ecosystem.

Pond Ecosystem : A pond as a whole serves good example of a freshwater ecosystem. A pond is self sufficient and self regulating system. It consists of both living (plants and animals) components as well as non-living components such as light, temperature and water in which nutrients, O_2, other gases and organic matter are dissolved.

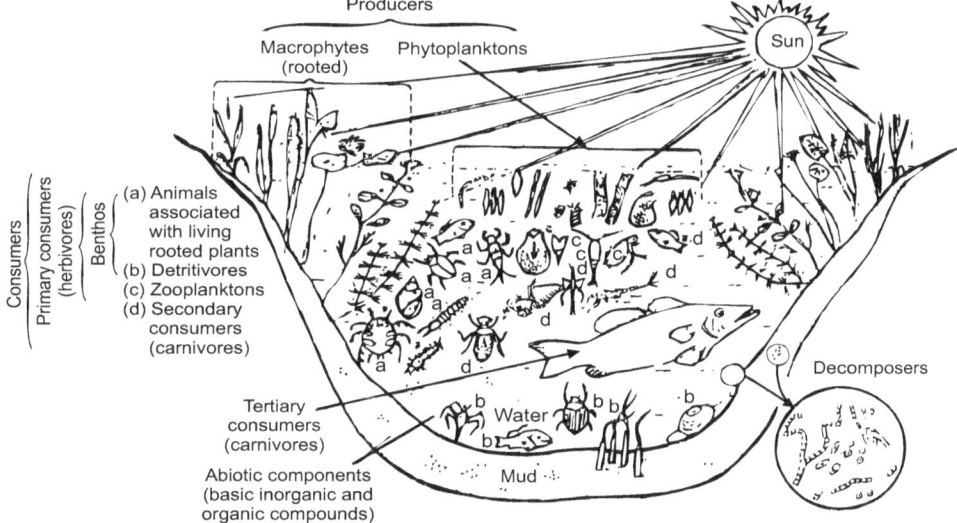

Fig. 1.11 : Diagram of the pond ecosystem, showing its basic structural units the abiotic (inorganic and organic compounds) and biotic (producers, consumers and decomposers) components

Biotic Components :

(1) Producers : The green plants and some photosynthetic bacteria are autotrophs. They fix the radiant solar energy and produce carbohydrates by the process of photosynthesis. Producers are of two types.

- (i) **Macrophytes :** These are rooted, larger plants which are partly or completely submerged, floating and emergent hydrophytes. The common plants are *Typha, Nymphaea, Chara, Hydrilla, Vallisneria, Utricularia, Eichhornia, Spirodella, Lemna.*

- (ii) **Phytoplankton :** These are small minute, floating or suspended lower plants. They are filamentous algae as *Zygnema, Ulothrix, Spirogyra, Diatoms, Volvox, Anabaena, Spirulina.*

(2) Consumers : These are animals and heterotroph which depends for their nutrition on producers. Most of the consumers are herbivores which feed on plant material, whereas insects, fish, frog etc. are carnivores as they feed on herbivores. Some organisms feed on both plants and animals called omnivores.

- (i) **Herbivores :** They directly feed on living plants. They may live at the bottom called benthos, e.g. insect larvae, beetles, mites, molluscs, crustaceans etc. Zooplanktons are small, microscopic forms live on the surface of water include rotifers, protozoans (*Euglena, Coleps*), Crustaceans (*Cyclops*). Herbivores are also called primary consumers.

- (ii) **Carnivores :** These may feed on herbivores e.g. insects, fish, water beetles. They are also called secondary consumers. Those feed on secondary consumers are called tertiary consumers, e.g. larger fish, frog, duck, aquatic birds.

(3) Decomposers : These are also called micro-consumers as they feed on dead organic matter. They bring about the decomposition of complex dead organic matter of plants and animals. They are chiefly bacteria, actinomycetes and fungi.

Abiotic Components : In pond, several non-living or abiotic factors are present for maintaining the ecosystem. They are water, temperature (heat), light, pH, inorganic compounds such as CO_2, O_2, calcium, nitrogen, phosphates, aminoacids, humic acid etc. These constituents are essential for the survival of living factors.

5. Biome :

A biome is a large community unit characterised by the kinds of plants and animals present e.g. Forest biome, tundra biome, grasland biome, desert biome etc.

In each biome, the kind of climax vegetation is uniform-grasses, confiers, deciduous trees but the particular species of plant may vary in different parts of the biome. The type of climax vegetation depends upon the physical environment and the two together determine the kind of animals present. Thus, biome exhibits the following features :

(1) A biome is a major terrestrial community containing distinctive plants and animals.
(2) There are many biomes present in geographical realm.
(3) The dominant community of biome is also called *climax community* which forms the matrix of the biome. The biome is named after the climax community. For example, in forest biome trees form climax community.
(4) In biome, several intermediate communities are present.
(5) There is no sharp line or demarcation between adjacent biomes.
(6) The broad transition region between two biomes is called ecotone, e.g. the extensive region in North Canada where tundra and coniferous forest blend in the tundra-conifens ecotone.
(7) There is difference between biome and ecosystem. Ecosystem consists of both biotic and abiotic factors, but in biome includes only plants and animals.

Ecologists have recognised some of the following biomes : Tundra biome, Alpine biome, Forest biome, Grassland biome, Desert biome.

(1) Tundra Biome : Tundra is also called marshy, treeless plain of arctic region. It is characterised by absence of trees, the presence of dwarf plants, remains marshy in summer and frozen hard in winter. The land is poorly drained and hence remains wet and spongy. About 5 million acres of tundra stretch across Northern America, Northern Europe and Siberia. There is variation from place to place. Tundra biome shows the following features :

(1) Temperature, rainfall and evaporation in tundra biome is low.
(2) The wormest month has average temperature 10°C and rainfall is 25 mm.
(3) Water is not limiting factor because of low rate of evaporaiton.
(4) Ground remains frozen except uppermost 10 to 20 cm which melt during brief summer seasons.
(5) The permanently frozen deeper soil layer is called permafrost.
(6) The vegetation forms thin carpet in summer only.
(7) There are no trees but dwarf plants, grasses and sedges, lichens (raindeer moss), mosses and shrubs are found.
(8) The fauna of this biome include Arctic fox, hare, reindeer, lemmings, polar bear, caribou, selas, walruses, migratory birds and insects generally found during summer.

(2) Alpine Biome : It is the region of mountain above the timber line contains typical flora and fauna. The peaks of mountain are covered by snow like Himalayas. The alpine zone lies between timber line and snow zone. There are extreme environmental conditions greatly influence the biota of this region. This biome exhibits the following features,

(1) This zone has low air density, low oxygen and carbon di-oxide contents and water vapour.
(2) It has high ozone content, greater penetration of light, high cold, snow cover, high mind velocity and increased rate of desication. Due to high ionizing radiation trees are absent.
(3) Alpine zone includes frog, crow, snow leopard, yak, sheep, insects etc.

(3) Forest Biome : It is the biome which includes complex assemblage of different kinds of biotic communities. The land is covered by thick growth of trees. Due to optimum conditions of temperature and ground moisture the growth of trees enhanced. Depending on the nature of forests and geographical regions they are classified into three types namely.

(a) Coniferous forests.

(b) Tropical forests.

(c) Deciduous forests.

(a) **Coniferous Forests :** These are evergreen thick forests populated with pine trees characterised by needle like leaves. These forests are confined to the northern hemisphere at high altitudes. Which stretches across both North America and Eurasia, just South of tundra. They are also called *taiga* because they give thick shade and prevents the growth of herbs and shrubs. They include flora spruce, fir, pine and fauna snow hare, Hlynx, wolf, fox, squirrels, Hyla, Rana. The trees range up to 40 m in height and large animals such as moose, caribou, elk, bear etc. Trees supply good timber and seeds as a food for animals.

(b) **Tropical Rain Forests :** The leaves of these trees are broad and ever green and they occur near equator in central and South America, Central and Western Africa (Congo), Southeast Asia (India, Malaysia) Malaya, New Guinea, Australia. These forests contain diverse communities. Temperature and humidity are high and constant. The annual rainfall is 200 to 225 cm. They show diverse flora tall trees covered with vines, creepers, orchids. Some trees grow 25 to 35 metres tall. The fauna of this biome is snails, worms, spiders, frogs, geckoes, snakes, parakeets, leopords, flying squrrels, sloths, tigers, deer etc.

(c) **Deciduous Forests :** These forests are characterised by tall trees with broad and thin leaves which fall during winter and grow new foliage in the spring. These forests occur in North America, Europe, Easter Asia, Australia and Japan. The climatic condition are warm in summer and cold in winter. Annual rain fall is 75 to 150 and temperature 10 – 20°C. The fauna includes deer, bear, squirrel, racoon, wild boar, snake, hawks, fly catchers, wood peckers and insects.

(4) Grassland Biomes : These biomes found where rainfall is about 25 to 75 cm per year. The plain land is occupied by grasses and hence grasses are climax community. They are also called tall or short grass *prairies* (North America) and *steppes* (Eurasia), the veldt of Africa and Pampas of South America (Argentina). The grass land biomes are open land communities with limited moisture, irregular rainfall and high radiation. There are no trees or thick vegetation and provide natural pasture for grazing animals. The soil is rich in humus. The fauna includes Antelopes, Bison, Zebra, Prairie dogs, Kangaroos, Ass, Wild horses etc.

(5) Desert Biome : This types of biomes are formed in the driest of environments, where there are no trees, no water and the large land is covered by sand. In hot deserts the temperature is very high whereas in cold deserts the temperature is very low. These deserts are characterised by extreme high or low temperature, low or no rainfall, scarcity of water, dust storms are common. The most important hot deserts of world is the Sahara, Kalahari of Africa, Gobi (China), Rajasthan (India). The cold deserts occur at high elevations where temperatures are low and rainfall scanty. Cold deserts occur in Ladakh regions of Himalayas, Tibet and Bolivia Arctic. In hot deserts, plants are mostly sacculent type e.g. Cactus, Palo verde trees, creosote bush etc. Most cold deserts have sage bush.

The animals found in desert biome are *Uromastix*, rattle snakes, quils, bustard, bats, hedgehog, ant eater, mouse, porcapine, wild boar, red foxes, jungle cats, panthers, camel etc.

7. Biosphere :

Biosphere is defined as the part of earth and atmosphere in which many smaller ecosystems exists and operate. So far as it is known, life exists on earth because it has all the physical conditions necessary for sustaining it. In other words, it is the environment of earth which makes it possible for the origin and survival of living organisms. Even on the earth, the optimal, conditions for the sustainance of life are only found in certain areas. Also, all types of environments are not favourable to all kinds of organisms. For example, aquatic organisms can not survive on land and terrestrial organisms can not live in water. The biosphere includes many distinct biomass, such as tropical evergreen forests, tropical and temperate deciduous forests, taiga, grass lands (prairies, plains, steppes, veldt) savanna, deserts, tundras etc. and aquatic biomass like marine and large fresh water bodies. In other words, the biosphere is a narrow sphere of earth where the atmosphere (air), hydrosphere (water) and lithosphere (soil) meet, interact and make the existence of life possible.

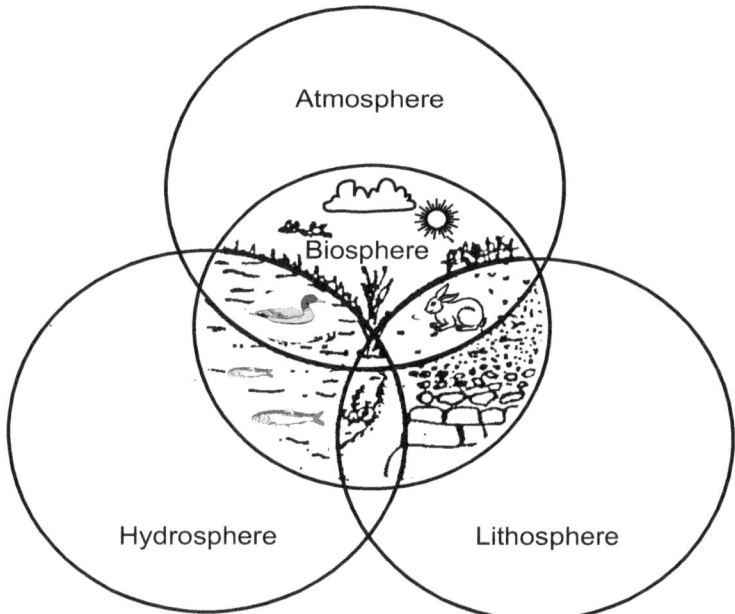

Fig. 1.12 : Inter-relation of environmental components

Three main sub-divisions of the biosphere are lithosphere (solid matter), hydrosphere (liquid matter) and the atmosphere or gaseous envelope of the earth, which extends upto a height of 22.5 km. The Fig. 1.12 shows the idealised scheme of biosphere in relation to hydrosphere, atmosphere and lithosphere. The area of the contact and interaction between these components is really important for life, because the entire life is confined and the basic processes of life like photosynthesis and respiration occur.

Living organisms are mostly confined to the parts of biosphere that receive solar radiation during the day. As stated above, this includes atmosphere, the surface of land, the few metres of soil and the upper layers of water of oceans, lakes and rivers. The illuminated zone may be a few centimetres in turbid water of a river, and upto about 100 metres in clearest part of an ocean. In the ocean, the biosphere does not end where light ceases, as gravity enables the energy flow to continue downward, since fecal pellets, cast skins and organisms dead and alive are always falling from the illuminated regions into the depths.

In addition to the extension of the biosphere downwards, there is limited extension upwards also. On very high mountains, like Himalayas, the limit above which chlorophyll bearing plants cannot live appears to be above 6,200 metres. In simple words, biosphere can be viewed as the part of the earth consisting of oceans and the surface of the continents, together with the adjacent atmosphere (i.e. the troposphere). However, polar ice caps and the higher mountains slopes above the snow line are known as parabiosphere.

Since, living organisms require inorganic metabolites from each of the subdivision of biosphere, enter from hydrosphere, mineral from lithosphere and chemical elements from atmosphere, a brief discussion on the nature and working of each sub-division will help us to know the mechanism which influences metabolic activities of living organisms.

Atmosphere : Atmosphere may be defined as a transparent gaseous envelope surrounding the earth. The vertical profile of the atmosphere shows several concentric layers. These layers vary in density, temperature, composition and properties. The density is highest near the earth's surface and decreases with lattitude. The atmosphere is divided into four distinct layers. The main layers from the surface of the earth upwards are :

(i) Troposphere   (ii) Stratosphere
(iii) Mesophere   (iv) Thermosphere (Ionosphere)

(i) Troposphere : It extends from the surface of the earth upto a height of 8 to 10 km. In this layer, the percentage concentration of different gases in air does not vary with an increase in height. But the water vapour content in air depends upon the weather, it decreases sharply with an increase in height as does the air temperature. The vertical temperature gradient of the troposphere is 5°C per km in the lower troposphere and 7°C per km in the upper troposphere. However, the upper region of the troposphere has a narrow boundary called tropopause which has a constant temperature. The upper troposhpere is almost transparent to the rays of sun, which do not heat it very much in passage. Most of the solar energy is absorbed by the earth's surface, and heat radiates from the lower troposphere to the middle and then to the upper troposphere. Hence, there is a gradual decrease in temperature with height. Besides, the non-uniform heating of the ground surface produces ascending and descending air currents which results in turbulence and mixing of air masses vertically. The air pressure at 11 km altitude is 225 millibars. Solar radiation causes water to evaporate from the earth's surface. The bulk of evaporation occurs at the ocean surface, since oceans form more than two-thirds of the earth's surface. Therefore, the part of the troposphere over an ocean carries more moisture than that over a land surface. The mass of water vapour decreases rapidly with an increase in height. It is the layer in which we live and it contains 90% of the air in the atmosphere. Here the clouds are formed and carried by winds.

(ii) Stratosphere : This layer is lying above the troposphere and free from clouds and aeroplanes usually fly in lower zone. Its thickness is about 50 to 55 km and it consists of a rich layer of ozone, which absorbs the harmful ultraviolet radiations from sun. There is a serious threat to this layer now due to the harmful effects of gaseous pollutants. Due to depletion of ozone, a big hole (thining of the layer) has occurred in it, above the Antarctic region. In this layer, temperature increases up to 90°C with height and it is limited by stratopause.

(iii) Mesosphere : This layer lies above 50 km upto 100 km. It is characterised by decrease of temperature upto – 80°C.

(iv) Thermosphere : It lies beyond the mesosphere. Here temperature rises upto 1000°C. It is also called ionosphere which contains several layers of ionised air. There are large number of ions and free electrons. It reflects the radio-waves signalled from the surface of the earth, helping in long distance radio communication. Most of the man made satellites used in modern communication and for diverse research purposes, more around or are stationed at different attitudes in the thermosphere. It extends to a height of 400 km.

(v) Exosphere : It lies beyond 400 km. The air density is very low in this layer in temperature eases at this layer. There is no boundary between the atmosphere and outer space.

The atmosphere is a mixture of several gases. Near the earth's surface, it contains mainly two gases :

Nitrogen - 78% and Oxygen - 21%

Atmospheric Regions Based on Temperature :

The remaining 1 per cent includes argon (0.93 per cent), carbon dioxide (0.03 per cent) and small quantities of hydrogen, helium, neon, crypton and traces of many other gases. Various quantities of water vapour, dust particles, smoke and salts are also found. There is sufficient movement of air upto a height of 100 km which keeps it well mixed of homogeneous. The general circulation of the air is responsible for specific climatic conditions and is responsible for the water cycle.

Much of the atmospheric air is present in troposphere, atmosphere is an essential part of the life supporting system, as it supplies oxygen, carbon dioxide and nitrogen. It provides medium for long distance radio communication. It also acts as shield against UV radiation and modern industrial activities and aviation technology are polluting the air and are disturbing the balance of gases in the atmosphere, causing a threat to the environment and climate.

The green plants convert solar energy into chemical energy in which atmospheric carbon dioxide enters the living world. By the process of photosynthesis plants produce glucose and oxygen. After decomposition of living matter, the CO_2 returns to the atmosphere to complete the cycle. O_2 is an important constituent of the atmosphere, enters the living world through respiration. Through it, glucose is, converted into energy for various activities. N_2 is also an essential component of living systems. It is essential for organisms for the synthesis of proteins, nucleic acids and other nitrogenous compounds. In nature, atmospheric nitrogen is fixed by specialised organisms. Many elements are circulated through living organisms.

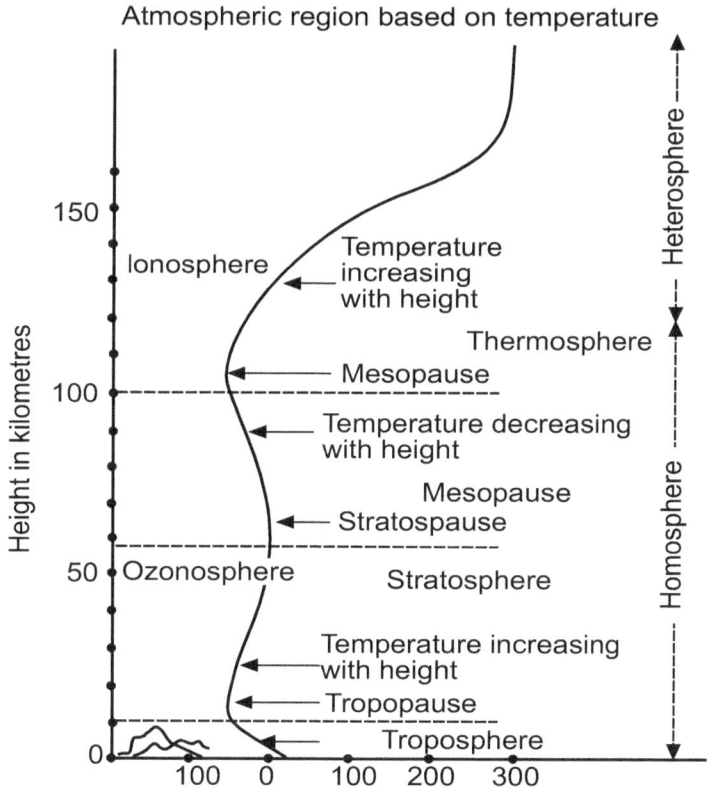

Fig. 1.13 : Different layers of atmosphere

Hydrosphere : The layer of water at or near the surface of the earth is called hydrosphere. Hydrosphere is formed by the oceans, lakes, rivers, streams, polar ice caps, water vapour etc. The water remains in solid (snow), liquid (water) and gaseous (water vapour) forms. Water is an important component of protoplasm, hence it is essential for life in all living organisms. Water is used as a raw material for various metabolic processes and it is obtained from hydrosphere. Water is also a source of hydrogen and oxygen.

The earth is sometimes called the watery planet, as it is the only planet in the solar system which has abundant supply of water. Water is the major constituent of hydrosphere and covers four-fifths of earth's surface. In fact, water is all around us. Every cubic millimetre of air, even over dry deserts, has water vapour. Water is present in the soil beneath our feet and also hidden in underground pools.

The total volume of water in the hydrosphere is 1.4 billion cubic kilometres (km^3), about 97 per cent is ocean water, unsuitable for human use. Only 3 per cent is available as freshwater. About 77.2 per cent is stored in ice caps and glaciers and 22.4 per cent is ground water and soil moisture. The rest (about 0.36 per cent) is distributed in lakes, swamps, rivers and streams.

Water is most essential substance for the continuation of life processes. It regulates climate. The oceans acts as giant heat bank for the coastal regions releasing and absorbing heat. Water falls, tides and river currents are used to move machines and generate power. Water is essential for agricultural and industry. It also provides surface for navigation.

Fresh water is a finite resource out of the water evaporating from the oceans, 90 per cent returns to the ocean and remaining 10 per cent falls on land surface to support natural and human ecosystems. An ocean is a reservoir of many substances of biological cycles and many other minerals. It provides richest and productive environment for diverse kinds of organisms.

Water is being polluted by human activities in various kinds.

Lithosphere : The solid component of the earth or body of the earth is called lithosphere. It was formed some 5-6 billion years ago. It has three main layers :

(1) **The Earth's Crust :** It is in solid state and outermost layer with a thickness of 16 to 50 km. It is composed of soil of thickness ranging from a few inches to a few feet. It offers shelter and food for the living organisms.

(2) **The Mantle :** Mantle is the middle layer of lithosphere, with about 2880 km thick and is made of hard rock containing iron and magnesium and form about 84% and 67% of the earth's volume and weight respectively.

(3) The Core : The core is the innermost layer of the earth composed of high density solid material, mainly iron and nickel with a temperature of about 8000°C.

Lithosphere helps in the metabolic activities in two ways. (i) It is the only source of most of the minerals for organisms both terrestrial or aquatic animals. (ii) It forms the soil required mainly by the terrestrial plants.

The metabolic activities of organisms occur only in few inches to few feet of the earth's surface containing soil. This is formed by the interaction of the complex, physical, chemical and biological processes of weathering of parent rock, which provides the mineral substrate for soil formation. In summary, the climate, vegetation, parent rock material and living organisms play an important role in the formation of soil and its profiles.

In normal mineral soils, the profile has three main horizons, usually called the A, B and C layers. These horizons are differentiated by texture, physical structure, colour, porosity and nature of organic material, root growth and distribution of living biomass.

Soil which is important non-renewable resource is being polluted by man-made activities. The variety of soil pollutants affect the physical, chemical and biological properties of soil and thus, seriously affect its productivity.

1.4 Energy Flow, Food Chain and Ecological Pyramids with Reference to Pond and Grass Land Ecosystem

1.4.1 Functions of Ecosystem

Plants use solar energy for their production of food, obtained from solar radiation. Very limited amount i.e. about 1/50 millionth of the total solar radiation reaches on the earth's surface. The solar radiation travels through the space in the form of waves. During travelling most of solar energy is lost in the space. The solar energy which reaches on the earth surface is largely of visible light (45%) and infrared components (45%) and ultraviolet rays (10%). Plants mostly absorb red and blue light.

Thus, in ecological energetic we study the following aspects :
(1) Amount of solar energy reaching in an ecosystem.
(2) Amount of solar energy used by green plants for the process of photosynthesis and
(3) Path and amount of energy flow from producers to consumers.

While travelling solar radiation through space about 34% sunlight reaching the earth's atmosphere is reflected back into its atmosphere. 10% is absorbed by ozone layer, water vapour and other atmospheric gases. The remaining amount of solar radiation 56% reaches the earth's surface. Very small about 1-5% fraction of solar energy is utilized by the plants for photosynthesis from energy reaching the earth's surface. The remaining energy is absorbed as heat by ground vegetation or water. In true sense, only about 0.02% solar energy is used by the plants for photosynthesis. But still on this small fraction survival of living organisms depends on an ecosystem.

Energy Flow in an Ecosystems :

The behaviour of energy in ecosystem is called energy flow. The flow of the energy is unidirectional. In ecological energetic, we can study the following aspects :
(1) The efficiency of the producers in absorption and conversion of solar energy.
(2) Use of this chemical energy by the consumers.
(3) The total input of energy in the form of food and its efficiency of assimilation.
(4) The loss through respiration, heat excretion etc.
(5) The gross net production.

The principle of food chains and working of thermodynamics can be explained by energy flow diagram.

The transfer of energy from one trophic level to another trophic level is called *energy flow*. The flow of energy in an ecosystem is unidirectional, i.e. it flows from the producer level to the consumer level and never in the reverse direction. Hence, energy can be used only once in the ecosystem.

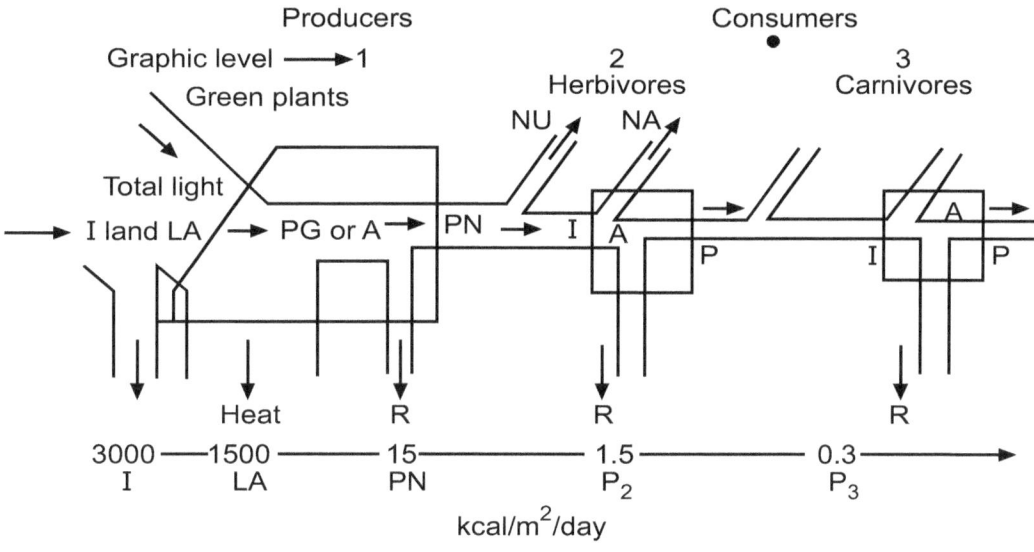

Fig. 1.14 : Simplified energy flow diagram depicting three trophic levels (boxes numbered 1, 2, 3) in a linear food chain

I – Total energy input; LA – light absorbed by plant cover; PG – gross primary production; A – total assimilation; PN – net primary production; P – secondary (consumer) production; NU – energy not used (stored or exported); NA – energy not assimilated by consumers (egested); R – respiration, Bottom line in the diagram shows the order of the magnitude of energy losses expected at major transfer points, starting with a solar input of 3,000 kcal per square metre per day.

(After E.P. Odum, 1963)

The figure represents a very simplified energy flow model of free trophic levels, from which it becomes evident that the energy flow is greatly reduced at each successive trophic level from producers to herbivores and then to carnivores.

Thus, at each transfer of energy from one level to another level, major part of energy is lost as heat or other form.

In the figure, the boxes represent the trophic levels and the pipes depict the energy flow in and out of each level. Energy inflows balance outflows as required by the first law of thermodynamics and energy transfer is accompanied by dispersion of energy into unavailable heat i.e. respiration as required by the second law.

Thus, as shown in figure, about 3000 kcal of total light falls on the green plants, of this approximately 50% i.e. 1500 kcal is absorbed, of which only 1 per cent (15 kcal) is converted at first trophic level. Thus, the net primary production is merely 15 kcals. Secondary productivity (P_2 and P_3 in diagram) tends to be about 10 per cent at successive consumer trophic levels i.e. herbivores and the carnivores although efficiency may be sometimes higher as 20%, at the carnivore level as shown (or $P_3 = 0.3$ kcal) in the diagram.

1.4.2 Food Chain

In an ecosystem, various living organisms such as plants and animals are arranged in a definite sequence according to their food habits. Plants are producers which are eaten by herbivores. The herbivores which in turn are eaten by carnivores. This transfer of food energy from producers (plants) through a series of organisms (herbivores to carnivores to decomposers) with repeated eating and being eaten is known as the food chain.

Plants convert solar energy into chemical energy i.e. carbohydrates by the process of photosynthesis. The producers always remain in any ecosystem at the first trophic level or producers level. The food energy stored in the body of plants is utilized by herbivores or plant eater which form second trophic level called *primary consumers*. In an ecosystem, the herbivores are eaten by carnivores which constitute the third trophic level or *secondary consumers* level. These carnivores in turn may be eaten by other carnivores at the tertiary consumers level i.e. by *tertiary consumers*. In an ecosystem, there are number of organisms which eat both plants as well as animals at their lower level in food chain called an omnivores. Such organisms occupy more than one trophic levels in the food chain.

For example, plants are eaten by insects, who are eaten by frogs, these frogs are eaten by fish, who are eaten by human beings. In this food chain, there are five trophic or feeding levels. Several factors are important in determining an animal's place in a food chain. Each species occupies a specific place and has flow of energy in ecosystem, from sunlight through photosynthesis in autotrophic producers, to the tissues of herbivores, the primary consumers, to the tissue of carnivores, the secondary consumers, determines the number and biomass of organisms at each level in the ecosystem. Flow of energy is greatly reduced at each successive level of nutrition, because of the energy utilization by the organisms and heat losses at each step in transformation of energy. This largely accounts for the decrease in biomass at each successive level. In addition no predator is completely efficient at capturing its prey; some energy is lost in the hunt.

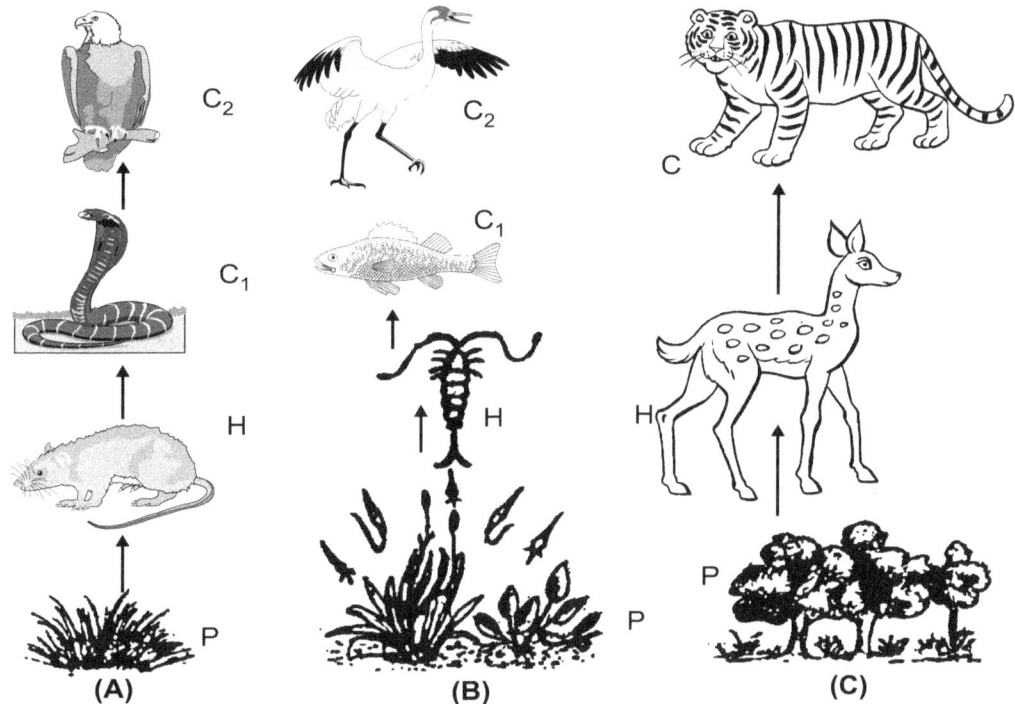

Fig. 1.15 : Food chains in nature

A – food chain in a grassland; B – food chain in a pond; C – food chain in a forest. The base of the food chain is always formed by autotrophs (producers). The links are usually 3 to 5 and the arrangement is mainly, producer → herbivore → carnivore (P = producer, H = herbivore, C_1 = carnivore order - 1, C_2 = carnivore order - 2)

An animal may be a primary consumer in one chain, eating plants but a secondary or tertiary consumer in other chains, eating herbivorous animals or other carnivores.

Food chain in grassland ecosystem starts with :

Grasses → Grasshopper → Frogs → Snakes → Hawk.

In pond ecosystem food chain starts with :

Phytoplanktons → Water fleas → Smaller fish → Bigger fish → Birds or Man.

In nature three types of food chains have been distinguished.

(1) Grazing Food Chain :

The consumers which start the food chain, utilizing plants or plant parts as their food, constitute the grazing food chain. The food chain begins from green plants at the base and the primary consumer is herbivore.

For example : Grass → Grasshopper → Birds → Hawk.

(2) Parasitic Food Chain :

It also begins from green plant base, then goes to herbivores which, for example, may be the host of a huge number of lice which live as ectoparasites.

(3) Detritus Food Chain :

This type of food chain goes from dead organic matter into micro-organisms and then to organisms feeding on detritus (detrivores) and their predators. Such ecosystems are thus less dependent on direct solar energy. These mainly depend on the influx of the organic matter produced in another system. For example, such type of food chain operates in the decomposing accumulated litter in a temperate forest. A good example of this food chain is based on mangroove leaves.

Leaves fallen in shallow water → Saprotrophs (fungi, bacteria, protozoa etc.) → eaten and re-eaten by small organisms like crabs, copepods, insect larvae, grass shrimp, mysid, nematodes, bivalve molluscs → Small carnivores → fish → birds (Top carnivores).

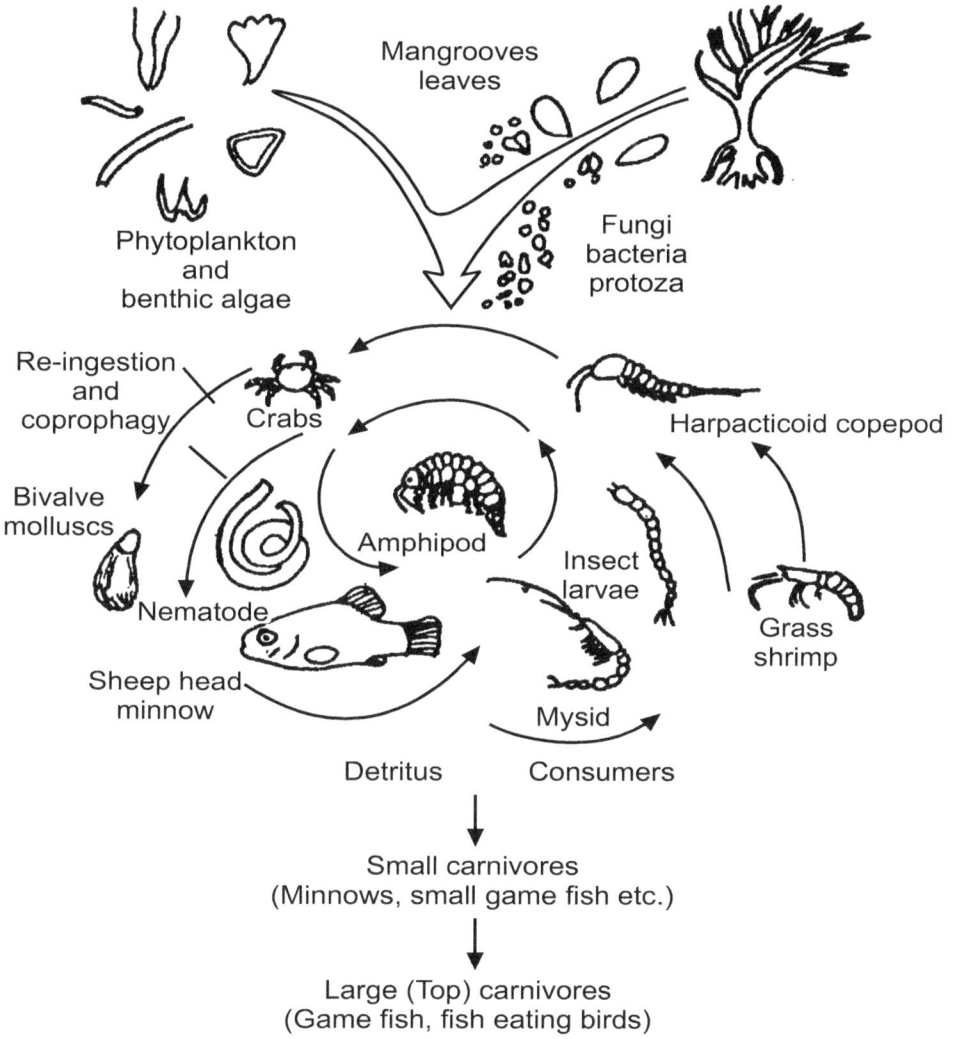

Fig. 1.16 : Detritus food chain based on mangrooves leaves falling into shallow estuary waters. Leaf fragments acted on by the saprotrophs and colonised by algae are eaten and re-eaten (coprophagy) by a key group of small detrivores which in turn, provide the main food for game fish, herons, storks and ibis

1.4.3 Food Web

Food chains in natural conditions never operate as isolated sequences, but in an ecosystem the various food chains are interconnected with each other forming some sort of interlocking pattern called **food web**. Simple food chains are very rare in nature this is because each organism may obtain food from more than one trophic level. In other words, one organism forms food for more than one organisms of the higher trophic level. For example, in grazing food chain of grassland, in the absence of rabbit, grass may also be eaten by mouse. The mouse in turn may be eaten directly by hawk or snake first which is then eaten by hawk.

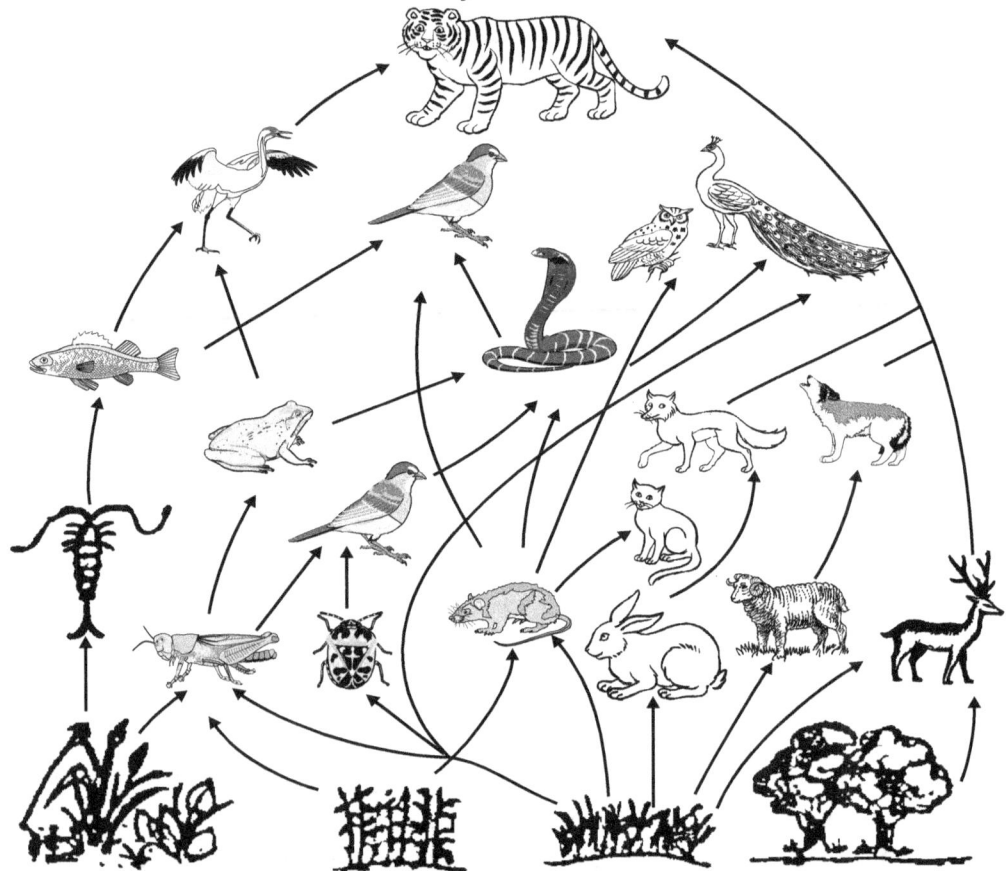

Fig. 1.17 : A food web shows the main food links and interconnection of many food chains. An organism may form a food source for many other organisms thus forming a web

The grass is eaten by grasshopper, rabbit and mouse. Grasshopper is eaten by lizard which is eaten by hawk. Rabbit is eaten by hawk. Mouse is eaten by snake which is eaten by hawk. In addition,

hawk also directly eats grasshopper and mouse. Thus, there are fine linear food chains which are interconnected to form a food web.
(1) Grass → Grasshopper → Hawk
(2) Grass → Grasshopper → Lizard → Hawk
(3) Grass → Rabbit → Hawk
(4) Grass → Mouse → Hawk
(5) Grass → Mouse → Snake → Hawk

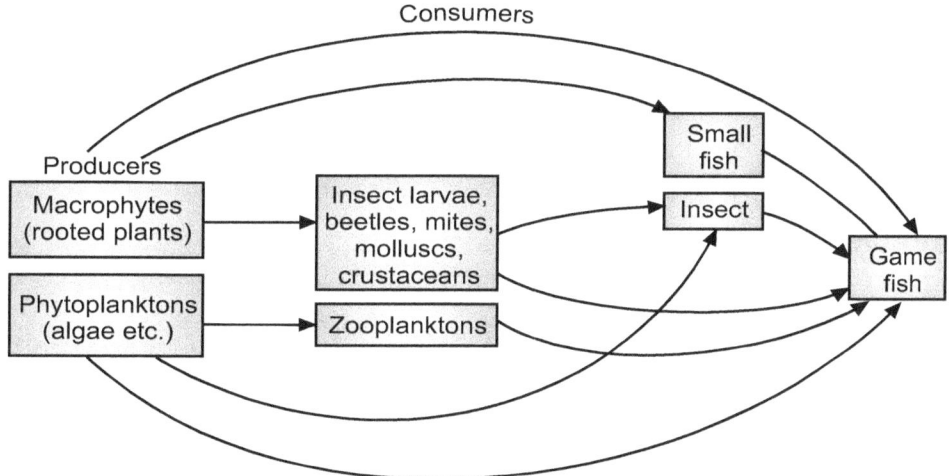

Fig. 1.18 : Diagrammatic sketch showing the food web in a pond

Food webs are very important in maintaining the stability of an ecosystem. For example, decrease in population of rabbit would naturally cause an increase in the population of alternative herbivore, the mouse. This may decrease the population of the consumer (carnivore) that prefers to eat rabbit. The alternatives or substitutes serve for maintenance of stability of the ecosystem. When one type of herbivore becomes extinct, the other types of herbivores increase in number and control the vegetation. Similarly, when one type of herbivorous animals becomes extinct, the carnivore predating on this type may eat another type of herbivore. Thus, each species of any ecosystem is indeed kept under some sort of a natural check, so that the system may remain balanced. The complexity of any food web depends upon the diversity of organisms in the system.

1.4.4 Ecological Pyramids

The number, biomass and energy of organisms gradually decrease from the producer level to the consumer level. These few steps of tropic level can be expressed in a diagrammatic way and are referred to as ecological pyramids. Ecological pyramid is the graphic representation of the number, biomass, and energy of the successive trophic levels of an ecosystem. **Charles Elton** in 1927, first used and described the term ecological pyramid. In the ecological pyramid, the producers forms the base and the final consumer occupies the apex. The ecological pyramids are of three types :

(1) Pyramid of numbers
(2) Pyramid of biomass
(3) Pyramid of energy

(1) Pyramid of Numbers :

They shows the relationship between producers, herbivores and carnivores at successive trophic levels in terms of their number. The number of individuals at the trophic level decreases from the producer level to the consumer level. The number of producers in an ecosystem is very high. The number of herbivores is lesser than the producers.

Similarly number of carnivores is lesser than the herbivores. For example, in crop lands the producers or crops are more in numbers and the grasshoppers feeding on crop plants are lesser in number. The frogs feeding on grasshopper are still lesser in number. The snakes feeding on frogs are fewer in number. In pond ecosystem, the number decreases in the following order :

Phytoplankton → Zooplankton → Fishes → Snakes

Thus, the pyramid is upright. In a forest ecosystem, however, the pyramid of numbers is somewhat different in shape. The producers are large sized trees are lesser in number and form the base of pyramid. The herbivores, fruit eating birds, elephants, deers etc. are more in number than the producers. Then there is gradual decrease in the number of successive carnivores, thus making the pyramid again upright.

However, in a parasitic food chain, the pyramids are always inverted. This is due to the fact that a single plant may support the growth of many herbivores and each herbivore in turn may provide nutrition to several parasities which support many hyper-parasites. Thus, from the producers towards consumers, there is reverse position, i.e. the number of organisms gradually shows an increase making the pyramid inverted in shape.

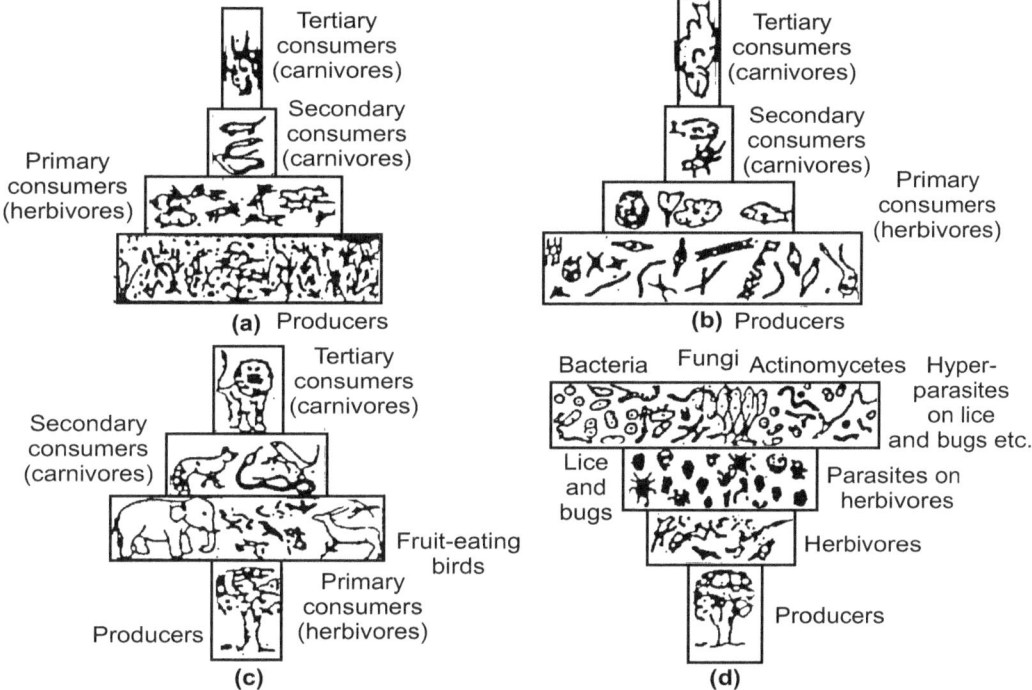

Fig. 1.19 : Pyramid of numbers (individuals per unit area) in different kinds of ecosystem/food chains (a) Grassland ecosystem, (b) Pond ecosystem, (c) Forest ecosystem. In (a) – (c) parasitic micro-organisms and soil animals are not included, (d) parasitic food chain.

Actually the pyramids of numbers do not give a true picture of the food chain as they are not very functional. They do not indicate the relative effects of the 'geometric', 'food chain' and size factors of the organisms. They generally vary with different communities with different types of food chains in the same environment. It becomes sometimes very difficult to represent the whole community on the same numerical scale (for example; forest).

(2) Pyramid of Biomass :

Biomass refers to the total weight of living matter per unit area.

Therefore, the pyramid of biomass is to weigh individuals in each trophic level instead of counting them. This would give us a pyramid of biomass i.e. the total weight of all organisms at a given level. In an ecosystem, the biomass decreases from the producer level to the consumer level. For most ecosystems on land, the pyramid of biomass has a large base of primary producers with a small trophic level perched on the top. In grassland and forest, there is generally a gradual decrease in biomass of organisms at successive levels from

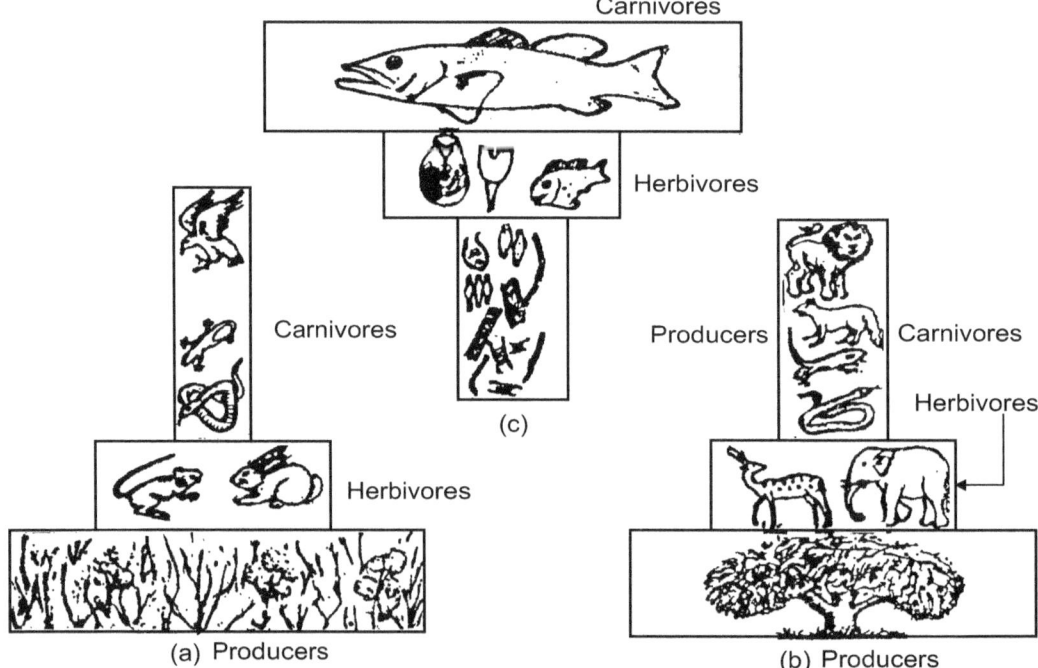

Fig. 1.20 : Pyramids of biomass (g dry wt. per unit area) in different kinds of ecosystems (a) Grassland, (b) Forest, (c) Pond

the producers to the top carnivores. Thus, pyramids are upright. However, in a pond or aquatic ecosystem as the producers are small organisms, their biomass is least, this value gradually shows an increase towards the apex of the pyramid, thus pyramid becomes inverted in shape.

(3) Pyramid of Energy :

Of the three types of ecological pyramids, the pyramid of energy is most informative and give the best picture of overall nature of the ecosystem. The energy flows in an ecosystem from the producer level to the consumer level. At each trophic level 80 to 90% of energy is lost. Hence, the amount of energy decreases from the producer level to the consumer level. This can be represented by pyramid of energy. An energy pyramid more accurately reflects the laws of thermodynamics, hence the pyramid is always right side up, with a large energy base at the bottom. A pyramid of energy must be based on the determination of the actual amount of energy that individual make in, how much they burn up during metabolism, how much remains in their waste products and how much they store in the body tissue. The energy inputs and outputs are calculated so that energy flow can be expressed per unit of land or water per unit time. For example, an ecosystem receives 1000 calories of light energy in a given day. Most of the energy is not absorbed; some is reflected back to space; of the energy absorbed only a small portion is utilized by

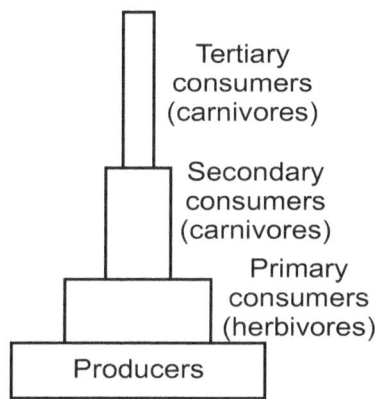

Fig. 1.21 : Pyramid of energy (kcal per unit area within unit time, season or years) in any ecosystem

green plants, out of which the plant uses up some for respiration and of the 1000 calories, therefore only 100 calories are stored as energy rich materials. Now suppose an animal, say a deer, eats the plant containing 100 calories of food energy. The deer uses some of it for its own metabolism and stores only 10 calories as food energy. A lion that eats the deer gets an even smaller amount of energy. Thus, usable energy decreases from sunlight to producer to herbivore to carnivore. Therefore, energy pyramid will always be upright.

1.5 Ecological Succession

The biotic communities are not stable. They are changing into different communities or forms in a longer time span. The changes which occur in community composition and structure are larger. Thus in a particular geographical area, one community may be replaced by another community or by a series of communities. This can be explained with the example of pond or lake community which fills with silt and changes gradually from a deep to a shallow pond or lake then transformed into a marshy land community if it is filled with sand and mud. In the course of time, the marshy land may be converted into grassland or a dry land forest community. If forest is completely burned over, it remains as a plot of bare ground, on which after some period series of plant communities grow up and replace one another first annual weeds, then perennial weeds and grasses, then shrubs and trees and formation of forest community. Thus, the process of formation of new communities is called ecological succession. It is defined as an orderly and progressive replacement of one community by another till the development of a stable community in that area. The stable community is called climax community. Thus, succession is the birth of ecosystem and subsequent aging process of its biotic and abiotic factors.

Characteristics of Ecological Succession :
(1) It is an orderly process of community development that involves changes in the species structure and community processes within time.
(2) It is directional and predictable.
(3) Succession results due to the modifications of physical environment by the community.
(4) It is transformed into a stabilized ecosystem with maximum biomass and symbiotic functions between organisms.
(5) Due to increase in biomass new habitat niches are created.

(6) There is continuous change in plants and animals in succession.

(7) The diversity of species tends to increase with succession.

Types of Succession : In the succession, formation of stable or climax community takes place by several communities which replace one another in an orderly sequence. The various development stages of a community are called *sere,* and each stage where change take place is called *seral* stage, which represents community although temporary with its own characteristics and may of short or long life. The final stable community is called climax community.

The ecological succession may be of the following two types in any of the two basic environments such as terrestrial and aquatic environments.

(1) Primary Succession : If the development of the community begins on a sterile area which has been not occupied by any community previously. Then the succession is called *primary succession.*

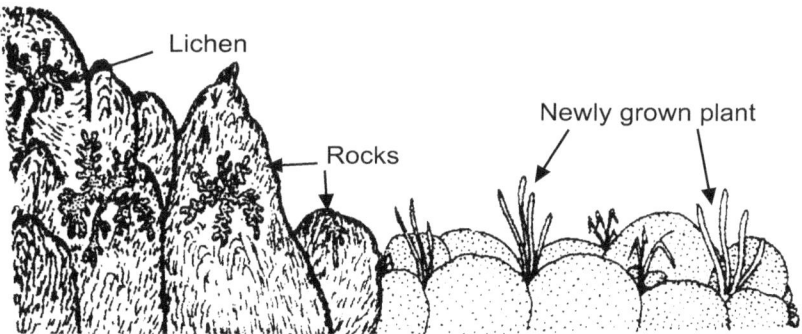

Fig. 1.22 : Primary succession on an island

For example, on newly exposed island the first organisms which start the ecological succession are called *pioneer community.* The process starts with base rock or sand dune or river delta or glacial debris and it ends when climax is reached. This is also example of primary succession. Suppose landslide exposes a surface of rock in the mountains, on which first of all lichens, the pioneer community will develop. Then in course of time spreading moss mat appears and moss is followed by grasses, herbs, shrubs and finally by larger trees. The trees become dominant community and forest community is formed.

(2) Secondary Succession : When community development starts on the areas or sites previously occupied by well developed communities called secondary succession. In this situation, organic matter and some organisms from the original community will remain. For example, areas burned by fire or cut by farmers for cultivation, cut over forests, abondoned crop lands and ploughed fields are the examples of secondary succession.

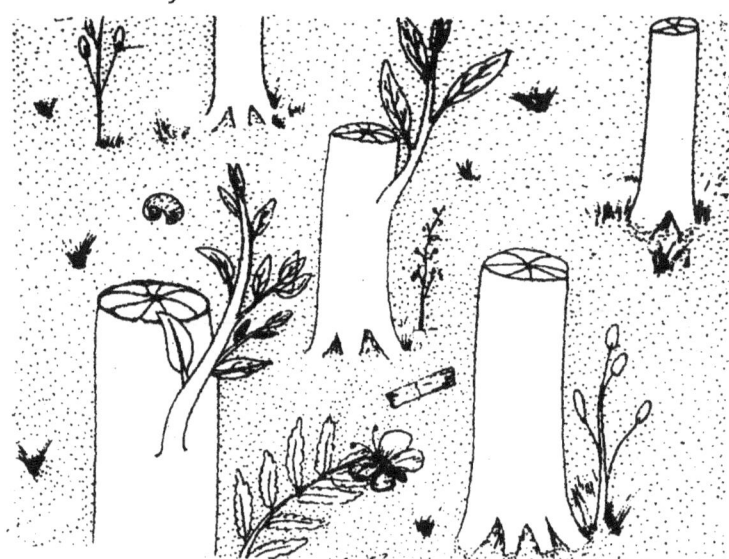

Fig. 1.23 : Secondary succession in a forest

Depending on the moisture contents the succession may be of the following types :

(a) **Hydrach or Hydrosere :** The succession when starts in aquatic environment like ponds, lakes, streams, swamps etc. called *hydrach* or *hydrosere*.

(b) **Mesarch or Mesosere :** The succession which begins in an area where adequate moisture is present called mesarch.

(c) **Xerach or Xerosere :** The succession when starts in dry habitat like deserts, rock etc. in which moisture is very scanty, it is called *xerach*. On the basis of community metabolism succession is of two types, namely *autotrophic succession* (dominance of plants) and *heterotrophic* succession (bacteria, fungi and animals).

Process of Succession :

Following sequential steps involve in the process of succession.

(1) Nudation : The process starts with formation of a bare area or nudation by several causes, such as flooding, erosion, volcanic eruption, fire etc. There are many new lifeless areas are created by man e.g. stone quarrying, walls, burning, digging, flooding large land areas under dams etc.

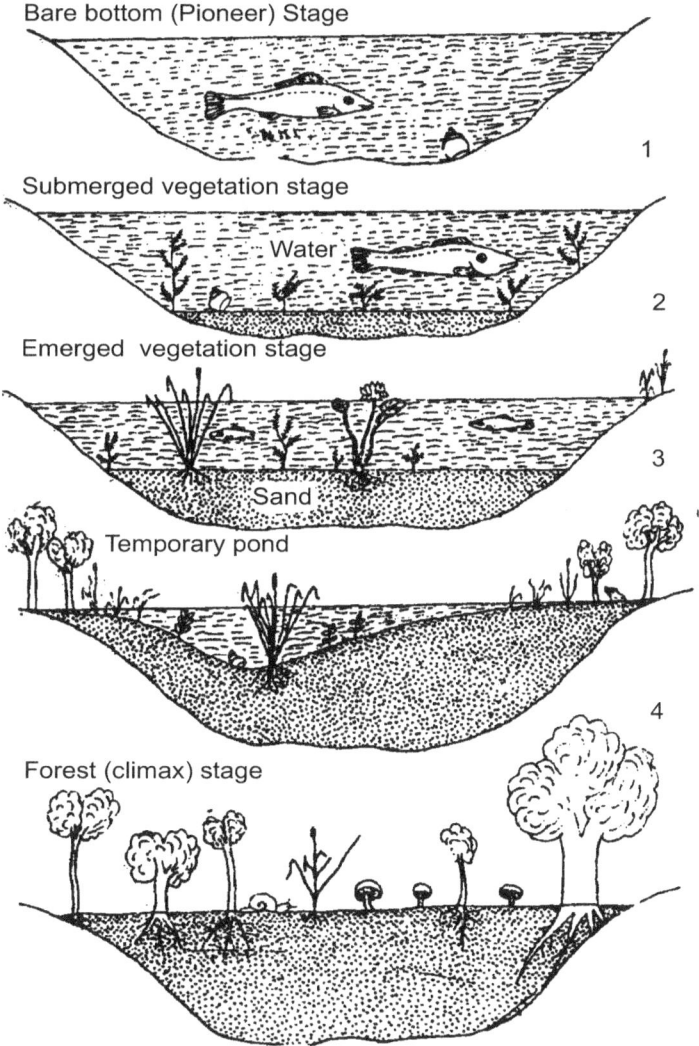

Fig. 1.24 : Ecological succession. A pond community is replaced by a forest community through ecological succession

(2) Invasion : It involves the arrival and settlement of various organisms on bare area. The plants are the first invaders hence called pioneers in this area. The seeds, spores reach on base area through air, water or animals. This is called *dispersal* or migration. When new migrated species establish on the new area by germination and start reproducing. This is called *ecesis*. Very few species can establish in new and hard environment and remaining disappear. The successful immigrants establish propogate and increase their number forming a large population in the area called aggregation. This the final stage of invasion.

(3) Competition and Reaction : In the limited area, the number of species or individuals increase due to reproduction, multiplication which ultimately results into competition for food and space.

This competition is of two types namely *intraspecific competition* in which competition is in between the individuals of same species and *interspecific competition* i.e. competition between the individuals of other species. The individuals interact with each other as well as with environment. Due to interactions the individuals modify the environment and it becomes unsuitable for the existing community. In the course of time they are replaced by another community members who find this environment more suitable. These new inveders compete with previous occupants and ultimately they are eliminated or brought to subdominant level. The small plants enrich the environment for larger plants or trees by organic matter, moisture and nutrients. The animal community also develops in the area because of availability of food. Again interactions among individuals further modify the environment and allow to invade another species of plants and animals which move the process of succession.

(4) Stabilization or Climax : The final terminal community becomes permantly stable in the area which is mature and self maintaining and self reproducing. This community is tolerent to the environmental conditions and it shows equilibrium as well as species diversity. This dominant and stable community is called climax community.

Points to Remember

- Ecology is important branch of science and divided into autecology and synecology.
- There are several branches of ecology like habitat ecology, conservation ecology, radiation ecology, paleoecology, human ecology, gene ecology, space ecology etc.
- Ecology uses the knowledge of different subjects.
- Biotic factors are living factors and abiotic factors are non-living factors.
- Animals, plant and microbs are biotic factors.
- Animal associations are of two types, intraspecific and interspecific associations.
- Intraspecific associations are always among the animals of same species.
- Interspecific associations are always among two animals of different species.
- Symbiosis, commensalism, mutualism are beneficial associations.
- Parasitism is harmful animal association.
- In predatism there is immediate killing of the prey.
- Parasites are of two types namely ectoparasites and endoparasites.
- Further parasites are classified into temporary, permanent facultative, obligatory, occasional, wandering, stationary and periodic parasites.
- Hosts are also of different types such as definitive host intermediate host, paratenic host, vectors and reservoir host.
- Water, temperature, light, gases, humidity and soil are the abiotic factors.
- Species, community, ecological niche, ecosystem are various ecological terms.
- Autotrophs, heterotrophs and decomposers are the components of ecosystem.

- Different types of ecosystems like pond, grass, land ecosystems are the types of ecosystems.
- Different types of biomes like Tundra, Alpine, Forest, Desert biomes are classified.
- Biosphere is made up of hydrosphere, lithosphere and atmosphere.
- Atmosphere has different components.
- Lithosphere has also different parts.
- Plants absorb solar energy for food production.
- The behaviour of energy in ecosystem is called energy flow.
- In food chain, animals are arranged in a definite sequence according to their food habits.
- In case of food web many food chains are interconnected with other forming interlocking pattern called food web.
- Pyramid of numbers, pyramid of biomass and pyramid of energy are the ecological pyramids.
- Ecological succession is the process of formation of new communities and it is of types namely primary and secondary succession.

Exercise

1. Define the term ecology. Describe the different branches of ecology.
2. Describe the various biotic and abiotic factors and their importance in study of ecology.
3. Give an account of animal associations.
4. What is mean by intra and interspecific associations? Describe with suitable examples.
5. What is parasite? Describe different types of parasites.
6. What is host? Describe different types of hosts.
7. Give brief account of the following terms :
    (a) Species,

(b) Community,
(c) Ecological niche,
(d) Ecosystem,
(e) Biome,
(f) Biosphere,
(g) Atmosphere,
(h) Lithosphere,
(i) Hydrosphere,
(j) Intraspecific associations
(k) Interspecific association
(l) Symbiosis
(m) Mutualism
(n) Commensalism
(o) parasitism
(p) Predatism
(q) Host.

8. Define ecosystem. Describe the structure of ecosystem and give an account pond ecosystem.
9. What is biosphere? Describe the different components of the biosphere.
10. What is food chain? Give an account of different types of food chains.
11. What is food web? Describe food web with suitable diagram.
12. Write short notes on :
    (a) Scope of ecology,
    (b) Temperature as a abiotic factor,
    (c) Abiotic factor light,
    (d) Atmospheric gases,
    (e) Abiotic factor soil,
    (f) Grass land ecosystem,
    (g) Energy flow in ecosystem,

(h) Food chain,
(i) Food web,
(j) Ecological pyramids,
(k) Pyramid of biomass,
(l) Pyramid of energy,
(m) Pyramid of numbers.

13. What is ecological pyramids? Give an account of different types of ecological pyramids.
14. What is ecological succession? Describe different types of succession.

UNIT 2...
Ethology

Contents ...

2.1 Introduction
2.2 Mimicry
2.3 Camouflage in *Chameleon*
2.4 Courtship Behaviour in Scorpion and Weaver Bird
    2.4.1 Courtship Behaviour in Scorpion
    2.4.2 Courtship Behaviour in Weaver Bird
    2.4.3 Courtship Behaviour in Birds
2.5 Social Behaviour in Honey Bees
    2.5.1 Life History of the Honey Bee
    2.5.2 Bee Behaviour
    2.5.3 Communication in Bees
* Points to Remember
* Exercise

2.1 Introduction

The main aim of evolution is the adaptation of an organism to its environment. Thus, the evolution is nothing but progressive adaptation. Successful and continuous existence of any species depends on good adaptations. *Colouration* and *mimicry* are two important aspects of adaptations and hence evolution. *Camouflage* is a trick used by animal to deceive an enemy. Such tricks are used by various animals to protect themselves. Mimicry is a protective resemblance of an animal to an inanimate object or the simulation for self preservation by a harmless species in the form, appearance, colour, and behaviour of another species which is unpalatable or dangerous. In camouflage colouration plays an important role for the protection of an animal.

Colouration : It is a biological phenomenon where the animals develop different colours and colour patterns for protection, warning, frightening the enemies, capturing prey, recognising mates and so on.

The colour appears in animal due to physical and chemical factors. Retration and defraction are physical factors while chemical factors are pigments. Melanin, carotene, pterin etc. are the various pigments found in animals. On the basis of the purpose of colouration it is divided into the following types :

(1) Protective colouration   (2) Aggressive colouration
(3) Warning colouration   (4) Alluring colouration
(5) Recognition colouration.

(1) Protective Colouration : Most colours of animals have a protective value for hormonizing with the surroundings to evade enemies. The animals develop colour patterns to conceal themselves from the predators. It is also called concealing colouration or cryptic colouration. There are several examples of this type such as : snow animals are white, forest animals are striped or spotted for concealment, desert animals are sandy or dull in colour. Counter shading is a colouration where the upper surface of the body is dark and lower surface is light.

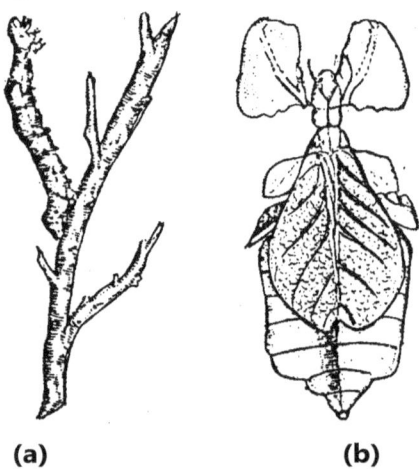

(a)   (b)

Fig. 2.1 : (a) Geometrid caterpillar (b) *Phyllium*

As a result when animal is looked from below, it merges with the colour of the sky, when looked from above, it merges with the darkness of the depth especially in the aquatic habitat.

Countershading is effective in camouflage and helps the animals to escape recognition.

A number of stick caterpillars, the larvae of moths resemble twigs in their colour, shape and posture.

Their colour remarkably resembles their background. Birds could not distinguish at sight the larva of the moth from the twigs of the tree on which the caterpillars were feeding.

Spiders and insects living on the bark of trees resemble the bark or mosses or lichens growing on it. Fishes living in sea weeds often have leafy outgrowths of body surface. *Phyllopteryx* is an Australian fish related to the sea horse *Hippocampus*. It lives in sea weeds and its body has cutaneous ribbon like outgrowths which disguises the animal in the weeds.

Certain varieties of moths and butterflies have conspicuous large markings on the wings. These markings represent imitations of vertebrates eyes.

Fig. 2.2 : *Phyllopteryx*

These eye spots are used by some insects as defence mechanisms. The true eyes of an animal is more conspicuous and indicates the position of head which is more vulnerable to the attack by predators. The insects develop eye spots in parts of the body which are not vulnerable to attack. Thus the predators attack the eye spot area assuming that it is head and vulnerable. Hence, the insects escape from attack is affected. For example, the owl, butterfly, eyed hawk moth.

The wings are provided with prominent eye spots. The predators attack the wings instead of head. Certain insects display flash colouration to confuse the predators and thus protect them.

For example, Insect large yellow underwing, *Triphaena pronuba*, has marking on the body. These marking are concealed when at rest. When it files away in an erratic manner the colour is very conspicuous and gives a flashing effect as the insect moves. This device helps the insect to escape from the predators when chased.

The cuttle fish *Sepia* uses a dark smoke screen to escape from the predators. The ink gland releases granules of melanin pigment when predator attacks. In the dark smoke cloud, predator is unable to detect prey, thus allowing the cuttle fish to escape.

(2) Aggressive Colouration : In aggressive colouration, the animals develop colour pattern to threaten or frighten other animals. For example, the eyed Hawk Moth, uses the eye spots to threaten the predator.

(3) Warning Colouration : Certain animals are provided with certain unpleasant or dangerous attributes like unpleasant taste, unpalatability, poison, abnoxious odour, sting and so on. These animals are couspicuously coloured and they advertise their unpleasant or dangerous attributes to the predators. For example, blue spots on the electric ray Tarpedo are for advertising the awaiting dangers of an electric shock. *Porcupines* have black and white quills, it takes no pains to conceal itself, and some have a rattle of hollow quills on the tail which is used for warning.

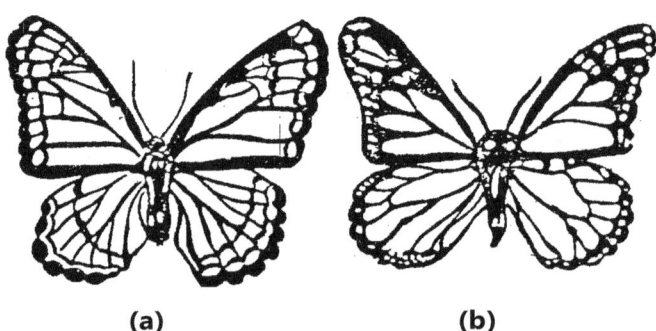

(a)   (b)

Fig. 2.3 : *(a) Basilarchia* **(Victory butterfly)**
(b) Danais **(Monarch butterfly)**

Rattle snake is brightly coloured and has a rattle on the tail to keep intruders away.

The victory butterfly is edible and resembles in colour pattern to the monarch butterfly.

Heloderma has conspicuous black brown, yellow and orange colours. It moves with safety because it is the only known poisonous lizard.

2.2 Mimicry

Mimicry is also a protective adaptation. The concept of mimicry was first introduced by **Bates (1862).** Mimicry is defined as the resemblances of one organism to another or to any natural object for the purpose of concealment, protection or for some other advantages. The animal resemble other unpalatable or dangerous animals in form, appearance, colour and behaviour, which resemble inanimate objects to escape from its enemies. The organism which exhibits mimicry is called *mimic* or *mimetic* and to which it imitates is called *model*.

On the basis of mimicry, it is classified into two types namely.

(1) Protective mimicry

(2) Aggressive mimicry.

There is another classification of mimicry based on the views of two scientists. They are (1) Mullerian mimicry and (2) Batesian mimicry.

(1) Protective mimicry : When mimicry gives protection to the mimic, the mimicry is called protective mimicry. In this mimicry, the animal imitates with an animal or inanimate object which is inedible or poisonous. According to **Wallace**, for this mimicry the imitative form must occur in the same locality and occupy the same station. Moreover, imitators should not possess defensive mechanism. This device is possible either by concealment or by warning.

(a) Concealing Device : This is very common mimicry in which the mimic tries to conceal it from its predators by mimicking the model or search a background which resembles their colour or to adjust with the existing background.

(i) Mimicking the Objects : The stick caterpillars of geometric moth *Solenia tetralunaria* resembles young twigs in colour and shape. Again its posture on the twig is fantastic. It is attached to the main twig by its posterior end and the entire body stands oblique to the twig so that it appears like a small branch; its pointed head resembles the terminal bud. The stick insects of walking stick insects also resembles the twigs in having slender bodies, sympathetic colouration and attenuated limbs. The pointed head and feet resemble terminal buds.

The leaf insect *Phyllium* lives among green leaves on the trees. Its wings and legs are green like the colour of leaves. The small yellowish white spot resembles the fungus or rust developed on the leaf.

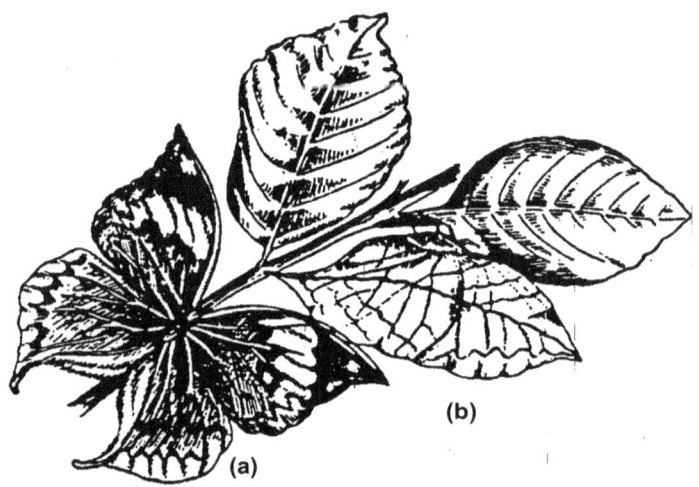

Fig. 2.4 : *Kallima paralecta.* **A-with wings spread.
B-with wings floded**

The dead leaf butterfly *Kallima paralecta* has very bright coloured wings on dorsal side while ventral side of the wings is dull brown which resembles with dry, dead leaves. When it settles on the dried leaves, the wings are folded and kept vertically upwards and the dull brown colour is exposed, which resembles the dry leaf of the twig. The wings show the midrib and the lateral ribs of the leaf.

The Australian sea horse *Phyllopteryx eques* resemble sea weeds because it bears numerous leaf like cutanous outgrowths.

(ii) Search of New Matching Background : Many animals move from one place to another in order to find out suitable matching background. This type of mimicry is shown by animals which are not able to change their colour. For example, caterpillar of *Noctuid* moth is blue green in colour with six long longitudinal white stripes. This colour resembles the pine needles. The colour of the animal becomes brown after last moult hence it move towards the brown twigs.

(iii) Change in Colour According to the Environment : Some animals protect themselves by changing their body colour according to the environment. For example, the white crab *Cryptolithodes* resembles a white quartz pebble on the beach with smooth rounded form and texture. Its colour matches with quartz so that it becomes difficult to notice it.

(b) Warning Mimicry : There are some harmless or palatable animals which mimic the harmful or non-palatable animals. Similarly, non-poisonous organisms mimic the poisonous animals. By this the mimics warn the enemies and protect themselves. For example, certain non-poisonous coral snakes exhibit colour pattern of coral snakes which are poisonous. The non-poisonous snake *Lycodon* mimics the poisonous krait (*Bungaris*) in its colour pattern. The non-poisonous snake *Heterodox* (hog-nose snake) possesses triangular, flattened head. The snake produces frequent hissing and strikes to exhibit its dangerousness. In addition to such mimicry many palatable animals simulate non-palatable forms and are saved from the predators. The edible butterfly, *Basilarchia archippus* resembles inedible immune monarch butterfly, *Anosia plexippus*. It is mistaken by the birds and thus saved. Certain spiders resemble ants in colour pattern and general appearance. They live in association with these ants and hence are mistaken as ants by their predators.

(c) Cryptic Structures : Some forms like south American butterfly, caterpillars, fishes, peacock etc. possess dark brown or black spots with light brightly coloured rings around them. These spots are generally present on the wings or body and acts as deflective. In this case, the pursueing enemy is generally attracted towards the prominent eye spots which infact is less vulnerable part of the body.

There are certain snakes which maintain their heads still but move the terminal parts of their tail in order to divert the attention of the predator. In many animals, the true head is either inconspicuous or concealed below the body. In such cases, the posterior part simulates the head in almost all respects. This head is called as dummy head which is generally attacked by the predators. For example, Lantern fly from Thailand possess dummy head.

(2) Aggressive Mimicry : In this type of mimicry, the mimic is the aggressive and it preys upon the model. Mimics possess some lure to attract the prey. For example, if a predator resembles its prey, the predator may be able to approach its victim more easily than it could otherwise do.

2.3 Camouflage in Chameleon

Different animals exhibit different body colours. These colours are useful to protect the animal. Concealment is often achieved either by hiding under the cover provided by the soil or vegetation or by specific colouration. Due to colours in the form of lines or bars on the body, the animal cannot be recognised. The most colourations form the morphological character of the species and these are due to pigments. Pigments occur in nearly all parts of an animal, not only on the surface but also in the deeper parts of the body. The colour is produced due to the absorptive powers of the chemical substance of which the tissues are composed. For example, haemoglobin, haemocyanin. This type of colouration is of no significance to the animals.

The pigments which is situated in the superficial layer gives a colour to the organism which may have a real value in the struggle for existence. The chromatophores or changeable pigment spots. The chromatophores produce the flushes of colour which pass over the skin of **Chameleon**. The chromatophores are influenced by the eyes and skin through the pituitary gland produce colour change as in African lizard.

How and why do *Chameleon* Change Colour ?

It is believed that *Chameleons* change colour in response to their environment. Sometimes they change colour based on temperature, light intensity and mood. Some scientists consider that there is myth that *chameleon* change colour to blend in with their surroundings, but this is actually not true. Most of the reasons *Chameleons* change colour is as a signals, a visual signal of mood and aggression territory and mating behaviours. Different *chameleon* species are able to vary their colouration and pattern through combinations of pink, blue, red, orange, green, black, brown, yellow and purple. Colour change in *Chameleons* has functions in social signaling and in reactions to temperature and other conditions, as well as camouflage colour change signals a chameleon's physiological condition and intentions to other *chameleons*. *Chameleons* tend to show darker colours when angered or attempting to scate or intimidate other, while males show lighter, multicoloured patterns when courting females. Some species, such as Smith's dwarf *Chameleon*, adjust their colours for camouflage in accordance with the vision of the specific predator species (bird or snake) by which they are being threatened. The desert dwelling Namaqua chameleon also uses colour change as an aid to thermoregulation, becoming black in the cooler morning to absorb heat more efficiently, then a lighter gray colour to reflect light during the heat of the day. It may show both colours at the same time, neatly separated left from right by the spine.

Mechanism of Colour Change : The way that *Chameleons* actually do this is really molecular. Chameleons have specialised cells, called chromatophores, which contain pigments in their cytoplasm, in three layers below their transparent outer skin. These are the cells that change colour. The chromatophores in the upper layer, called Xanthophores and erythrophores, contain yellow and red pigments respectively.

Below the chromatophores is a second layer, of chromatophores called iridophores or guanophores these contain quanine, appearing blue or white. The deepest layer of chromatophores, called melanophores, contain the dark pigment melanin, which controls how much light is reflected. Now how does the chameleon change colour? Well those chromatophores are connected by nerves to the nervous system.

Fig. 2.5 : *Chameleon*

They are sensitive to chemicals that are washing around the blood stream of the *Chameleon*. What happens is that the colours are locked away in tiny vesicles, little sacs inside the cells that keep them in one place, so the cell do not look coloured. But when a signal comes in from the nervous system or from the blood stream, the granules or vesicles can discharge, allowing the colour to spread out across the cell. It is rather like giving the cell a coat of paint. By varying the relative amount of activity of the different chromatophores in different layers of the skin, it is like mixing different paints together. So if you mix red and yellow, you get orange, for example, and this is how chameleon do this. They mix different contributions of the chromatophores. It is a bit like on your television screen. When you mix different colours together on the screen to get the colour that the eye ultimately perceives and so, that is how the chameleon changes colour and usually does so to convey mood.

The calm *Chameleon* is a pale green colour. When it gets angry, it might go bright yellow and when it wants to mate, it basically turns in every possible colour it can which shows that it's in the mood. This is not unique to Chameleons. Other animals also have these chromatophores.

2.4 Courtship Behaviours in Scorpion and Weaver Bird

The simplest definition of behaviour is movement, and it may be movement of legs in walking, wings in flying or heads in feeding. In another words, the animal behaviour consists of a series of muscular contractions. Thus, animal behaviour is the branch of zoology which deals with study of animal interactions with their living and non-living environments. It is also called as ***behavioural ecology***.

Reproductive behaviour possess a set of related questions about mating and the rearing of offspring. Before conception, there may be a struggle among males, and a characteristic sequence of behaviour patterns in which sexes court each other.

The term **courtship** is used by ethologists refers to all the behavioural interactions of male and female, which come before and lead upto the fertilization of eggs by sperms. The courtship behaviour brings two animals of different sexes of the same species under conditions where mating is likely to occur and to be successful. In courtship there is a complex sequence of interacting signals which ensure that an animal mates with an appropriate partner. For successful reproduction timeing is an important part i.e. both male and female must be in appropriate physiological condition of mating. Therefore, it is ensured by the synchronization of cycles that results from the interactions of environmental stimuli and two partners themselves. According to ethologists, many courtship patterns contain elements of conflict, it is because of initial response of an individual to a stranger in its vicinity may be aggressive.

The form and display of courtship vary from species to species. In some species, there is no courtship seen, whereas in some species courtship lasts for few minutes. In others, it may last for months. In case of waved albatrosses *Diomede irrorata*, inhabitants of Isla Espanola of the Galapagos islands may court each other with an extensive repertory of stero typed movements of neck and bill, for several hours a day, day in day out for much of the year. The question arises, why courtship exists and why in some species ?

The answer of this question is that courtship ensures that animal mate with other individual, of the same species, sex and condition. It is exhibited by the animals in form of numerous energetic and colourful displays. These are extreme structural modifications in males. These things are not easily explained.

Mating systems vary greatly from species to species. For example, the species of swans and geese one monogamous and pair for life. Many migratory birds form pair bonds that last for a single season. There are primates who are polygamous in which they pair with several individual partners for a particular period of time. In case of simultaneous polygamy, individual maintains simultaneous pair bonds with several individuals of the opposite sex. There are several mammalian species show many copulations and no pair bonds.

Different animals from different taxa show unique patterns of courtship and this behaviour has been studied by different ethologists.

Reproductive behaviour involves first the location of mate, followed by courtship and mating, oviposition and sometimes brood care.

2.4.1 Courtship Behaviour in Scorpion

Seasonal patterns of mating for most scorpion species are rather poorly known. Some species appear to exhibit fairly extended mating periods; for example, *Centruroides vittatus* and *Smeringurus mesaensis* have been observed mating througout the warner months of the year. Other species are known to have shorter mating periods ranging from two weeks to three months in mid-to-late summer (**Polis and Sisson, 1990**). It seems to be a general rule, however, that make scorpions (even burrowing species that tend to be sedentary during other parts of the year) become vagrant during the mating period in order to search for females. There is recent evidence that the male locates the female by encountering and following phenomones (attractant substance) that she releases at appropriate times of the year. The male senses the females pheromones with his pectines.

Fig. 2.6 : Scorpion courtship and mating

Mating in scorpions involves a highly ritualized series of behaviors that comprise the courtship dance. Upon contacting the female, the male will grasp her pedipalps with his own and begin leading her on the 'dance'. If she resists, he attempts to appease her with a 'kiss' this behaviour consists of touching and kneading the females chelicerae. Resistance by the female takes several forms, she may attempt to sting him, push him away with her stinger tucked in or simply refuse to dance. In some species, the male stings the female during the initial stages of courtship, slowly and deliberately inserting his aculens into the soft area of her body, leaving it in for as long as 10 minutes (**Francke, 1979**). It is not known if he is actually injecting her with venom or some other chemical substance. Almost invariably, however, her response is a passive one.

Because sperm transfer is not direct, the pair does not copulate. The males ultimate goal is to locate a suitable place to deposit a spermatophore, a structure carrying the sperm pocket; that is extruded from his body and glued to some hard surface. If he is successful, he will pull her over the spermatophore so that she can pick up the sperm packet in her genital pore. After this the male releases his grip and the two (usually) go their separate ways. On, occasion, however, the male ends up being the victim of canabalism, supplying his mate with her first meal to nourish his unborn offspring.

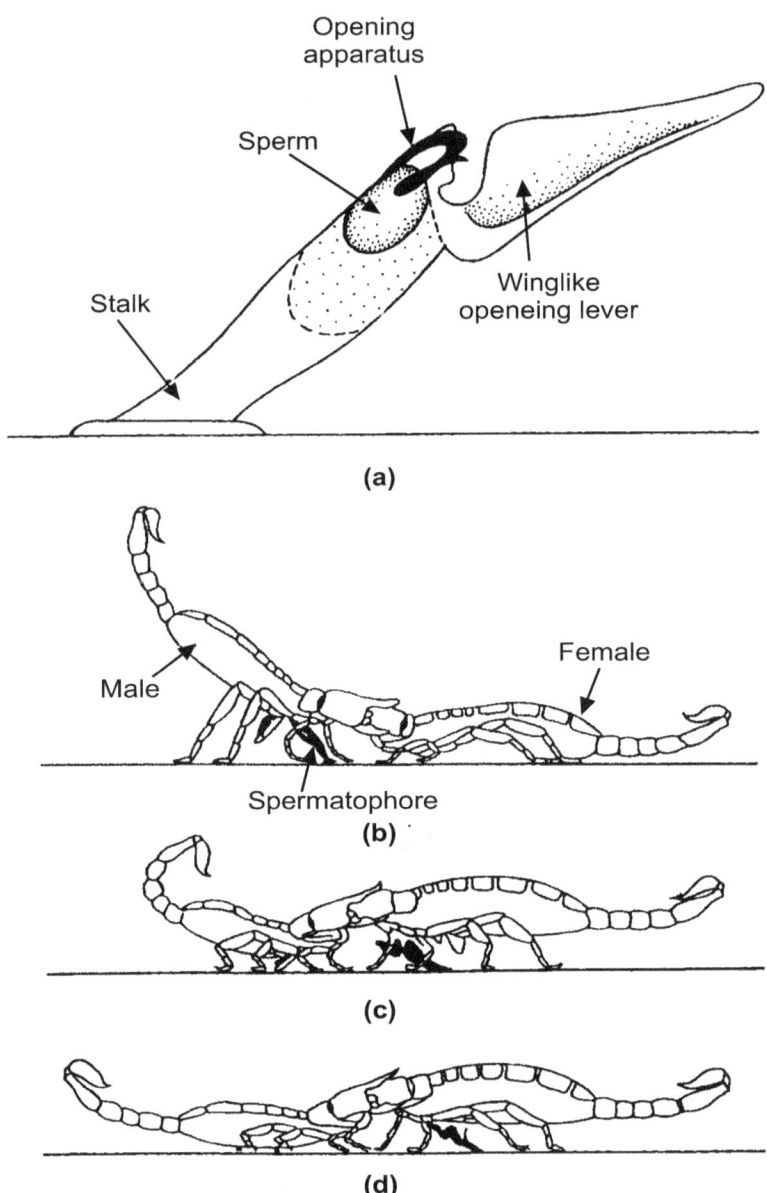

Fig. 2.7 : Courtship and mating in Scorpion (a) A spermatophore; (b) Sperm transfer in scropion. (c) While holding the female's pedipals in his own, the male (on the left) deposits the spermatophore on the ground. (c) The female is pulled over the spermatophore. (d) The spermatophore is taken up into the female's gonopore.

2.4.2 Courtship Behaviour in Weaver Bird

The Baya Weaver (*Ploceus philippinus*) is a weaver bird found across south and south east Asia. Foods of these birds are found in grasslands cultivated areas, scrub and secondary growth and they are best known for their hanging retort shaped nests woven from leaves. The nest colonies are usually found on thorny trees or palm fronds and the nests are often built near water or hanging over water where predators cannot reach easily.

(a) Male race *philippinus* displaying at nest

(b) Male of burmanicus race with the bright yellow crown

Fig. 2.8

Baya weavers are social and gregarious birds. The breeding season of the Baya weaver is during the monsoons. Weavers are best known for the elaborately woven nests constructed by the males. These pendulous nests are retort-shaped, with a central nesting chamber and a long vertical tube that leads to a side entrance to the chamber. The nests are woven with long strips of paddy leaves, rough grasses and long strips from palm fronds. Each strip can be between 20 and 60 cm in length. A male bird is known to make up to 500 strips to complete a nest. The birds use their strong beaks to strip and collect the strands, and to weave and knot them while building their nests. The male take about 18 days to construct the complete nest with the intermediate "helmet stage", taking about 8 days. The nests are partially built before the males begin to display to passing females by flapping their wings and calling while hanging from their nests. The females inspect the nest and signal their acceptance of a male. Once a make and female are paired the male goes on to complete the nests by adding entrance funnel. Males are almost solely incharge of nest building, though their female partners may join in giving the finishing touches, particularly on the interiors. Females may modify interiors or add biobs of mud. A study has found that nest and nest location is more important than nest structure for the female when it selects the nest and mate. Females prefer nests high in trees, those over dry land, and those on thin branches.

Fig. 2.9 : Male *burmanicus* at half-built nest in "helmet stage" without the entrance funnel

Both male and females are polygamous. Males build many partial nests and begin courting females. The male finishes the nest only after finding a mate. The female lays about 2 to 4 white eggs and incubate them for about 14 to 17 days. Males may sometimes assist in feeding the chicks. The chicks leave the nest after 17 days. After mating with a female, the male typically court other females at other partially constructed nests. Intraspecific brood parasitism is know that is, females may lay their eggs in the nests of others.

The green heron exhibits elaborate courtship behaviour which includes songs with stereo-typed movements. Courtship beings when the male advertises himself by posturing on a treetop with up pointed bill and giving a call that sounds like skow. Females are attracted to the male's call and one female soon perches nearby and answers with

(a) Male of race philippinus   (b) Female of race philippinus

Fig. 2.10

slightly different call, skeow. The duct continues for some time, until the male allows the female to approach. Both birds then perform aerial dance above nest. Showing unique colours of the plumage of their species to one another. The pair returns to the treetop, male enters the nest, displays his coloured features. Male utters a soft song aaroo-aaroo. Then female enters the nest. They preen feathers of each other. Then mating takes place.

2.4.3 Courtship Behaviour in Birds

Various birds show various types of courtship behaviour. Initial features of the ritual is bird's song which attracts and excites the female. The male bird is generally aggressive in defense of his territory. Consequently, courtship in females often takes the form of reactions which tend to avoid provoking of the attack. For example, in case of female kestrel, a European falcon, show infantile behaviour reminding the appeasement employment by the young. Courtship ceremony begins by offering food to each other which is a behaviour pattern carried over from infancy.

Long legged shore birds called avocetes having webbed feet and slender up curved bill. Male and female both preen their features in a hosty fashion during courtship.

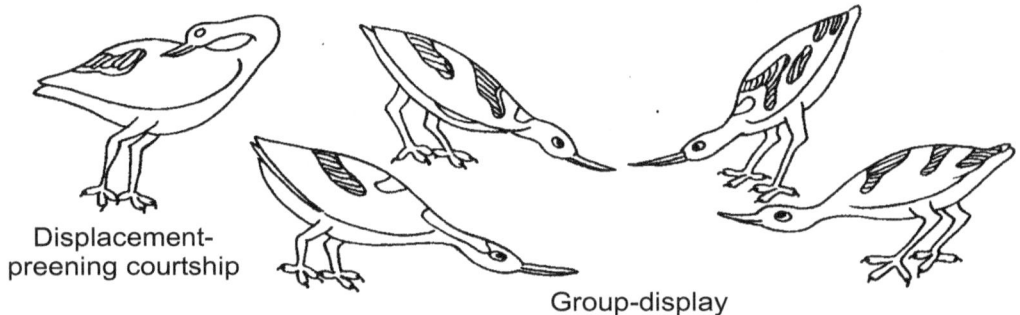

Fig. 2.11 : Displacement preening courtship and group display in avocete

In case of herring gull, the precoital displays are quite interesting. Both male and female bob their heads upward uttering a soft melodius call with each bob. After a series of such mutual head tossing the male takes the initiative in copulation and sudden mounts and mates.

Fig. 2.12 : Head-bobbing precoital display of herring gulls

Pair bounding and display of ritualised courtship dances in the great crested grebe are unique in animal kingdom. **Julian Huxely** (1914) studied it thoroughly. In their courtship ceremony includes a series of behaviours such as head shalking ceremony, dive and eat display, mutual greeting and eat displays, and penguin dance. In penguin dance, male and female birds dive and reappear with bunches of weeds in their bills. They swim towards one another, and then spring upright and move together shaking their heads from side to side, which crest and neck ruff raised. The weed or nest material is firmly held in the bill. This is called rituatlization for precoital displays of great-crested grebe.

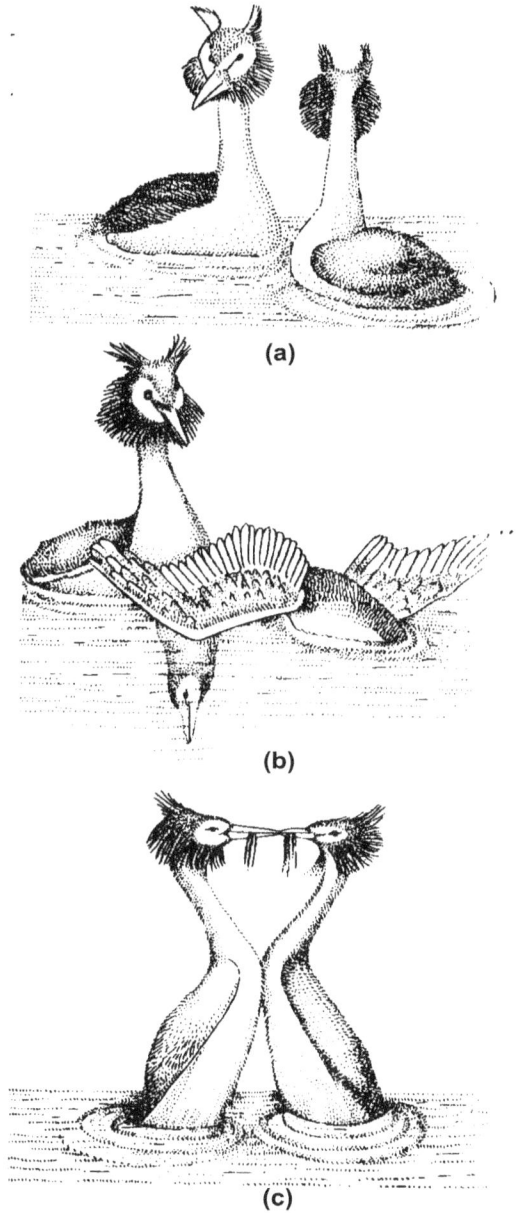

Fig. 2.13 : Penguin dance of great crested grebe

The bower birds are brilliantly coloured. They build display grounds and decorate them with various objects such as stones, flowers, shells etc. The satin bower bird found in East Australia constructs a power called rustic cottage with two parallel walls of arched twigs. On one side of bower is a display ground in which is found an assemblage of things and varieties of decorations such as blue parrot feathers, flowers, glass pieces, papers, shells, wasp nests etc. Display begins with sunrise and may occur throughout the day except during feeding; preening, bathing or calling. Male stands on his bower making a whirring noise, arches his tail in fan like manner stiffens his wings, keeping his neck low and erect. His plumage glistens magnificently while eyes bulge and become rose red. The dusky female utters sounds. She arranges the disordered twigs of the bower. Male makes sounds and many times males are rejected by females.

Then male copulates and female leaves to lay eggs and incubate them until they hatch, feed the hatchlings and take care around neighbourhood. Her partner stays at the bower and improves and decorate it. Some males who decorate the bower wall may copulate with more than one female.

Indian peacock is a polygymous bird. During breeding season cock forms a harem of 4 to 5 pea hens. The courtship behaviour of peacock is interesting. While courting the peacock spread its beautiful tail whenever a peahen approaches but as she comes near him he takes turn showing her his rear portion. If peahen is ready for mating, she would run swiftly around the tail to be able to see him from front again. The peacock responds by rustling his tail feathers. Then he will turn around again and this courtship game will be repeated several times. Finally the peahen will lie dow infront of him giving signals for mating.

2.5 Social Behaviour in Honey Bees

Caste, Colony Organization (Social Organization) and Division of Labour :

The highly evolved social organization of bees had been established before the existence of human race. Bees teach us the lesson of work and work with co-operation. A highly organised system of division of labour is found in colony of bees. The colony is highly polymorphic, comprising three varieties or castes - Queen, workers and drones. In a normal colony, there are one queen (Functional female). 25,000 - 35,000 workers (Sterile female) and 300-500 drones.

The queen after nuptial flight (mating) lays both fertilized and unfertilized eggs. From unfertilized eggs male bees are developed which are termed as drones, whereas from the fertilized eggs worker bees (sterile females) are produced. The workers when feed on royal jelly, develop in queen.

The Queen : The queen is the only perfectly developed fertile female. She is the mother of the colony and provided with well developed ovaries. Only one queen is present in each colony and feeds on royal jelly. Egg laying is the sole function of the queen throughout her active life span and lay 1,500 eggs in a day which is almost twice the weight of her body. The queen is 15 to 20 mm in length and can be easily distinguished by her long tapering abdomen, short legs and wings. She is unable to produce wax or honey or gather pollen, nector. She mates with the drone in the air (nuptial flight) only once in her life but in a single chance of fertilization, drone releases 2-crore sperms which are enough for the fertilization of the eggs at the time of laying by the female throughout her life span. In the whole life span of 2 to 5 years a queen lays about 15,00,000 eggs. When the queen loses its egg laying capacity, another worker of the same colony starts feeding on queen's diet i.e. royal jelly young and grubs develops into a new queen and is provided with the facilities of real queen. At the same time old queen may be driven out but sometimes some workers take objection that's why the mother of the colony be driven out so ultimately they also come out with the mother. Sometimes when 2 or 3 queens are developed in a colony, only one take the position of the real queen and the others come out with some workers to establish new colonies.

Queen provides the cohesive force which keeps the thousands of worker members of the colony together as a social unit. She does this by satisfying their demands for queen substance i.e. a substance secreted by the queen. This substance is most important in the maintenance of a colony and its social organization. It has been found that a scent of fatty acid 9-oxodecenoic acid produced by queen's mandibular glands attracts workers only over a very short distance which also inhibits queen rearing by the workers of her colony and development of ovaries of laying workers.

The Workers : These are imperfectly developed females from the fertilized eggs laid by the queen and live in a chamber called as "worker cell ". The workers take 21 days in the development from egg to the adult and the total life span of a worker is about 6 weeks. The workers are unable to reproduce; but possess all the maternal instincts. They are responsible for all the work necessary for the maintenance and welfare of the colony. Division of labour among the workers is on a physiological basis. The indoor and outdoor dutiets of the colony are performed by the workers only due to having special structures for particular work as : (1) Long proboscis for sucking the nectar. (2) Strong wings for fanning. (3) Pollen basket for the collection of pollen. (4) Powerful sting to defend the colony against enemies. (5) Wax glands for wax secretion.

Each worker bee performs different types of work in her life time and becomes fitted for various duties. During the first half of her life, she attends to indoor duties such as secretion of royal jelly, feeding of the brood, feeding the queen and attending on her, secreting bees wax, building combs, cleaning, ventilating, cooling and guarding the hive, evaporating nectar and storing honey. During the second half of her life lasting 3 weeks she attends to outdoor duties as collects the nectar, pollen, propolis (gum / bee glue) and water which are received and stored properly by the house bees.

The field force of colony is divided into searchers and gatherers. The searcher bees fly around the surrounding area and bring back news of available food and communicate to gatherer bees by performing a round or tail-wagging dance.

The worker bees has been compared to a storage battery which can not be recharged. She is capable of performing a definite amount of work and when that is accomplished she dies. For example, in

Chennai, due to a mild climate and plain variety *Apis indica* worker bee on average lives for 50 days.

The Drone (Fertile Males) : The drone is the male member of the honey bee colony which fertilizes the queen so called as ' King ' of the colony. These are stouter and larger than worker bees and have greatly enlarged eyes. They take 24 days to develop from the egg to the adult stage. The drones are unable to gather food, but they eat a lot.

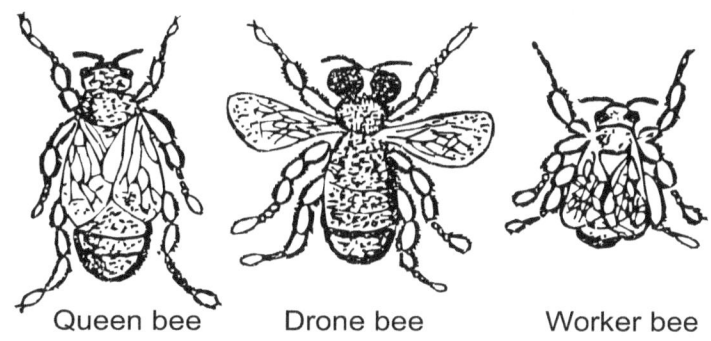

Queen bee   Drone bee   Worker bee

Fig. 2.14 : (a) Caste System in *Apis indica*

They spend their time in enjoying the sun and fresh air. The drones are reared from unfertilized egg in large drone cell during the breeding season in spring and autumn when new queens are to be mated. They are driven out of the hive to die of starvation before the monsoon and winter. The normal life span of drones of *A. indica* is 57 days in Chennai state. Drones are dependent and begging honey from the workers. During the swarming period, the drone follows the queen, copulates and dies after compulation.

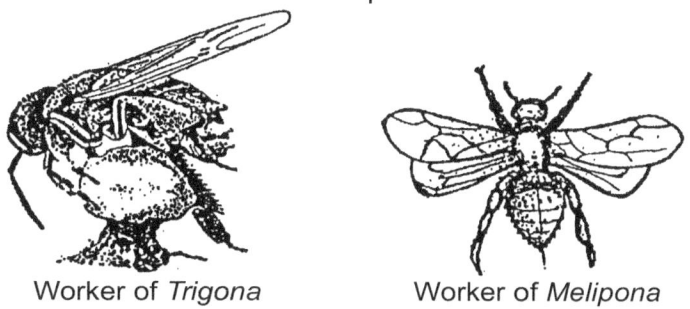

Worker of *Trigona*   Worker of *Melipona*

Fig. 2.14 : (b) Workers of *Trigona* and *Melipona*

2.5.1 Bee Behaviour

Swarming : The phenomenon of leaving off the colony by the queen and other members is known as swarming. It is taking place towards the end of spring or early summer but the true reason is of swarming is still not well known. In the summers when plenty of food is available and hive is overcrowded by the bees the queen leaves the hive on a fore-noon with some old drones and workers and establishes a new colony at some other place.

Supersedure : When the egg laying capacity of the old queen is lost or is suddenly dies, a new young and vigorous queen takes the position of the old queen is called supersedure.

Absconding : The migration of the complete colony from one place to another place due to some unfavourable conditions of life, such as destruction of the comb by termites or wax-moths and scarcity of nectar producing flowers around the hive. This phenomenon is quite different from swarming.

Nuptial Flight : After swarming, the new virgin queen is followed by the drones in clear, sunny days is called nuptial flight. One of the drones starts copulating with the queen in the sky and fertilizes the queen and dies during the course of copulation. The queen receives sperms and store them in spermathea and reaches to the hive. This whole phenomenon is known as nuptial flight or marriage flight.

2.5.2 Communication in Bees

Honey bees have an unique and one of the best understood animal languages with which they inform each other the distance and direction of the source of food. This system of communication (language) was identified and discovered by Austrian zoologist **Karl-Von-Frisch** at the University of Munich, Germany.

Prof. Karl Von Frisch has spent many years to study the behaviour and experiments in the early 20s. He kept a dish of sugar solution near its hive, the bees start arriving there, goes back to the hive; the first bee must have informed others in the hive. After long experimentation, Karl Von Frisch put colour dots on the thorax of bees to identify them from their fellows and observed their behaviour after they returned from the sugar solution dishes kept at varying distances from the frame hive which he kept in glass hive for easy observation. He found that the Forager bee on return to the nest makes two kinds of dances on the vertical surface of the comb.

   (i) Round dance (Rundtanz)

   (ii) Tail-wagging dance (Schwanzeltanz).

(i) Round Dance : The round dance is used to direct a short distance i.e. less than 50 metres (i.e. *A. mellifera*). This dance performed by the bees indicate or tells their sisters that the source of food is close to the hive but when they did a shuffle on returning to the hive, the foraging bees prepared for a long flight.

In the round dance, the bees run in circles, first in one and then in opposite direction (clock and anticlockwise). In fact, she traces out a figure of eight with its two loops more or less closely superimposed upon one another. The performer bee do this dance for half a minute or more on same part of comb and latter repeats, it on the another part of comb to demonstrate other group of bees. Some of the workers in the hive closely follow the dance and may partly join it. Eventually, they leave the hive to secure more of the honey.

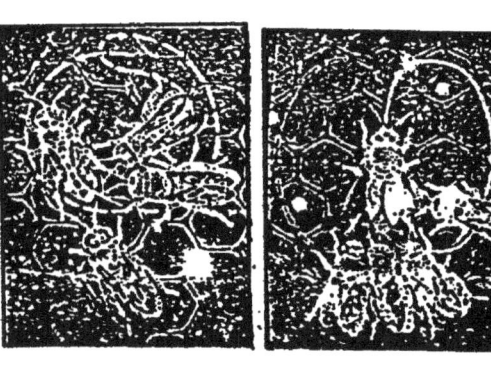
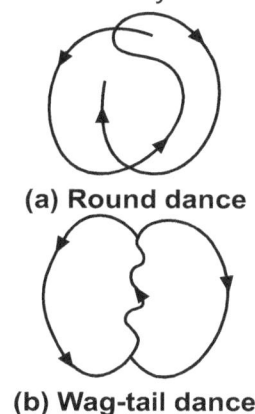

(a) Round dance

(b) Wag-tail dance

(a) Round dance   (b) Tail wagging dance

Fig. 2.15 : The 'language' ('dances') of bees (after von Frisch)
(a) 'Round dance' of nectar foragers; (b) Successive stages of the 'shuffle' of bees foraging nectar and pollen

(ii) Tail-wagging Dance : If the source of food discovered by a forager is more than about 50 metres away (i.e. an case of *A. mellifera*), it performs a different dance on its return. In which, the bee runs along semicircles, alternately left and right, ending each turn with a straight run back to her starting point. During the straight run, the bee shakes (wags) its abdomen from side to side so called Tail wagging dance. Karl Von Frisch found that the aumltes of wags per unit time was related to the distance the food was located. more the wags-indicate that the food source was nearer. For example *A. indica* perform, 10.5 shakes (wags) in 15 seconds, indicated a distance of 60 feet and 4.4 wags showed 1000 feet. These figures vary with different bees species.

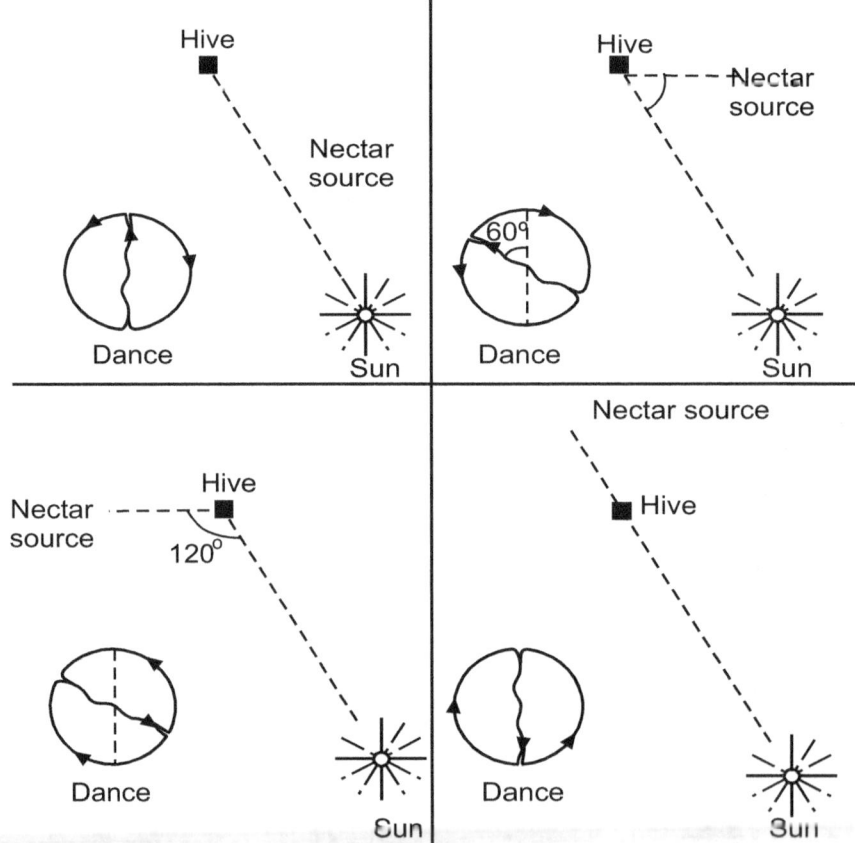

Fig. 2.16 : How the foraging bee's dance conveys information on the direction to plants according to the position of the sun (after von Frisch)

The tail-wagging dance also indicates the direction of the food supply. The signal depends upon the bees use of the sun as a compass and of polarized light, if the sun is obscured. If the wagging dance run is carried out in vertically upwards on the comb the feed place lies in the same direction as the sun, while if it is carried out downwards the feeding place is situated away and opposite direction from the sun. The performer runs upwards to the left at a certain angle to the vertical, the feeding place lies at the same angle to the left of a straight line between the hive and the sun and so on. It is also shown that the majority of recruits do not change more than 15° from the correct direction.

(iii) Massage Dance : When bees are sick or tired then massaging is required. The sick bee requiring massaging bends her head in a peculiar way with mandibles wide open and tongue protruded out which is dry. Then other bees (neighbouring bees) get excited, climb over and under her, then pull the joints of fore, mid and hindlegs, touch the sides with antennae and mandibles, clean the tongue and sometimes lick the bee. During massaging the tongue may be unfolded or completely distorted and cleaned. After several minutes, the cleaning activities ceases and the bee starts working normally. This dance is observed usually in the fall or during the winter. The same treatment is given to the chilled bees in early spring placed on the entrance of their lives.

(iv) DVAV Dance (Joy dance) : DVAV dance first observed by Haydak (1945) among bees. The DVAV is a short form of dorso-ventral abdominal vibration, this name is proposed by Milium (1955). Originaly, it was named as 'Joy dance' by Haydak (1945). While performing this dance, the dancer bee places her front legs on some part of the body of another bee, then makes 5-6 shaking movements up and down with the abdomen. There is a simultaneous slight swinging forward and backward. This been then goes to various locations, touches other been and perform the same dance. The field bees perform this type of dance either on a sealed queen cell, after the emergence of virgin queen (new) from queenless colony or when the conditions in the hive are optimum. Many bees (workers) perform this dance during field duties. The dance is observed on many occassions, at all hours of the day and night, at all seasons, even in queenless colonies. Many times DVAV dance may be intermixed with wag-tail or crescent dances.

(v) Alarm Dance : This type of dance is performed by bees when the condition in the colony is critical. Different substances or disturbances cause these dances. While performing alarm dances, the bees ran in spirals or irregular zig-zags with vigorously shaking their abdomen sidewise (vibrations). The flight activity of bees is stopped completely and neighbouring bees began to respond to dancers. Schneider (1949) observed alarm dances when the sugar solution is contaminated with dinitrocresol in hive box, because the bees get excited and show increased dancing activity with the spread of poison. After about 3-4 hours the colony returned to normal activities and flight activity was resumed again.

(vi) Intermediate Sickle or Crescent Dance : In one of races of bees, this dance is performed. The bees show a rapid transition from the round dance to the wag-tail dance, but in other races there is a slow transition called the sickle dance. Variations are performed when the food source is between 25 to 100 meters from the hive.

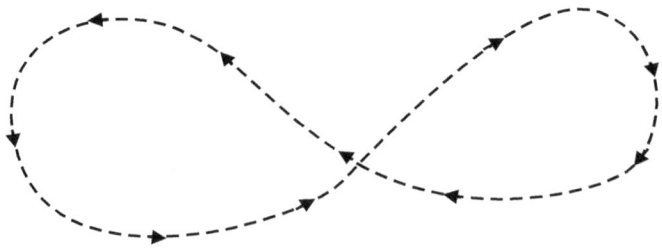

Fig. 2.17: Cresent or Sickle Dance

(vii) Cleaning Dance : The bee begins to dance when it requires cleaning. During dancing the bee shows rapid stamping of the legs and swinging of the body with cleaning the bases of the wings. The cleaner attempts the dancer. The dancer stops dancing when the cleaner touches the base of wings of dancer bee. The cleaner works with mandibles by raising the forelegs in the air. She cleans wings, thorax and head from one side then climbs to the other side. The dancer may then clean its body in general. The cleaner bees are less in number, on an average ten at one time in a colony.

Points to Remember

- Colouration is important for protection, warning, frightening the enemies, capturing pray and recognising mates.
- Types of colouration are protective, warning, recognising, aggressive, alluring colouration.
- Mimicry is a protective adapation.
- Mimicry is of two types namely protective and aggressive mimicry.
- Chromatophor cells of chameleon contain pigment.
- Colour change mechanism in the lizard chameleon is under the control of nervous system.
- Scorpions shows courship behaviour throughout warmer months of the year.
- Courtship in scorpions involves a highly ritualized series of behaviour that courtship the courtship dance.
- Weaver bird or baya also shows distinct courtship behaviour.
- Various birds also exits courtship behaviour in which group-display, preening, neadbodding, penguin dance activities are exhibited by the males and females.
- Honey bee colony is polymorphic coutaining three casts, queen, workers and drones.
- Queen is functional female, workers are sterile females drones are fertile males.
- From unfertilized eggs drous or males are developed.
- Lifecycle of honey bee contains egg, larva, puepa, and adult stages.

- Bee shows swarming, supersedure, absconding, nuptilial flight.
- Bees communication is based on round dance and tail wagging dance.

Exercise

1. What is colouration ? Describe the different types of colouration occurs in animals.
2. Define the term mimicry. Describe different types of mimicry.
3. Describe the camouflage and mechanism of colour change in chameleon.
4. What is courship behaviour ? Describe it in scorpion or weaver bird.
5. Give an account of courship behaviour in birds.
6. Writ short notes on :
    (a) Protection colouration,
    (b) Aggressive colouration,
    (c) Mimicry,
    (d) Types of mimicry,
    (e) Mechanism of colour change in chameleon,
    (f) Courship behaviour in scorpion,
    (g) Courship behaviour in weaver bird,
    (h) Courship behaviour in birds.
7. Give an account of colony organisation and division of labour in honey bees.
8. Describe the life history of honey bee and add note on bee behaviour.
9. What is bee communication. Give an account of bee communication.
10. How does bees communicate with each other ? Explain in brief the communication by bees for source of food.

UNIT 3...
Evolution

Contents ...

3.1 Formation and Dating of Fossils
    3.1.1 Formation of Fossils
    3.1.2 Essential Conditions for Fossilisation
    3.1.3 Types of Fossils
    3.1.4 Dating of Fossils
3.2 Connecting Links
    3.2.1 *Peripatus*
    3.2.2 *Archaeopteryx*
3.3 The Living Fossils
    3.3.1 *Spenodon*
    3.3.2 *Limulus*
3.4 Organic Evolution Concepts & Origin of Life (Solapur University)
3.5 Drawin's Theory of Evolution
3.6 Evidences from Palaeontology
3.7 Anatomical Evidences
* Points to Remember
* Exercise

3.1 Formation and Dating of Fossils

The term 'fossils' is derived from the Latin word 'fossilium' meaning something dug out. Fossils are defined as the remnant of previously existing animals and plants preserved in the earth's crust. According to **Huxley** Fossils are defined as the plants and animals which become dead rather longer than those which died yesterday. The fossils are regarded as the written documents of evolution. The fossils include whole body of the animal or plant, bones, teeth, shells and also the impressions left by bodies or body parts, foot prints etc.

Leonardo Da vinci (1452 - 1519) first recognised the importance of fossils as an evidence of evolution. The significance of fossils as an evidence of evolution was also realised by **Charles Darwin**.

3.1.1 Formation of Fossils

When animals die, they lie scattered on the earth. Generally, the soft parts of the dead animals are destroyed by predator animals, scavengers, insect larvae, bacteria and so on. These destructive forces also act on the hard parts like bones, shells, teeth etc. but slowly. The dead bodies which are protected from these destructive forces alone are fossilised. It is necessary for the formation of fossil the dead bodies should be quickly buried in the earth. But generally quick burial rarely happens and the bodies which are quickly burried are fossilised. Most of the time majority of the dead animals are attacked by the several destructive forces and are destroyed.

Several natural agencies are responsible for burial process. They are water, wind, ice, volcanoes, duststorms, amber, asphalt, minerals etc. The floor of oceans and large water bodies are ideal places for the process of fossilisation. Most of the aquatic animals are fossilised in such areas. The dead aquatic animals sink into deep sedimentary deposits. Under these sediments dead bodies are protected from scavengers and oxidation. The soft parts of dead body gradually undergo decay and this process is enhanced by water.

The hard parts like shells, bones, scales remain as such or may be replaced by particle minerals. More and more sediments are deposited over the dead bodies. Thick layers are formed by continuous deposition of sediment. During the process of deposition simultaneously sedimentary deposits gradually harden into rocks. The dead bodies which are embedded in the sedimentary, stratified rocks form the fossils.

The process of fossilisation differs on the land. The terrestrial animals are fossilised by dust-storms. The deposits of dust-storm and are formed like sediments in the ocean. Volcanoes are also responsible for the process of fossilisation. Volcanic ashes, magma also quickly bury the organisms and thus preserve them as fossils.

3.1.2 Essential Conditions for Fossilisation

For successful fossil formation five important conditions are essential. They are as follows :
1. The dead bodies should be quickly buried.
2. They should be protected from destructive forces.
3. The dead bodies should be prevented from oxidation.
4. The dead body should possess some hard parts.
5. The material, where the dead body is buried, should be good preservative.

3.1.3 Types of Fossils

The fossils obtained so far are classified into five groups : They are as follows:

1. Actual Remains : In rare cases, the dead animals are preserved as such even with the soft parts of the body. This type of fossil occurs in icelands, deep sea sediments, volcanic ashes, amber, asphalt etc. In Siberia about 50 huge fossils of elephants, called *Woolly Mammoths* were preserved in the ice even with the hairs, flesh etc. It is estimated that these elephants lived about 20,000 years ago. Similarly, insects are preserved as such in amber.

Fig. 3.1 : Actual remains of a *woolly mammoth*

2. Petrified Fossils : When animals die, the organic matter of the body is replaced in the water. This method of fossil formation is called petrification or petrifaction and the fossils are called petrified fossils. In this type of fossil, the entire plant or animal is deposited with minerals. The mineral content vary from fossil to fossil and place to place. Generally, the minerals like silica, calcium carbonate, iron pyrites, sulphur, dolomite, gypsum etc. are deposited. Depending on the type of mineral deposition petrification fossils are classified into the following types.

Fig. 3.2 : Actual remains : Ant in amber

(a) **Silicification :** In this type of petrification, the original matter of dead body is replaced by silica. e.g. fossils sponges.

(b) **Pyritization :** In pyritization, the original material is replaced by iron pyrites.

(c) **Carbonization :** It is a fossilization where carbon compounds are deposited. For example, Chitinous skeletal parts, leaves etc.

(d) **Dolomitization :** It is another kind of petrification where the original material is replaced by the double carbonate of calcium and magnesium. This type occurs at the sea floor.

3. Moulds : A mould is hollow cavity left in the mud by the dead body of buried animal, the surrounding material or sediment becomes hardened. The original material of the body decay, disintegrate and disappear completely leaving a cavity. This forms the mould of the body of the buried animal. The cavity gives the size, shape and the exact external features of the animal, but it does not give the internal structures of the body. Jelly fishes, wings of insects and leaves of plants are formed by moulds.

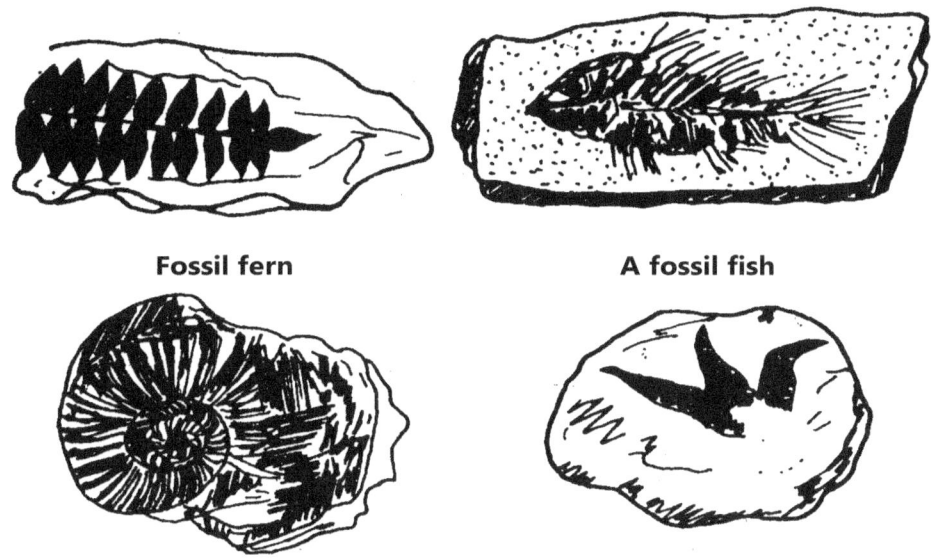

Fossil fern   **A fossil fish**

A Fossil ammonite petrified fossil   Dinosaur foot print (Tracks)

Fig. 3.3 : Some fossils

4. Casts : Casts are similar to moulds, but in casts the cavity is filled with minerals. These minerals harden to form casts; in casts also none of the original parts of the animal is preserved. It reflects the internal replica of the animals. When a snail is burried, the cavity of the shell is gradually filled with minerals; later the shell disappears completely and the mineral is hardened to form a cast.

5. Tracks and Trails : Tracks are the foot prints left by the walking animals on the wet sand and mud. These prints are preserved by sedimentation and hardening. Tracks of amphibians and reptiles are recognised.

Trails are produced on the soft sediments by the crawling worms and snails by the dragging tentacles of jelly fish etc.

3.1.4 Dating of Fossils

Dating of fossils, refers to the finding out of the age of fossils. The age of the fossil indicates the age of the strata and the rock from which it is collected. Palaeontologists use three main methods for dating fossils. They are as follows:

1. Stratigraphy
2. Biostratigraphy
3. Radiometry

1. Stratigraphy : The basis of this method is that the earth's crust is formed of a number of strata arranged one above the other. These strata are formed one above the other by the deposition of sediments. In this process, the lowest strata is the oldest and the upper strata is formed recently. Stratigraphy consists of analysis of the succession of strata that have been laid down, one after another in a more or less regular fashion.

Actually, it is a crude method of dating, it does not give the age accurately. This method can be used in places where erosion by streams has cut deep rashes on the earth's surface. This method can also be applied in places where the strata have been tilted so that one can pass over the earth's surface from older to progressively younger strata. Stratigraphy shows only which strata are older and which strata are younger. It does not give the actual age of the strata.

The dating of the different strata was originally based on the rates at which geological processes are known to occur. Many strata originated as deposits in the sea at the mouth of rivers, the length of time required to produce a deposit of a given thickness can be measured by the rate at which modern rivers are depositing sediments in the sea.

This method has two difficulties:

(i) First of all the deposition of strata is not uniform in all the places. For example, in places of violent volcanic eruptions, a layer of several feet in thickness can be laid down in a few days. On the other hand, at the bottom of oceans the deposition is so slow that the thousands of years are required to produce an inch of sediment. Then there are areas where the rate of deposition is intermediate as in the case of shells and sandstones.

(ii) The second difficulty is that there were floods alternating with elevation of land. So in most of the parts of the earth there were erosion rather than deposition.

2. Biostratigraphy : This method consists of recognizing strata having similar fauna and flora in different parts of the world. In this method, the different strata of the earth are identified by comparing the fossils available in the strata of the different parts of the earth.

3. Radiometry : This is now universely accepted method. After the discovery radioactive decay of certain elements in the 18th century, geologists discarded the stratigraphic and biostratigraphic methods of dating fossils. Now-a-days the age of fossils is sensitively calculated by radioactive isotopes. This method of dating fossils is called radiometry or radioactive clock method. The main principle underlying this method is that many rocks have natural 'clocks' in the form of radioactive isotopes and these radioactive isotopes change into-stable elements slowly, but at a steady rate. For example, one gram of radioactive element changes into half gram in a particular duration of time. This duration is called half life of the element. Half life is defined as the time taken for the activity of a radioactive element to decay to one half of its original value. The duration of half life varies from element to element. The commonly used radioactive elements for dating the fossils are uranium, carbon 14, potassium, rubidium etc.

The following different methods are used in radiometry:

1. Lead Method : This is devised by **Boltwood** in 1907 for dating the fossils. In this method, uranium^{238} (the number represents the atomic weight) is considered for dating the fossils. It continuously but slowly disintegrates into lead^{206} (i.e. Pb^{206}). The rate of disintegration is uniform and is unaffected by any factor in the environment. One half of the total number of uranium atoms will break down, forming lead^{206} in a period of 4.51 billion (4,510,000,000) years. This period is called half life of uranium because in 4.51 billion years one gram of uranium disintegrates into half a gram of uranium. The age of the rock or fossil can be calculated by present in the rock.

The dating of fossils with uranium has three limitations. They are :
(i) Uranium is not common element, so certain rocks may not contain uranium. In such case this method becomes useless for dating the fossil.
(ii) This method can be used only for old rocks, the age of which should be of lakhs of years, it can not be applied to and rocks with lesser years of age.
(iii) It is not known whether the lead produced is lost or retained in–the aquatic rocks; for example, the lead formed may be washed away by the water current and hence calculation may not be accurate.

Table 3.1 : Isotopes and their half life

Sr. No.	Isotopes	Half life
1.	Rubidium^{87}	6 Billion years
2.	Uranium^{238}	4.51 Billion years
3.	Carbon^{14}	5568 years
4.	Potassium^{10}	1350 years

2. Carbon Method : This method was devised by **Libby (1956)**. The living organisms contain a definite amount of C^{14} in their tissues, bones etc. When organism dies the C^{14} disintegrates into C^{12} at a constant rate. The half life of C^{14} is 5568 years; i.e. one gram of C^{14} disintegrates into half a gram in 5568 years. The age of the fossil can be calculated by measuring the amount of C^{14} still present in the fossil. The difference in the amount of C^{14} present in the living tissue and in the fossil can be taken as being due to disintegration and the age of the fossil is calculated from the half life.

This method can not be used for fossils which are more than 70,000 years old. Hence, the age of recent fossils can be calculated accurately and sensitively with 30 years plus or minus by this method. Another limitation of this method is that it is applicable only when the fossil contains at least some of the organic materials.

3. Potassium : Argon Method : Natural potassium contains a small amount of radioactive isotope K^{46}. The half life of K^{46} is 1350 years. It decays into 88% $Calcium^{40}$ and 12% $Argon^{46}$. By calculating the amount of Argon gas emitted in a particular unit of time, it is possible to calculate the age of fossils.

4. Rubidium : Strontium Method : $Rubidium^{87}$ is another radioactive isotope and it decays into $strontium^{88}$. The half life of $rubidium^{87}$ is 6 million years. By this method the age of good old fossils can be calculated.

5. Fission Track Method : It is some what different method used when rock contains glass or crystal. When $uranium^{239}$ is present in the rock, it undergoes spontaneous fission. This radiation damage causes the appearance of tracks in the rock. When such a rock is etched with hydrofluoric acid, the tracks are revealed. These tracks can be seen through a microscope and counted. From the count the age of the glass or rock can be computed. This method may be used for glass as young as 2000 years **(Rainey and Ralph, 1966)**.

3.2 Connecting Links

3.2.1 *Peripatus*

Peripatus belongs to the group *Onychophora* (Greek, *onychos*-claws; *phoros*-bearing) which has been of special phylogenetic interest. The Onychophora is a small group of peculiar worm-like creatures with characteristics of both the Annelida and the Arthropoda. Therefore, it is often referred as '*connecting links*' between these two great phyla. Previously, this group was considered as a class of phylum Arthropoda but now it is treated as subphylum.

Peripatus is a small, caterpillar-like animal commonly called the 'walking worm'. It has cylindrical, bilaterally symmetrical body measures about 50 mm in length. The body of *Peripatus* is covered by a thin, flexible cuticle. The integument bears all over transverse rings of minute papillae, each bearing little spine. Body of the animal is not divided into definite segments. The anterior part of the body shows head which is not distinct. It bears pair of anntennae, eyes, jaws and oral papillae. The antennae also called pre-antennae are anterior in position and are formed by several short rings with minute spines. Eyes are dorsal in position and simple showing resemblance with chaetopod eyes. The jaws lie on the sides of the mouth enclosed by a

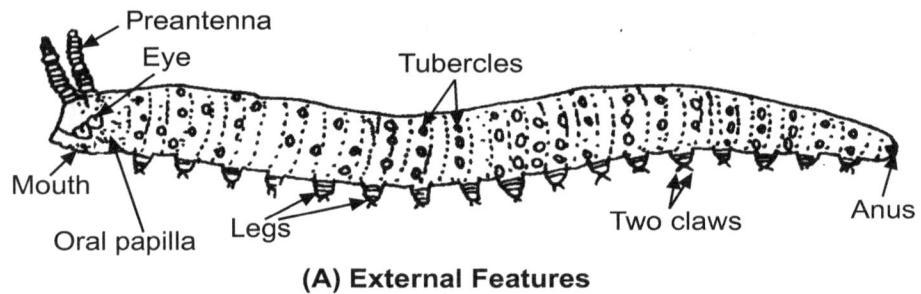
(A) External Features

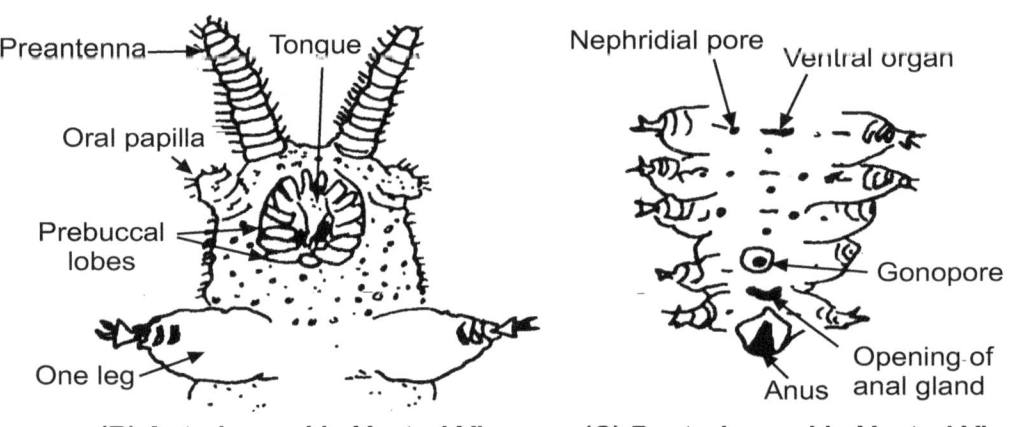
(B) Anterior end in Ventral View   (C) Posterior end in Ventral View

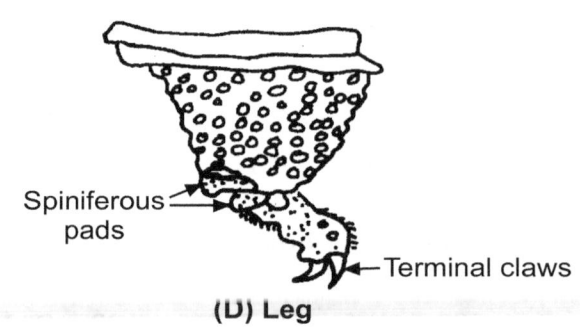
(D) Leg

Fig. 3.4 : *Peripatus*

fleshy, ridged, circular lip. Each jaw terminates into two hook like teeth. The oral papillae are short, blunt out growths on the sides of the mouth. They are ringed and bear large tubercles distally. Each papilla bears an opening of a slime gland. A jet of slime is ejected through this opening in defence and for capturing the prey. Mouth is lying ventrally surrounded by circum oral fold or circular lip. The anus is located at the extreme posterior end, somewhat ventrally, and the genital aperture lies infront of the anus.

The body lacks external segmentation but it bears ventro-laterally a series of paired short, stumpy, unjointed conical legs at intervals, each ending in a pair of horny claws. The legs bear rows of papillae that give them a ringed appearance. At the base of each leg on the innerside lies a minute nephridiopore. The colour of the body is blue or black.

Peripatus is terrestrial nocturnal and shy creature lives under stones, logs, bark, in crevices of rocks and leaf litter in damp tropical forests of Australia, Asia, South and Central America. It is predaceous, feeding on insects.

The body wall of the animal has circular, longitudinal and transverse muscle layers. The body cavity is a haernocoel known as mixocoel. The true coelom is reduced to cavities in the gonads and nephridia. The digestive tract is complete. Salivary glands are present. Respiration occurs by tracheae whose spiracles are irregularly scattered over the body surface. Circulatory system is open and has tubular heart with paired valvular ostia. Nephredia are the excretory organs. It is uricotelic, excreting chiefly uric acid. The nervous system is primitive and ladder-like. Ventral nerve cords are separate without ganglia and connected by transverse commissures giving ladder-like appearance. Sexes are separate. *Peripatus* is viviparous. Young ones resemble the adults, except in size and colour.

Affinities of *Peripatus* :

Peripatus exhibits both annelid and arthropod characters as well as its own pecularities, therefore it is called as connecting link.

[A] Annelidan characters :
1. Body is vermiform with truncated extremities.
2. True head is absent.
3. Body wall covered by thin flexible cuticle and underlying circular and longitudinal muscles.
4. Locomotion slow and by peristalsis like earthworm.
5. Eyes are simple like polychaetes.
6. Appendages are unjointed, hollow, stumpy like parapodia of polychaeta.
7. Alimentary canal is straight and complete.
8. Paired nephridia are segmentally arranged.
9. Slime and coxal glands correspond with glands of chaetopoda.
10. Excretory and reproductive ducts are with cilia.

[B] Arthropodan characters :
1. Antennae are present.
2. Jaws are modified appendages.
3. Legs are usually provided with claws and useful for locomotion.
4. Cuticle and contains thin deposit of chitin like that of arthropoda.
5. Body cavity is haemocoel or mixocoel.
6. The true coelom is reduced to cavities in the gonads and excretory organs.
7. Heart is dorsal, tubular with lateral ostia.
8. Respiration by spiracles and trachea.
9. Nervous system consist of large brain.
10. Reproductive organ and development is like arthropoda.

[C] Onychophoran characters :

Peripatus shows distinct characters which differ from phylum Annelida and Arthropoda.

1. The body lacks external segmentation.
2. Cuticle is having many velvety processes not seen in other phyla.
3. Head is three segmented.
4. Antennae are not similar to that of Arthropoda.
5. Legs are jointed with claws.
6. Spiracles and trachea are irregularly distributed.
7. Two ventral nerve cords are separate without ganglia and ladder like.
8. Eyes are simple.

Taxonomic-position :

Since *Peripatus* shows more close resemblance with arthropods than annelids and perhaps it might have arose as an offshoot; from near the base of arthropod line. Therefore **Manton (1958)** and others classified Onychophorans in the phylum arthropoda as a class or subphylum. Some Zoologists are still of this opinion that it is definitely annelid. But onychophorans are neither worms nor arthropods but they have their own distinctive characters and hence onychophora is treated as separate phylum.

3.2.2 *Archaeopteryx*

Archaeopteryx is an extinct bird and is a transitional stage showing characters of both reptiles and birds. Hence, it is considered as the connecting link between reptiles and birds. This is also called as Lizard bird and was found in 1861 by **Andreas Wagner** from the upper Jurassic limestone rocks of Solenhofen in Bavaria, Germany. Archaeopteryx was about the size of crow and dwelt in forests. Its body was covered with feathers and body axis was elongated like that of a lizard.

Archaeopteryx shows following important characteristics of both birds and reptiles.

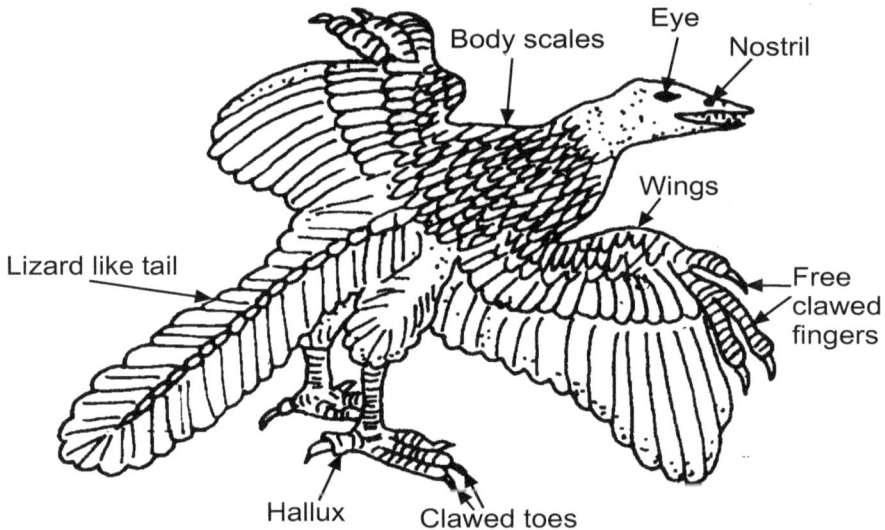

Fig. 3.5 : *Archaeopteryx* : Restoration Showing Detailed Structure

1. The bones are solid, strong and stout without air spaces.
2. The skull is large and skull bones are fused. Frontals and premaxillae are small.
3. Beak is short and blunt
4. Teeth are small conical, enamel crowned and thecodont and present only in the front part only. The upper jaw has 26 teeth and lower jaw with only 6 teeth.
5. The eyes are large like birds with a ring of sclerotic bones.
6. The fore limbs are reptilian but form wings of small area and round shape. Flight feathers are attached to the back of the ulna and manus. There are 6-7, primaries and 10 secondaries. Each fore limb has three well formed digits with separate phalanges. The first digit is with two phalanges, second with three phalanges. The digits are without feathers and project from anterior margin of the wing and beam curved claws. There are three free metacarpals, no carpometacarpals but the third metacarpal is fixed to a carpal.

7. The humerus shows that biceps were not strong, the radius and ulna are well developed.
8. The hind limb has separate tibia and fibula of equal size. The proximal tarsals are free but the distal ones fused with the fused metatarsals to form a slender tarsometatarsus. Each hind limb has four clawed digits with 2, 3, 4, 5 phalanges with backwardly directed small hallux.
9. In the pectoral girdle coracoid is small, scapula is slender and curved and they are at right angles as in birds. Furcula is U-shaped formed by clavicles. Keel bone is absent.
10. The bones of pelvic girdle are not fused into an innominate bone. The ilium is long and pubis is directed posteriorly and probably there is an ischiac symphysis. The pelvic girdle and hind limbs show both avian and reptilian characters.

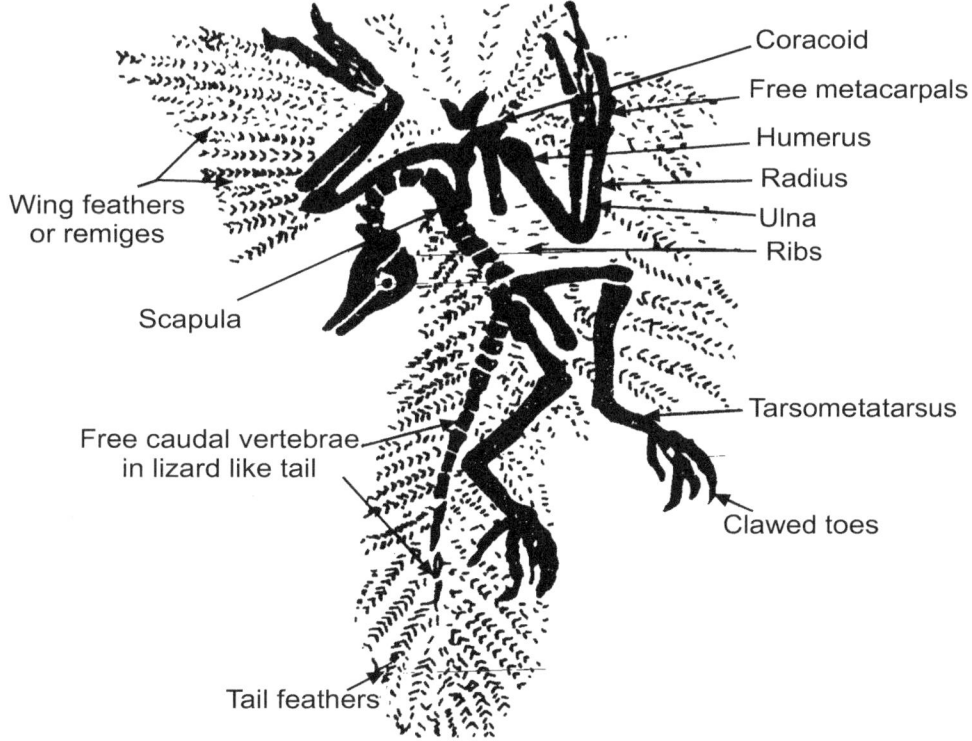

Fig. 3.6 : Fossil *Archaeopteryx* Berllin Specimen

11. The vertebral column is elongated and vertebrae are amphicoclous with simple concave articulation as in reptiles. Sacrum is formed by 5 or 6 vertebrae like some dinosaurs.
12. The ribs are thin, single headed with no uncinate processes attached to vertebrae. Besides the cervical and thoracic ribs there are abdominal ribs or gastralia in the ventral wall of the abdomen as in Sphenodon and crocodilians.
13. Tail is elongated with 20 free caudal vertebrae which shows tapering towards the distal end. Pygostyle is absent.
14. Recent studies revealed that *Archaeopteryx* was warm blooded (endotherma) as like other birds.
15. Brain was with smooth long and narrow cerebral hemispheres and small cerebellum showing reptilian characters.
16. *Archaeopteryx* could not fly efficiently but could only volplane, free tree to tree in forests. It is because small sternum without keel bone. Wings were small and tail was long lizard like with feathers.

Thus, *Archaeopteryx* shows both avian and reptilian characters hence it is connecting link between these two groups.

3.3 The Living Fossils

3.3.1 *Spenodon*

Spenodon which is also called Tuatara is the only living representative of the Reptilian order Rhyncocephalia. It is one of the ancient reptiles was very common about 200 million years ago. It is found living in burrows and confined to one or two islands near New Zealand. *Spenodon* has remained unchanged for 200 million years and rewincd many primitive features hence it is called living fossil. It shows the characters of diapsids of late Permian. *Sphenodon* is nocturnal and carnivorous feeding on insects, molluscs and small vertebrates. It is dull olive green in colour with white and yellow spots. It grows to about 60 to 90 cm. The dorsal surface has with granular scales and median row of scales forming spines from the head to the end of the tail except on the neck region. The ventral surface has squarish plates arranged in transverse rows. The tail of the *Spenodon* is thick and laterally compressed.

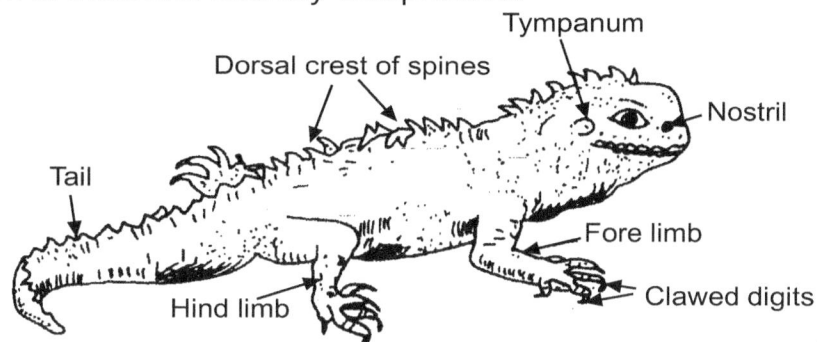

Fig. 3.7 : *Sphenodon punctatum*

The limbs are primitive, but shows pentadactyl condition. The radio and ulnar bones of fore limbs are not fused and there are 10 carpals in each. There are two complete temporal fossae in the skull, quadrate is fixed and pterygoids extends forwards separating palatines. The unique feature of this tetrapod is presence of postfrontals. The teeth are acrodont pointed, triangular arranged in two rows, one along the maxilla and other along the palatine. The lower jaw teeth bite between the two upper rows. Sternum is present. The vertebrae are amphicoelous type with presence of intercentra and notochord and notochord between the vertebrae. Each vertebra has single headed rib and abdominal ribs are also present with uncinate processes. The pro-atlas vertebra is present between skull and atlas like crocodiles and chameleons. The caudal vertebral are with chevron bones. The centrum of each caudal vertebra has an unossified transverse zone. From where the tail can break off, but it regenerates as in many lizards. There is well developed parietal eye with lense, retina and nerve connection. It is located in a parietal foramen covered with skin having a transparent scale. This eye is photosensitive. Another important character of this animal is absence of penis in male. Female lays about 10 hard shelled eggs. Incubation period is about one year. *Sphenodon* is known to live for 28 years. It is now in danger and rapidly approaching extinction and is protected by law.

3.3.2 *Limulus*

Limulus or king crab or horse-shoe crab is a marine animal but it occasionally occur in fresh and brackish estuarine waters. It is marine arachnid burrowing in the sand. It lives in shallow waters along muddy shores. This animal is nocturnal and becomes active and swim through the water at night.

Systemic position :

Phylum – Arthropoda

Class – Arachnida

Order – Xiphosura

Genus – *Limulus*

The body of the animal is depressed, dark brown in colour and measuring about 60 cm in length. They are called king crabs but neither they are kings nor crabs. The body of the animal is horse shoe shaped and divisible into cephalothorax, abdomen and a caudal spine or telson. The body is covered by smooth chitin. The cephalothorax is semicircular and consists of a pair of median eyes which are very close to each other. The median eyes lie on median ridges whereas the lateral eyes on lateral ridges. Seven spines are present. On the ventral side of the cephalothorax there is a mouth and seven pairs of appendages. Infront of mouth there is a flattened longitudinal ridge called **camerostome** and beyond the mouth is oval structure called **promesosternite**. The mouth is surrounded by seven pairs of appendages. The first pair is called chelicera. Each chelicera is three segmented structure which is followed by 5 pairs of walking legs called pedipalps. Each pedipalp is made up of six segments. In female the 4th anterior pair of pedipalps is chelate in appearance whereas in the male the first pair has claws which are curved. There is difference in male and female in 5th pair. In male, there is a peculiar curved spine called **spatulate process** or **flabellum**. All the appendages are postoral in position but at later stages the first pair becomes pre-oral in position.

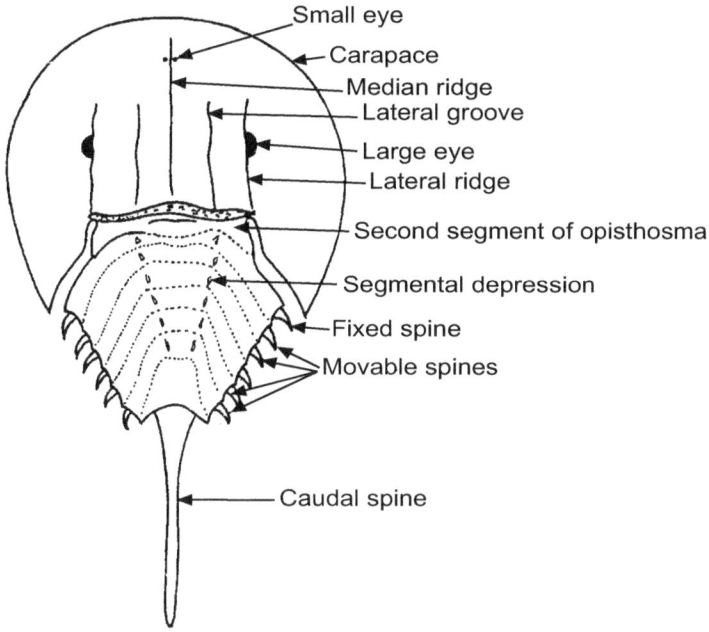

Fig. 3.8 : Dorsal view of *Limulus*

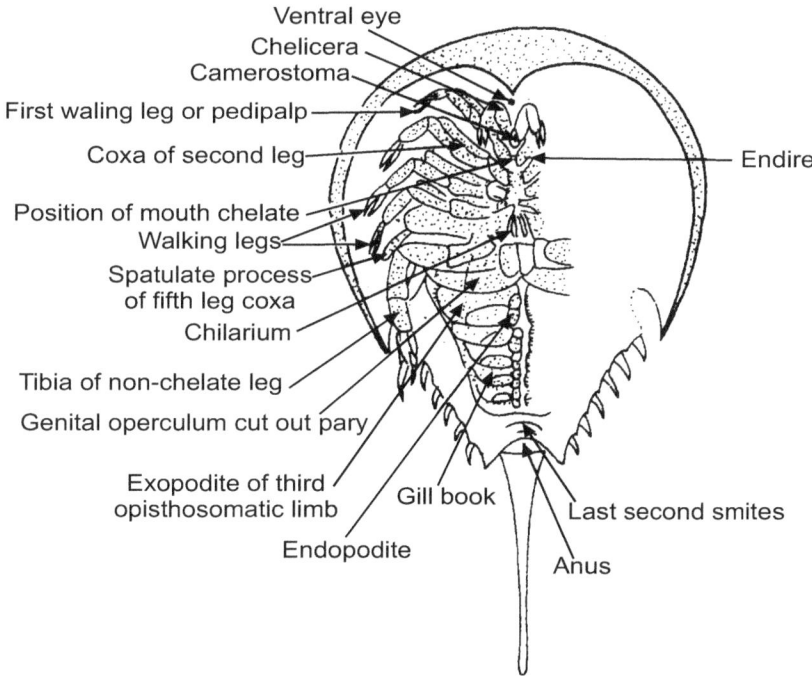

Fig. 3.9 : Ventral view of *Limulus*

The abdomen is jointed to cephalothorax or prosoma by a transverse hinge. It is broad, hexagonal with hardly any trace of segmentation. It is made up of fusion of an anterior six segmented mesosoma and a posterior three segmented metasoma. The mesosoma bears three spines in a single median row on dorsal side and two lateral row of 6 small pits. There are six immovable spines on each lateral sides which appear serrated. There are six pairs of appendages in abdomen. They are lamellar in form and resemble the crustacean limbs. The **genital operculum** is formed by anterior most abdominal appendages. The genital operculum acts as a protective cover over the gills. The 5 pairs of abdominal appendages are biramous because each consists of endopodite and exopodite. Each exopodite bears a lamellated structure known as **book gill**. In *Limulus* the book gills are external. Each book gill has 120-200 leaf like lamellae. At the posterior end the abdomen bears a pointed, triangular telson. The telson is not true as it does not bear the anus. It consists of fused tergites or dorsal plates of the abdominal segments. It consists of fused tergites or dorsal plates of abdominal segments. The telson is not of used for defence but is thrust into mud.

The *Limulus* is an ancient animal and the group now nearly extinct. These animals are usually referred to a **living fossils**. This animal show close relationship with scorpion. Such as presence of 6 pairs of appendages in cephalothorax, both bear medial and lateral eyes, structure of book gills and book lungs, presence of hepatopancreas, presence of coxal gland and similarities in development. There is also superficial resemblance to a fossible Trilobite. It is believed that *Limulus* like ancestors gave rise to air breathing arachnids like scorpions.

3.4 Organic Evolution : Concepts and Origin of Life

The earth is the only planet in the universe on which life exists. In the curious mind question always arises, How earth is originated ? How first life is originated on the earth ?

It is believed that the earth was cast off from some heavely body in the form of huge mass of extremely hot gaseous or molten mass. In the course of time, the mass condensed and gradually cooled and reduced in volume or size. Then there appeared a gaseous atmosphere with sufficient pressure which retained the water on the surface. The water formed oceans; the volcanoes released as a molten rocks on land. The sun provided heat and radiation to visible light. After complete cooling of lands and waters on the earth life might have appeared.

On our planet earth a variety of living forms exist. This living world includes microscopic unicellular organisms like bacteria, algae, and also gaint multicellular animals and plants. Living matter might not have existed all the time on the earth. The high temperature and dry climate of the early time of earth might have made life impossible to exist. But in the course of time, changes might have occured in the universe and on the earth and life could appear. Thus, evolution simply means, change or unfolding. It is a gradual and orderly change from one condition to another. There are ample ecological evidences which suggest that the planets and stars, the earth, topography, the chemical compounds of the universe are even the chemical elements and their subatomic particles have undergone gradual and orderely changes during the long history of universe. The evoluation is divided into two types : chemical or molecular evolution and biological or organic evolution.

(1) Chemical or Molecular Evolution : It delas with changes from atoms and molecules to simple and then complex substances and from these to still more complex ones capable of self-duplication. The most significant out come of chemical evolution is the origin of biologically imporant molecules (like proteins and nucleic acids DNA & RNA) origin of life and environment to sustain life on the planet earth.

(2) Biological or Organic Evolution : It deals with the origin of life. Different types of micro-organisms, plants and animals existing on the earth today have originated and gradually changed from their simpler ancestors which have become extinct. Specialisation in structure and function in an organism is the outcome of organic evolution. Species which changes show better adaptations to the environment and therefore survive whereas those poorly adapted are eliminated by nature.

About 2 million different species of organisms exist on the planet earth. All these life forms are characterised by diversity and unity. It can be explained by the concept of evolution. In short, the present day complex forms are derived from the simple ancestral forms through a gradual change by process called organic evolution.

Origin of life : The question of origin of life on our planet, earth has remained as the most complicated puzzling problem to man of modern as well as ancient times. Theory of evolution has not been able to explain how and from what first simple form of the life originated. Different thinkers, philosophers and evolutionists of different ages have forwarded the different views, theories concerning the origin of life. Most of them are not satisfactory and relevent. However, various theories have been put forward to explain the origin of life. These include the following theories :

(1) Theory of special creation.
(2) Theory of spontaneous generation.
(3) Theory of Eternity of life.
(4) Theory of catastrophism.
(5) Theory of Biogenesis.
(6) Theory of organic evolution and
(7) Theory of chemical evolution or Modern concept of origin of life.

(1) Theory of special creation : This theory was proposed by *Hebrew* and others and according to it all species of living things are created simultaneously by a supernatural force or creator or God. The whole world was specially created on 6th day. First man *Adam* was given soul and later the female *Eve* was created. This theory is purely based on religious thinking and has no scientific base hence it is not accepted.

(2) Theory of spontaneous generation : This theory is also called a theory at *abiogenesis* and according to it life is originated from non-living organic material. This theory was proposed by famous Greek Philosopher and Scientist *Aristotle*. To support this theory various famous examples such as appearance of maggots (largvae) in decaying meat, generation of fishes from mud and frogs and toads from rain are given. These examples can not prove the theory.

(3) Theory of Biogenesis : This theory explains that are living things are formed from other living things i.e. life begets from life. Thus each and every new organism simple or complex, would have at least one parent. This theory was proved by **Redi, Spallanzini** and **Pasteur**.

(4) Theory of Eternity of life : This theory was proposed by **Helmholtz Ritcher, Hoyle** who believed in the eternity of life. According to them life only changes its form but it is never created from dead matter. It has no origin and has always existed. They believe that life must have existed even at the time when earth was molten mass. **Richer** proposed a cosmozoic theory in which life came from other planet in the form of *celestial bodies* and small particles carrying viable germs or spores which came on earth and developed. **Helmholtz** is of the opinion that life might have came in form of germs along with the meteorites falling from other planets. All these theories are rejected because in extreme cold, radiation and dryness life was impossible.

(5) Theory of catastrophism : Accroding to this theory there had been several ups and downs in the history of the earth which made extinction of several forms. At the end of each period the organisms had been wiped out and new set of organisms created. This theory is also rejected. Accroding to **d'Orbigny** (1802–1857) catastrophes were world wide and destroyed the population as a whole and again repopulation by recreation after each. He believed that there were catastrophes occured 27 times.

Theory of organic evolution : According to this theory the present day organisms have arisen by natural evolution from their simple ancestors. This is ascending process from lower to higher, simple to complex form. This theory was explained by **Charles Darvin, Lamark, Wallace** and **Hugo De Vries**.

(6) Modern theory of origin of life or Chemical evolution : The experiments of *Redi, Spallanzi* and *Pasteur* proved that life originated from the pre-existing living forms and not spontaneously. But theory of biogenesis still leaves behind the main question unanswered, i.e if it requires life to produce life where did the first life come from ? To find an answer to this question means looking back billions of years in time and trying to imagine what conditions were present on the earth when life first appeared. To answer this question Russion biochemist **F. A. Oparin** and British biologist **J.B.S. Haldane** putforth in the year 1936, theory of biochemical origin of first living form on the earth.

Oparin - Haldane Theory : According to this theory life might have originated from a non living organic molecule. Oparin was the first scientist to suggest that a long evolution of chemical substances occured before life actually originated. This theory gives most scientific idea of origin of life and hence it is also called '*Oparin, hypothesis*'. He published the book 'Origin of life on earth' in 1936 in which he provided the biochemical explaination of origin of life. This theory is based on the following important events.

(i) Origin of earth : According to *Oparin* the origin of life occured along with the origin and evolution of the planet earth and its atmosphere. The earth has originated from sun due to collision with some other planet. The gaseous mass separated from sun provided material for the earth formation. Carbon from polar atmosphere passed to earth. The carbon clouds might have condensed into drops or solid particles mixed with earth in the form snow or carbonaceous rain.

(ii) Presence of Elements on Protoplanet : Whatever elements are present now in the protoplasm of organism were probably present as organic molecules on the hot earth. N, H and O were probably present in combined state as the temperature was about 5000 to 6000°C. Large amounts of H and O combined to form water vapours which remains in the form of super heated steam for ages.

After gradual cooling of earth the steam was condensed and there was rainfall on earth. This resulted into formation of large bodies of water like oceans in which several reactions occured. Thus, earth was a sort of gaint crucible for formation of compounds. Series of physical and chemical changes occured. Rocks and compounds were formed by condensation of hot gases and solidification of molten matter. The source of energy available for the formation of humerous types of molecules were cosmic rays, ultra violet radiations, electrical discharges such as lightening, radioactivity and heat from volcanoes and hot springs. Oxygen combined with calcium and carbon to form calcium carbonate, i.e. lime stone.

(iii) Formation of Hydrocarbons : C, N, O and H would be reacting with each other at random. The compounds of carbon and hydrogen were also formed sometimes along with nitrogen or oxygen. These are called hydrocarbons or organic compounds. Methane (CH_4), and Ammonia (NH_3) were formed.

(iv) Formation of complex organic compounds : Due to condensation, polymerisation, oxidation-reduction, the hydrocarbons form different aminoacids. The molecules of aminoacids combine together to form large complex molecules called proteins which are the building blocks of life.

(v) First living molecule : Many such proteins molecules formed colloidal solution in water. They have opposite electrical change and mixed mutually to precipitate as drops of complex, mixtures called *coacervates*. They have tendency to absorb water on their surface to form sort of membrane.

(vi) Primitive living organisms : The coacervates underwent some chemical reactions and produced special proteins or enzymes. These molecules were simple, self replicating called *free gene*. They were similar to free living virus and formed by nucleoprotein. Due to self replication and mutations these genes formed gene aggregates. They were called independently existing chromosomes. This stage might have represented by smallest bacteria in its evolution. Further changes occured around chromosomes by accumulation of metabolites around chromosomes and such complex structure

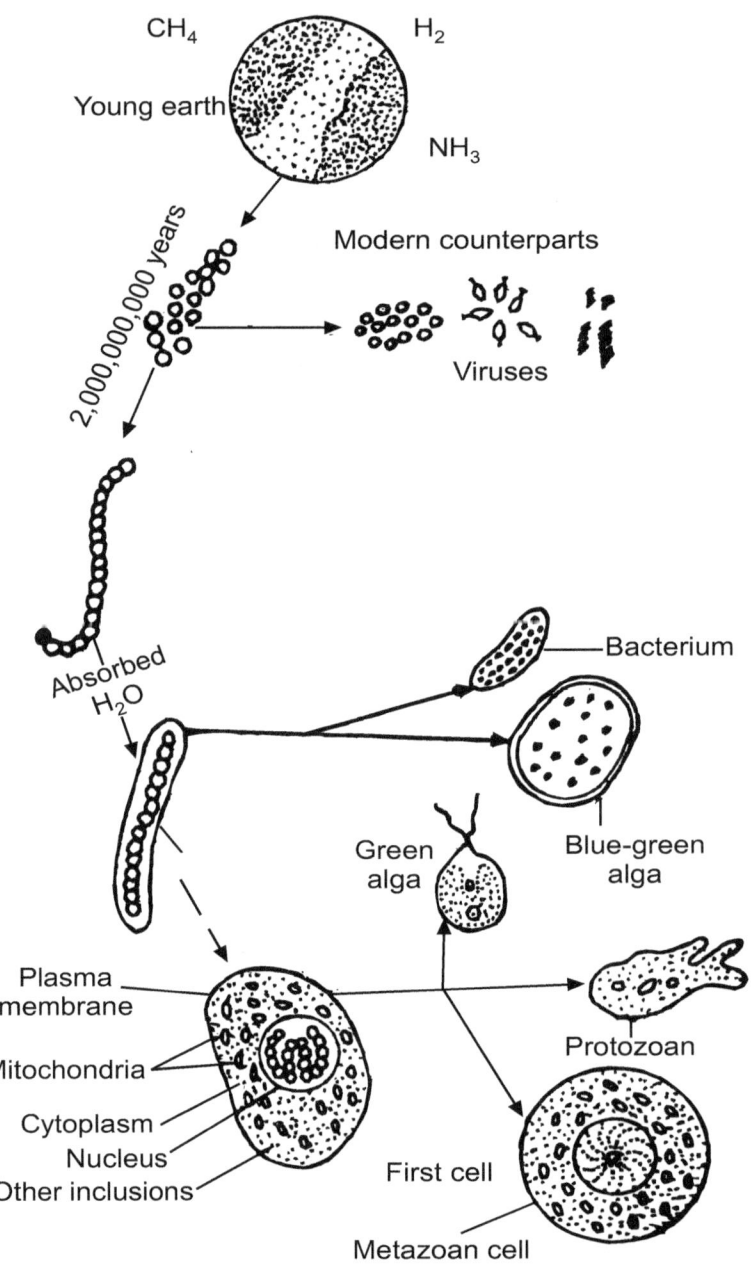

Fig. 3.10 : The first organisms

exhibits exposed nucleus. Some bacteria show this type of structure. Then cytoplasm might have been aquired, like blue green algae or large bacteria. Finally, after mutations there was formation of typical cell with nuclear membrane. These cells were having all potentialities like higher plant and animal cells.

This first organism was neither heterotrophic nor chemotrophic but lasted for long period. These organisms were first accidently originated in sea water. Because of property of self replication, they are called living organisms. They had limited food supply. In some forms by random combinations chlorophyll might have formed which could produce their own food by a process of photosynthesis. Sunlight helps to synthesize carbohydrates like sugar and starch from CO_2 and water. Due to Photosynthesis, Oxygen is given off. As such, organisms grew and photosynthesis produced atmosphere grew richer in free oxygen.

In the presence of ultraviolet radiation, oxygen forms ozone, a gas through which ultraviolet radiation can not pass. This occurs at a height of about 25 km above the surface of the earth giving protective layer. This allowed living organisms to come to the surface of water and to survive even on land. The cell developed organelles like mitochondria, Golgi complex etc. and thus eukaryote cells were originated.

(vii) Miller and Urey's experiment : The *Oparin Haldane* theory was experimentally supported by *Stanley Miller* and his guide *Harold Urey* in 1953. Miller, an American biolgist set up the apparatus as shown in figure and filled it with water vapour, methane, ammonia and hydrogen. The mixture was kept circulating at 80°C and then passed through the condensers. The gaseous mixture was subjected to high electric discharge like that of lightening. Thus, the conditions similar to those prevailed in the early atmosphere were duplicated in this apparatus. The experiment was conducted for a week. The contents of the flask were analysed by the end of the week. The contents showed the presence of aminoacids like alanine, glycine and many other organic compounds. Thus, it was proved that biological macromolecules could actually be formed under conditions present on the primitive earth.

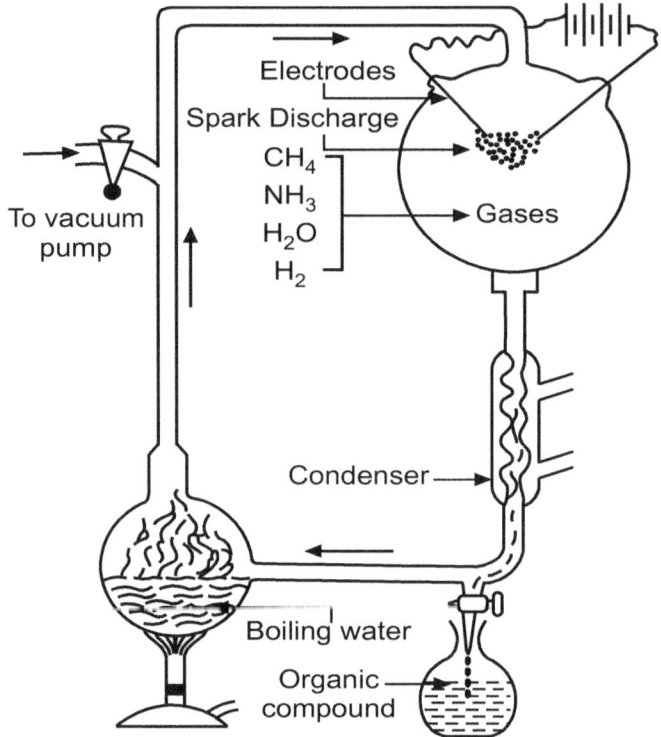

Fig. 3.11 : Miller's experiment

Besides Miller and Urey, many other scientists conducted various similar experiments using different energy sources and obtained variety of biological important molecules like Adenosine triphosphate (ATP), Purines, Pyrimidines, Ribose and Deoxy ribose sugars.

3.5 Drawin's Theory of Evolution

Charles Drawin (1809-82) was the naturalists and who first putforth the theory of organic evolution. **Drawin and Wallace in 1858** presented a paper putting forward the view that species had evolved by a process of natural selection of those races which are most fitted to survive in particular environment. In 1859, Drawin published his book. 'The origin of species by Natural selection' which was accepted by scientists and others.

Drawin's theory of evolution is based on the following six fundamental principles.

(1) Over production : Organisms reproduce rapidly and produce large number of individuals. But all the individuals can not survive. If reproduction remains unchecked there will be no space on the earth for a particular organism. For example, an oyster lays 60 million eggs per year, the offspring of one pair in five generations would have the shells eight times the size of the earth; if all of them lived. In case of *Drosophila* each female lays 200 eggs and fly completes the life cycle in 10–14 days. Therefore, if the production is continued, in 40 days there will be about 200,000,000 flies. A single *Ascaris* female lays 27 million eggs in her life span. The single codfish lays 10 million eggs, if all the eggs hatch, then in few generations the seas would be unable to hold the cod fish population. In case of very slow breeding elephant normally produces six young ones in one hundred years. If they are allowed to reproduce and if all offsprings survive then in the span of 750 years, single pair will produce 19 million descendents. But after a time an organism reaches condition of reproductive equilibrium in which its numbers are maintained at a constant level as long as environment remained unchanged. The high fertility of the animal is compensated by great destruction because there are natural checks like food, shelter, space, diseases upon increase, hence the total number of animals remains almost stationary. This is because; otherwise the food and land will be much less for over population.

(2) Stuggle for existence : It is the most important check for keeping the number of individuals constant. Because of large number there is competition or struggle for food, space among the individuals of the same or different species. This is called struggle for existence. In this struggle there is acute competition between organisms for shelter, food, mating spaces etc. Therefore, most species tend to remain constant due to this limitation. The competition or struggle for existence is of three types :

- **(i) Intra specific :** It is the competition between members of the same species, because they require the same conditions to live and hence it is more acute.
- **(ii) Inter specific :** This competition is among the individuals of different species of plants and animals. Any environment consist of different species and there is struggle for living space and food. For example, eggs and embryos are

destroyed as food, animals are attacked by parasites and diseases, and some are prayed by predator carnivorous animals.

(iii) Extra specific : It is the struggle with physical factors like extreme cold, heat, heavy rains, earth quakes, volcanoes etc. They play an important role in checking the number of individuals and causing population control.

Thus, competition or struggle of existence is continuous process in nature which eliminates some individuals.

(3) Variation and Heredity : Variations are the differences of an individual from its parents or related species and these are essential for evolution. The resemblance of an individual to its parents is called heredity. The variations are to be hereditary. The most suited variations are transmitted to the next generation while unsuited variations are eliminated. Variations help to fit an animal into its environment and better adjusted to survive.

(4) Survival of the fittest or Natural selection : According to Drawin, in the struggle of existence the individuals which are best adapted in the environment will survive and propagate, while the ill-adapted will perish in the process. This process is called survival of the fittest. Thus, favourable variations are useful for the individual to face conditions of life but those who lack favourable variations will not able to face the conditions and will perish or fail to reproduce and hence eliminated from the population. Therefore, favourable variations bring about natural selection whereby the individuals become more and more perfectly adapted to their environment. If there is any change in the environment the species gradually undergoes change to face the new environment and survive under natural selection. Drawin has given the example of cat, tiger, leopord, lion which possess number of similaries but they are different hence are classified separately. This indicates that these animals might have diverged from a common ancestor but through competitions, variations and natural selection. Thus according to Drawin nature selects the individuals which are best suited to the environment. This is called 'survival of the fittest' i.e. those individuals which are fit in nature will survive and unfit individuals are eliminated by the nature.

(6) Origin of new species : According to Drawin the organisms which adapt to new environment through variations may lead to the formation of new structures and modes of behaviours. Thus, these organisms generation after generation produce new and different types called new species. The modification in relation to changes of environment will lead to the 'origin of new species'. The newly formed species shows some few changes from parent species but in the course of time and due to changing environmental conditions there are several variations appear and thus from ancestor many new species are formed.

Objections to the theory of evolution : There are objections to Drawins theory of evolution and they are as follows :

(1) Theory does not satisfactorily explain the occurance of vestigial organs.

(2) It is not explaining the origin of non-useful variations.

(3) Natural selection is not a creating or initiating force but only directing and controlling factor for evolution. It operates after variations have appeared. It accounts for the preservation rather than origin of favourable variations.

(4) The geologic time has been to short to give selection opportunity to do its work.

(5) 'Upon what material does natural selection act in the formation of species' is very fundamental and important problem which was not solved by Drawin.

(6) There are no transitional stages in the formation of new species in the theory.

(7) The theory does not distinguish between heritable and non-heritable variations and it also does not explain the origin of variations, which must be present before any selection can operate.

(8) Natural section is not the main cause, but one of the causes of structural modification in an organism. Theory does not explain cause of natural selection.

3.6 Evidences from Palaeontology

Palaeontology is the study of ancient life of past geologic ages. This branch studies the remains of extinct animals and plants including traces of their existence such as impressions and foot prints. These remains of plants and animals were found in rocks, mud, snow or in sedimentes and they are called fossils. Therefore, fossils are the direct evidence that indicates evolution has occurred. So fossils deal with the actual animals or plants which lived on this earth in the past. But fossil studies remain incomplete because very few living forms had been preserved in nature and very few fossils have been dug and studied. Moreover, most of the animals and plants are soft and can only be preserved under exceptional conditions. Variety of fossils are obtained by palaeonotologists. This includes bones, wood, shells, teeth, skin, pollen, tracts, burrows and even faeces or dung. The fossil record provides us with evidence that there were organisms that have become extinct.

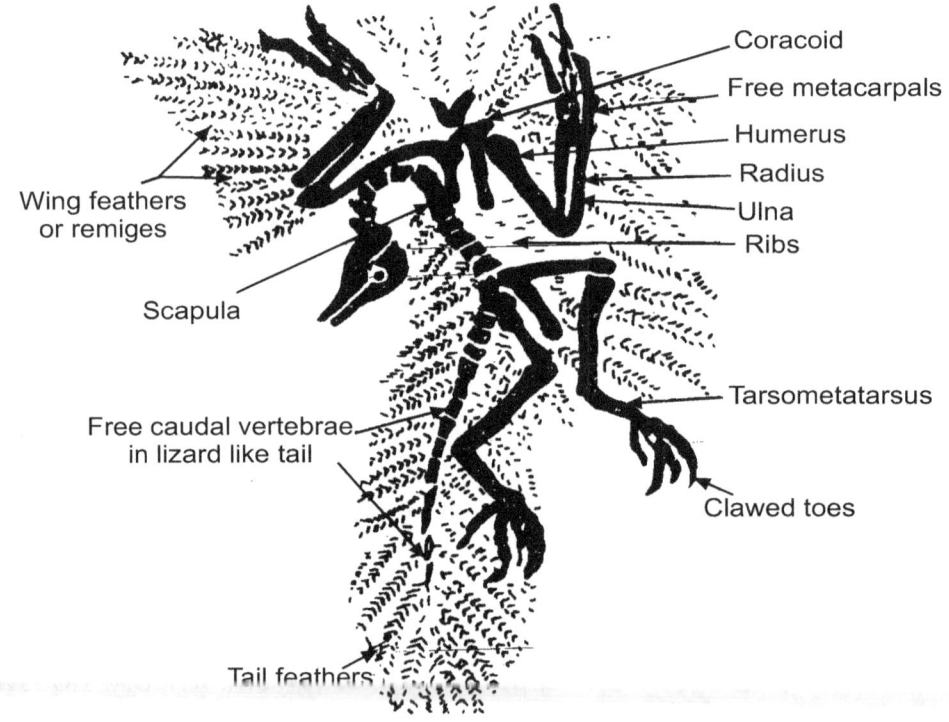

Fig. 3.12: Fossil of *Archeopteryx*

Formation of Fossil : The plants and animals are only preserved and fossilised when they are suddenly burried in the slit of water, lava, ice or sand. Decomposition is caused by several agents. Many parts are destroyed by action of fungi, bacteria, acids, water, wind and temperature. However, under very special circumstances some parts may be preserved with certain modifications to form fossils. Thus, shells which are inorganic in nature are usually preserved completely unultered, bones, and wood on the other hand, are often mineralised or petrified (i.e. turn to stone). The organic matter in wood or bone gradually disintegrates, leaving porous structure. Water seeps into the interior of the bone and minerals dissolved in the water are slowly deposited there. Thus, the porosites gradually become filled with deposits of such materials as lime or silica. Sometimes original inorganic structures may remain as it is or may be replaced by minerals.

Different types of fossils : The fossils are either original remains of extinct animals and plants or their traces of foot prints or impressions on clay, coal or rocks. Some of these fossils have been turned into stone of which strong casts or moulds have been made. Some animals are also found preserved in amber which is the petrified resin of the conifers.

As far as classification of fossils is concerned they are of the following type.

(1) Actual remains : These are original remains of organisms burried and embedded in soft sedimentation or in ice and there had been no change in the constituting material. For example, *Mammoths* and *Woolly Rhinoceroses* burried in ice or oil bearing layers.

(2) Petrified fossils : This type of fossils are formed when organisms are burried in hard sedimentation and due to petrification the organic matter of dead animals or plants is replaced totally by mineral material.

(3) Casts and Moulds : The animal or plant materials were embedded in the hard material, the entire body decayed and dissolved away by the water current under the strata and sometimes percolated by sand or something which become accumulated in that rock case. Such case or moulds and casts were formed in the Cambrian age.

Fig. 3.13 : Mammoth

(4) Trails and foot prints : The animals who walk over sand or mud left their foot prints in the sediment and after that when preserved forms the fossils in the form of foot prints. Sometimes, worms, molluscs left their movement line and formed their trails.

(5) Coprolites : When food particles in the food tract or excretory products are fossilized, they are called corpolites.

Palaentologist gather the fragments of fossils and reconstruct the appearance of extinct animals. Many times the fossils are quite different from the forms found today and indicate that evolution has taken place. The fossils of Archeoptery show that the birds are evolved from reptiles because this animal exhibits the characters of reptiles as well as birds. Thus, palaentological evidence supports the process of evolution.

3.7 Anatomical Evidences

A comparative anatomical study of any particular organ system in the different members of a given phylum reveals a basic similarity of form which is varied to some extent from one class to another. Such studies in comparative anatomy provide many evidences of biological evolution. The comparative forms and structure of various parts of organs of the body offered excellent evidence of evolution. These organs concerned fall into two categories, namely **homologous organs and analogous organs**.

Homologous organs : These are the organs which have the common origin and are built on the same fundamental pattern. But they perform different function and have different appearance. Homology is found in every organ system from pisces to mammals. For example, the arm of man, the leg of horse, the wing of bat, the wind of bird and the flipper of seal are apparently different from one another, both in appearance and function, yet all are pentadactyle limbs. Whatever deviation exists in them, is due to varied adaptation for flying in bat and bird, for running on hard surface in horse, for paddling in water in the seal. Similar homologies are found in vertebral column of vertebrates built on the same plan and derived from the same source of embryo.

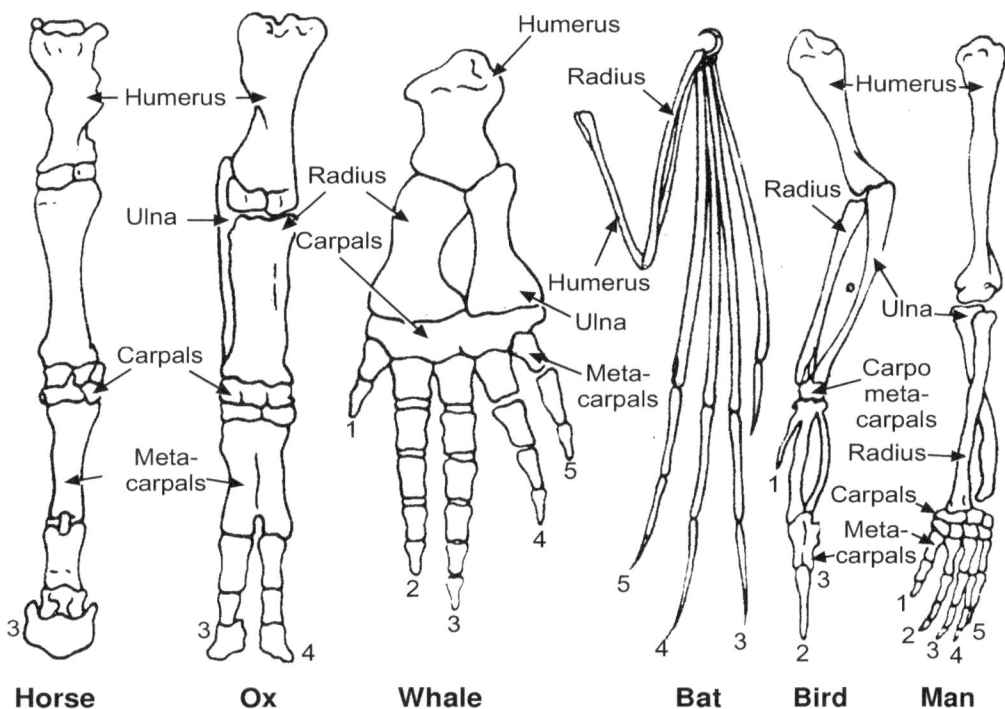

Fig. 3.14 : Homology in vertebrate limbs

The brain of vertebrates presents another good example of homology. The brains of vertebrates ranging from fishes to mammals, are constructed of similar parts like olfactory lobes, cerebral hemispheres, optic lobes, cerebellum, medulla and so on. As one moves higher through the series some lobes become more prominent than others. This happens due to adaptations and evolutionary change.

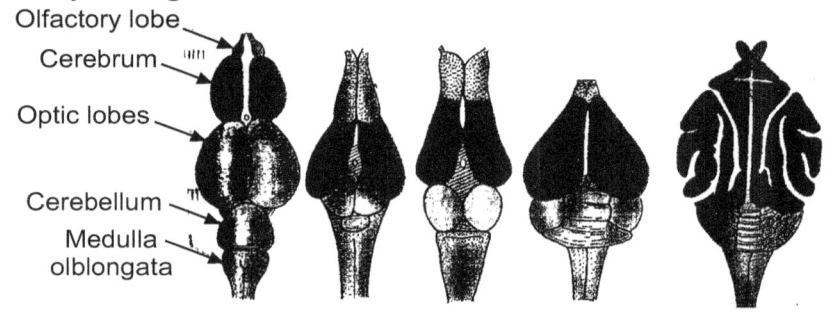

Fig. 3.15 : Brains of vertebrates showing homology

All mammals have seven vertebrae in neck. For example, rabbit, whale, and Giraffee. Their necks are of different lengths. The only conclusion to which one can arrive from these evidences, is that organisms having homologous structures must have a common ancestry and through successive generations extending over millions of years the organisms have time after time, diverged more and more ancestral types usually towards most perfect adaptations to their particular place in the world.

The wings of birds and wings of butterfly serve the same purpose of lifting them in the air but their basic structure has not the least similarity. Such structures which are non-homologous but with similar functions are said to be analogous organs or structures. They have arisen in the evolutionary process through adaptations of quite different organisms to similar mode of life. The analogy thus refers to the relationship between structures which though differ anatomically but have superficial similarity due to similar functions. Often analogous organs have little gross structural resemblance to each other. For example, the gills of palaemon and the lungs of man. Other analogous organs, such as the wings of insects, birds and flying mammals bats may have a superficial resemblance.

Vestigial organs: A special category of homologous organs is that of vestigial organs. These are the organs which were once fully developed and functional but later lost their significance and continue to linger on without purpose. From evolutionary point, they are important evidences for establishing relationship and in ancestors these organs were fully developed and functional.

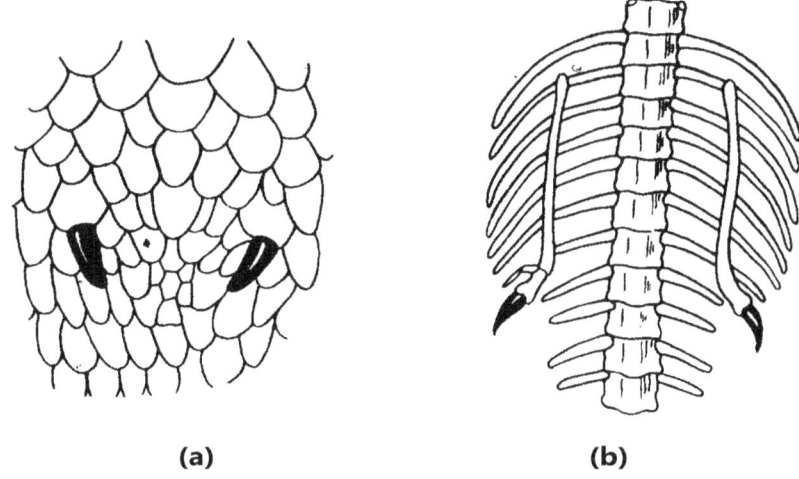

(a)   (b)

Fig. 3.16 : Vestigial limbs of Python

Most of the snakes do not have limbs but in the python there are vestigial hind legs projecting as bluent spines close to the cloaca, which indicates that the snakes have evolved from ancestors that had fully developed limbs. Cave dwelling forms have eyes usually covered with skin or entirely lost. There are about 180 vestigial structures present in man. Nictitating membranes in eyes, vermiform appendix, coccyx or tail vertebrae, tail muscles and muscle of ear pinna, third molar tooth, mammae on male etc. are the vestigial organs found in man. Many vestigial strucutres are more fully developed in embryo, then in the adult, for example, the hair in the whale which are almost completely shed before birth. Pineae eye tuatara lizard, wings of Kiwi, and other flightless birds are other examples.

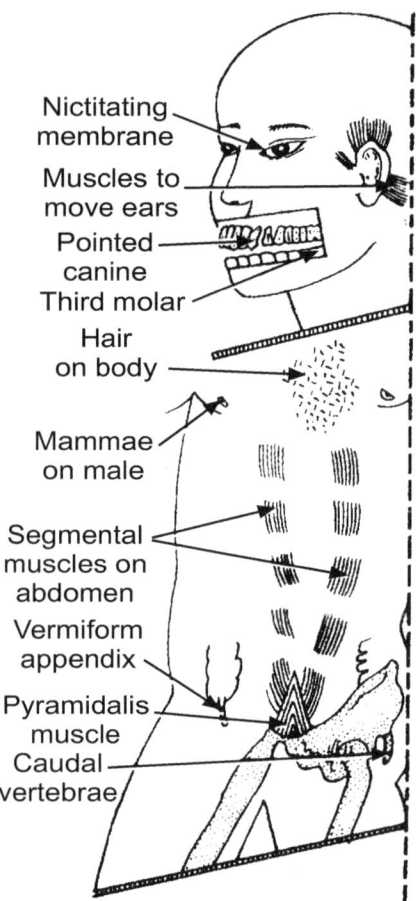

Fig. 3.17 : Vestigial organs in human being

Points to Remember

- Fossils are nothing but remnant of previously existing animals and plants preserved in the earth's crust.
- Different types of fossils are present like actual remains, petrified fossils, moulds, casts, tracks and trails.
- Dating of fossils is determined by stratigraphy, Biostratigraphy and radiometry.
- Under radimetry lead method, carbon method, potassium argon method, stontium method, fission tract method are used for fossil dating.

- *Peripatus* is the connecting link between phylum Annelida and Arthropoda as it shows affinities and with both groups.
- *Archeopteryx* is extinct bird and connecting link between reptiles and birds and it shows important characters of both reptiles and birds.
- *Spenodon* is also called Tuatara, and it is the only living fossil representative reptilian order rhyncocephalia.
- *Limulus* is also called living fossil of phylum arthropoda.
- Evolution is classified into two types namely chemical and biological evolution.
- These are several theories of origin of life.
- Charles Darvin, Lamark, Wallace and Hugo De Vries explained the theory of organic evolution. Oparin Haldane theory explains that life might have originated from non-living organic molecule.
- Oparin Haldane theory was experimentally supported by Stanley Miller.
- Darwin's theory of evolution is based on six fundamental principles. Like over production, struggle for existence variation and heredity, survival of the fitest or natural selection and origin of new species.
- Fossils and anatomical evidences are the palaeontological evidences support the process of evolution.

Exercise

1. What is fossil? Describe the types of fossils.
2. What is dating of the fossils? Give an account of the different methods of the dating of the fossils.
3. Write short notes on:
    a) Formation of fossils.
    b) Types of fossils.
    c) Dating of fossils
    d) Radiometry
    e) Stratigraphy

4. What is connecting link? Describe the *peripatus* as a connecting link between Annelida and Arthropoda.
5. Describe the extinct bird archaeopteryx connecting link between reptiles and birds.
6. What is meant by living fossil? Give an account of living fossil spenodon or Limulus.
7. What is evolution? Give an account of the theories of origin of life.
8. Give an account of Darvin's theory of evolution and add the objections raised on it.
9. What is palaeontological? Give an account of organic evolution.
10. Write short notes on:
    a) *Peripatus* as a connecting link
    b) Affinities of *Peripatus*
    c) Archeopteryx
    d) Living fossil *Spenodon*
    e) Living fossil *Limulus*
    f) Evolution
    g) Theories of origin of life
    h) Chemical evolution
    i) Darvin's theory of evolution
    j) Palaeontological evidence
    k) Anatomical evidence.

UNIT 4...
Applied Zoology : Sericulture
(For Shivaji University only)

Contents ...

- 4.1 Sericulture Industry in India
- 4.2 Species of Silkworms (Silk moths)
- 4.3 Types of Silkworms and their Distribution
- 4.4 External Morphology and Life Cycle of *Bombyx mori*
  - 4.4.1 External Morphology of *Bombyx mori*
  - 4.4.2 Life cycle of *Bombyx mori*
- 4.5 Cultivation of Mulberry
- 4.6 Harvesting of Mulberry
- 4.7 Silkworm Rearing
  - 4.7.1 Selection of Silkworm Variety
  - 4.7.2 Rearing House
    - 4.7.2.1 Disinfection of Rearing Room and Equipments
  - 4.7.3 Rearing Techniques
  - 4.7.4 Important Diseases and Pests
    - 4.7.4.1 Protozoan Disease
    - 4.7.4.2 Fungal Disease
    - 4.7.4.3 Bacterial and Viral Disease
    - 4.7.4.4 Viral Disease
- 4.8 Post Harvesting Process of Cocoons and Preparation of Cocoons for Marketing
- 4.9 Reeling Equipments
  - 4.9.1 Reeling of Multivoltine Cocoons
  - 4.9.2 Reeling of Bivoltine Cocoons
  - 4.9.3 Pressurized Cooking System
- 4.10 Raw Silk Yarn (4.1 to 4.10 only for Shivaji University)

4.11 Microscopic Examinations of Silk Fibre
    4.11.1 Silk Reeling Technology
    4.11.2 Stifling or Drying of Cocoons
    4.11.3 Storage of Cocoons
    4.11.4 Sorting of Cocoons
    4.11.5 Reeling Technique
    4.11.6 Reeling (Devices)
    4.11.7 Re-reeling for Making Standard Sized Hanks
    4.11.8 Skeining
    4.11.9 Book Making and Baling
4.12 Sericulture as Labour Intensive Agro-industry
4.13 World Silk Scenario
4.14 Indian Silk
4.15 Sericulture in Andhra Pradesh
4.16 Sericulture at a Glance
4.17 Rearing Appliances
4.18 Economics of Sericulture
4.19 Brief Idea (Definition and Scope) of Branches of Applied Zoology
4.20 Vermitechnology (4.19 to 4.20 only for Solapur University)
*   Points to Remember
*   Exercise

INTRODUCTION

    The rearing of silkworm for the production of raw silk is known as sericulture. It is the commercial product of silk which originating in the spittle of an insect is a natural fibrous substance obtained from pupal nests or cocoons spun by a large variety of caterpillars known as Silkworm.

    The earliest authentic reference to silk is to be found in the chronicles of **Chou-king** of China (2200 B. C.) where silk is reported to have played a prominent role in public ceremonies as a symbol of homage to emperors.

Legend attributes the unravelling of silk's secret to the Chinese Empress **XI Ling shi** when she was sitting under a mulberry tree with a cup of hot tea before her, a silk cocoon from the tree accidentally fell into the tea cup. Attempting to remove the cocoon she discovered that she could unwind a very fine glistening thread from the softened cocoon. Chinese emperors guarded the secret of silk in the province of *Chan-Tong* for hundreds of years and displayed its beauty to foreign visitors and fancied it as 'the hair of Sea-sheep'. Thus, was born silk which the Chinese called **Si** in honour of the Empress and the Empress **Si-Ling** her self was regarded as the diety of the silkworm. The silk was sold by the Chinese weight for weight in gold and its manufacture was kept a closely guarded secret for centuries. Leakage of the secret was punishable by death. Europeans becoming curious to know the mystery of silk, sent two spies to China in 555 A. D. in the garb of Buddhist monks. The 'monks' discovered the secret and smuggled out silkworms and cocoons in the hollows of their staff. The silk thus reached Europe where the first silk factory was established in the middle of the 6th century A. D. at Constantinople in Turkey, now called *Istambul*. Since, that time commercial production has sprung up in some of the warmer countries but the industry has been confined largely to China, Japan, India and Mediterranean region.

4.1 Sericulture Industry In India

Sericulture is a regular industry in India. It was **Lefroy** who first begun investigation on silkworm and sericulture in 1904-1905 at *Pusa* Institute, New Delhi. But the planned development of this industry was taken up only after the establishment of Silk Board in April 1949. Today, it is well known cottage industry achieving continued progress through improved technology. India has silk producing centres in Assam, Bengal, Chennai, Mysore, Karnataka and Jammu and Kashmir. India produces about 2.5 million pounds of silk as against the requirement of 4.2 million pounds per year. India is second in the world production of Tassar silk. Sericulture is a multidisciplinary programme which involves cultivation of food plants like mulberry, silkworm rearing and silk reeling, weaving and marketing. It is well known that sericulture is a labour intensive agro-industry, well suited for economically backward sections of the underdeveloped and developing countries which have an agriculture base and problems of providing employment not only to the agriculture poor but also to the landless labourers. This industry has a highly remunerative agro-industry with less investment and rich dividends.

The modern silk industry in India has grown to meet the domestic rather than export requirements. Further, this industry provides employment opportunities to about 6 million people in India and plays a key role in the uplift of rural economy besides earning considerable foreign exchange. Like Japan, India has a culture in which silk occupies a dominant position.

Table 4.1 : Silk producing moths in India

Family and Silkworm	Main Host Plant (s)	Domesticated or Wild	Cocoon and Silk	Producing States
Bombycidae Mulberry silk worm (*Bombyx mori*)	Mulberry (*Morus spp.*)	Domesticated	Reelable, white or creamy	W. Bengal, Kashmir, Karnataka, A.P.
Saturnidae Tassar silk worm (*Antheraea paphia*) A. mylitta A. pernyi minor A. royeli	Asan (*Terminalia tomentosa*) Arjun (*Terminalia arjuna*)	Wild	Reelable, brown or coppery	Bihar, Orissa, M.P.
A. proyeli Muga silkworm (*Antheraea assama*)	Som (*Machilus bombycina*) Soalu (*Listaea polyantha*)	Semi-domesticated	Reelable, golden yellow	Assam
Eri silkworm [*Philosamia* (= *Attacus*) ricini] A. (atlas) = minor	Castor (*Ricinus communis*) Kaseeru (*Heteropanax fragrans*)	Domesticated	Unreelable white	Assam

4.2 Species of Silkworms (Silk Moths)

Silk is prepared by the species belonging to family *Bombycidae* and *Saturniidae*. *Bombyx mori* is the well known silkworm belongs to *Bombycidae* while *Eri, Tassar* and *Muga* Moths belong to the family *Saturniidae*. The eri-silk moth was once a wild species, but is now completely domesticated.

1. ***Bombyx mori*** : This is the well known silkworm and is indigenous to *India* and *China*, from where it has been introduced into many parts of the world for commercial purposes. The natural food in all cases is the leaf of mulberry and hence they are commonly called as mulberry silkworms. The silk produced by *B. mori* is white or yellow. This species is used on large scale for obtaining silk.

2. ***Antheraea yamamai*** : This is commonly known as *Japanese Oak silkworm* and also reared on large scale in Japan. This species was introduced into Europe in 1861.

3. ***Antheraea pernyi*** : This is popularly known as the Chinese Oak silkworm which yields silk in large quantity. The colour of silk is pale buff.

4. ***Antheraea assama*** : It is a multivoltine semi-domesticated species chiefly found in Assam. It yields muga silk.

5. ***Antheraea paphia*** : This is known as the common tassar silk moth. It is bi-voltine and yields brownish tassar silk, which is readily reelable. The caterpillars feed on ber, sal, oak and fig.

6. ***Attacus ricinii*** : It is commonly known as castor silkmoth. It is reared on castor leaves and yields "*arandi*" silk.

Taxonomic Position:

Phylum	:	Arthropoda
Subphylum	:	Mandibulata
Class	:	Insecta
Subclass	:	Pterygota
Division	:	Endopterygota
Order	:	Lepidoptera

Family:	(1) Bombycidae	(2) Saturnidae	(3) Saturnidae	(4) Saturnidae
Genus:	*Bombyx*	*Antherea*	*Antheraea*	*Philosomia* (= *Attacus*)
Species:	*mori* (Mulberry silkworm)	*paphia* (Tassar silkworm)	*assama* (Muga silkworm)	*ricini* (Crisi silkworm)

4.3 Types of Silkworms and their Distribution

There are four kinds of natural silk which are commercially known and produced. Out of them *mulberry silk* is most important and it contributes about 95% of the world production. Other three kinds of commercially important silk are non-mulberry silk viz. *eri silk, tassar* silk and *muga silk*.

(a) Mulberry Silkworms

Bombyx mori or the Mulberry silkworm is completely domesticated insect and is never found wild, which has been exploited for over 4000 years. All the strains reared at present belong to the species *B. mori* which is originated from the original *Mandarina* silkworm, known as *Bombyx mandarina* Moore.

The adult moths of *B. mori* is seldom, fat and are primarily concerned with reproduction. Their larvae are voracious eaters. They feed on the leaves of mulberry trees. Some moths are single brooded or *univoltine* and others are many brooded or *multivoltine*. Owing to domestication, a large number of strains have evolved out, which produce cocoons of various shapes, sizes, weights and colours ranging from white to yellow. Only one generation is produced in one year by worms in Europe and other countries where the length of winters far exceeds the duration of summers. Some strains pass through two to seven broods and are cultivated in warm climates. In South India, particularly Mysore, Coimbatore and Salem, a strain which produces several generations, extensively utilized to produce silk.

Bombyx mori produces cocoons with continuous silk filament and therefore can be industrially reeled to produce raw silk. The mulberry silkworm may be further classified and identified as of Japanese, Chinese, European or Indian origin based on geographical distribution or as univoltine, bivoltine and multivoltine depending upon the number of generations produced in a year under natural conditions.

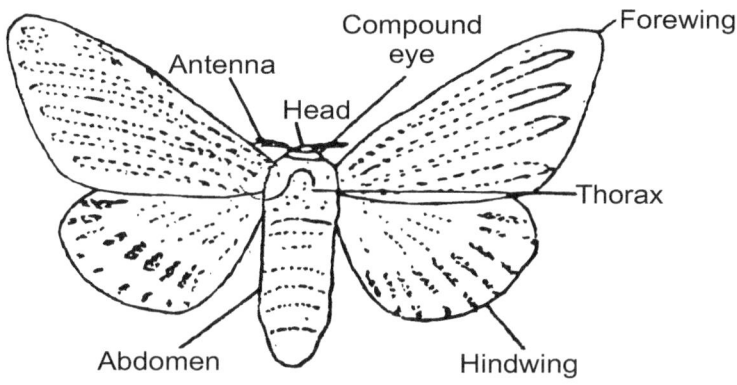

Fig. 4.1 : Moth (*B. mori*)

(b) Eri Silkworms

Eri silkworms *Samia cynthia ricini* (Huts) belong to family *Saturnidae*. The local name *eri* derives from its primary food plant 'era' (castor), so commonly known as castor silkworm is a domesticated and reared on castor oil plant leaves so as to produce a white or brick-red silk popularly known as *eri silk*. The filament of the cocoons spun by these worms is neither continuous nor uniform in thickness, the cocoons cannot be properly reeled and therefore, the moths are allowed to emerge and the pierced cocoons are used for spinning purposes to produce the eri silk yarn.

The distribution of eri silkworm in North eastern India is mostly confined to the Brahmaputra valley and the surrounding areas extending to the foot hills of Meghalaya, Mizoram, Nagaland, Manipur and Arunachal Pradesh upto about 3000 altitude. Manipur are predominantly eri growing areas of this region. Eri silkworm is polyphagous in nature. Its food plants are abundantly found in natural forests in the plains and hilly areas of north eastern India.

However, castor (*Ricinus communist* : Linn) is the major food plant; while Kesseru (*Heteropanox fragrans* Seem), Tapioca (*Manihot utilissima* Pohl) and Barkesseru (*Ailanthus excelsa*) are the secondary food plants of eri silkworm.

Both male and female have brown, black and green coloured wings with white "crescent markings and woolywhite abdomen". The male is smaller than female bearing bushy antennae and narrower abdomen.

This species is domesticated and multivoltine in nature having six generations in a year. *Samia ricini* exhibits several larval strains viz. plain, spotted, semizebra and zebra based on larval markings and white, blue and green based on larval body colour. These strains cross breed naturally.

Eri culture is a traditional practice among the Indo-Mongolid and Tibet Burman sub tribes of this region. This region accounts for more than 90% of the total eri-silk production. From time immemorial, the eri-culture remained a part of tribal's way of life. Hence, eri-fabric is commonly known as 'poor man's wool' or 'poor man's silk'.

(a) Eri Silkmoth   (b) Larvae

Fig. 4.2 : Silkworm larvae of *Attacus ricini*

(c) Tassar Silkworms

The tassar silkworms belong to the genus *Antheraea* and they are all wild silkworms. There are many varieties such as the Chinese tassar silkworm – *A. pernyi* G. The Indian tassar silkworm – *A. mylitta* Dury. The Japanese tassar silkworm – *A. yamamai* Guerin.

Tassar silk occupies the third position; next to mulberry and eri silk. China is the biggest tassar silk producer of the world; followed by India. In the North Korean provinces bordering China, a small quantity of tassar silk is also produced in Japan.

Traditional tassar silk of India is the one produced by the tropical tassar silkworm, *Antheraea mylitta* D. Its distribution extends along the tropical forest belt of India starting from West Bengal in the east, extending upto Karnataka in the South-East through Bihar, Orissa, Uttar Pradesh, Madhya Pradesh, Andhra Pradesh and Maharashtra. Extending along the Himalayas right from Arunachal Pradesh in the east Jammu and Kashmir in the west using the temperature breeds of Tassar silkworm like *A. pernyi*.

Fig. 4.3 : Tassar silk moth *Antheraea paphia* (after Lefroy)

Tassar silkworm is polyphagous, feeding on about two dozen host plants belonging from different families, genera and species but more commercial important are :

(a) *Terminalia* (Vernacular asan, ain)
(b) *Terminalia arjuna* (V. sal) (V. Arjun)
(c) *Shorea robusta* (V. sal)
(d) *Lagerstroemia* sp. (V. Sidha)
(e) *Ziziphus jujuba* (V. bar)

Unlike other silkworms, tassar silk worms being entirely wild, have to be fully reared on host plants. Tassar moths are fairly large insects, females being larger and yellowish brown in colour while males are smaller and brick red in colour but both having eye spots on their wings. Antennae of male are busy (branched) and narrowed abdomen.

The worms are either uni or bivoltine and their cocoons like the mulberry silkworm cocoons can be reeled into raw silk.

4.4 External Morphology and Life Cycle of *Bombyx mori*

4.4.1 External Morphology of *Bombyx mori*

The adult moth of *Bombyx mori* L. is about 25.00 mm long with a wing span of 40.00 to 50.00 mm from side to side and fat bodied. The male silk moths are smaller in size than females. The moth is quite robust and creamy white in colour. The body is distinctly divisible into three regions, viz., *head, thorax and abdomen*. The head possess a pair of *compound eyes*, a pair of bushy (branched) or feathery *antennae*. The females have smaller antennae and the mouth parts with long proboscis. The thorax is three segmented and bears three pairs of legs (five segmented each) and two pairs of wings the meso and meta-thoracic, the front pair overlapping the hind pair when the moth is in the resting position. The cream coloured wings are about 25.00 mm long and are marked by several faint or brown lines.

In the male, eight abdominal segments are visible and in the female, seven. There are six pairs of spiracles present laterally on either side of the body. Female has comparatively fatter and larger abdomen. At the caudal end, the male moth has a pair of hooks known as Harpes whereas the female moth has a knob-like projection with sensory hairs. The female is generally less active than the male. The entire body of both is covered by minute scales.

4.4.2 Life Cycle of *Bombyx mori*

The silkmoth is *dioecious* i.e. the sexes are separate. Fertilization is internal, preceded by copulation. Silkworms pass through a complete metamorphosis (Holometabolous) from egg to the adult stage through two intermediate stages of larva (caterpillar) and pupa (cocoon) (See Fig. 4.4).

Eggs : Each female can lay 300 to 400 small, smooth, subspherical yellowish eggs, either in free or agglutinated conditions. The eggs are tiny and weigh around 2,000 eggs in a gram. They measure 1 to 1.3 mm in length and 0.9 to 1.2 mm in width. The eggs of European races are comparatively larger and heavier. Silkworm eggs are of two types :

(a) **Hibernating eggs :** Deposited in spring, which undergo diapause and hatch out only in next spring.

(b) **Non-hibernating eggs :** Derived from successive generations without any pause in a year.

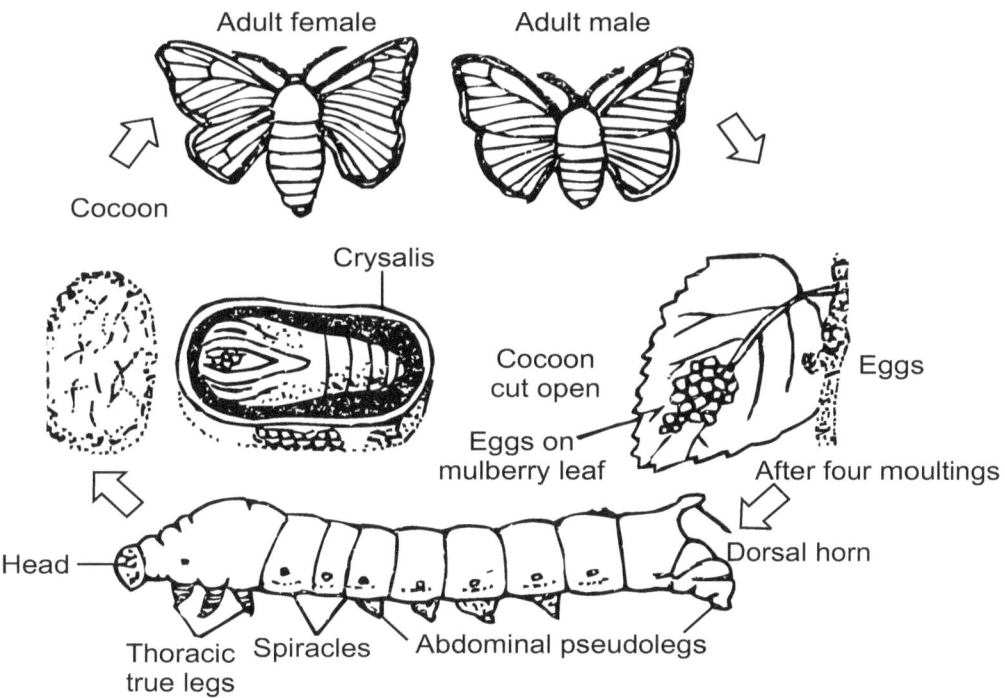

Fig. 4.4 : *Bombyx mori* (silkworm) - Life cycle

The egg contains a good amount of yolk and is covered by a smooth hard chitinous shell. After laying the eggs, the female moth does not take any food and dies within 4-5 days. In the univoltine (a single brood per year), they may take moths because over-wintering takes place in this stage but the multivoltine broods come out after 10-12 days. From the egg hatches out a larva called the caterpillar.

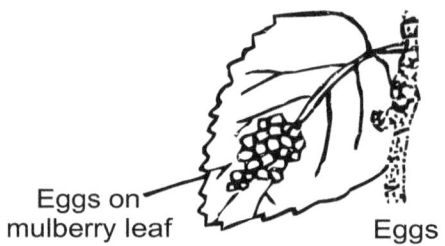

Fig. 4.5 : Eggs on leaves of *B. mori*

Larvae : Eggs when first laid, are bright yellow in colour and under the influence of suitable temperature, embryonic development takes place and the colour changes from yellow to brown, then to grey. At summer temperatures, the eggs hatch in 10 days. On the completion of development, the newly hatched caterpillar is black or dark brown. It has a large head and the body is rough, wrinkled and densely covered with bristles so that it looks like a hairy caterpillar and is polypod type. It measures about 4 to 6 mm in length. The full grown larva is about 6 to 8 cm in length. The body of larva is divisible into a prominent head, distinctly segmented thorax and an elongated abdomen. The head bears mandibulate mouth parts and three pairs of ocelli. A distinct hook like structure, the *spinneret*, is present for the extrusion of silk from the inner silk gland. [Please refer to Fig. 4.6 (a)].

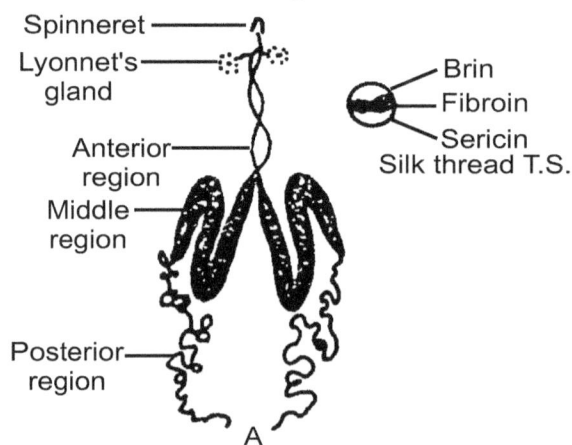

Fig. 4.6 (a) : Salivary gland

The thorax forms a hump and consists of three segments. Each of the three thoracic segments bears pair of jointed true legs. The tip of each leg has a recurved hook for locomotion and ingestion of leaves.

The abdomen consists of ten segments of which first nine are clearly marked, while the tenth one is indistinct. The 3rd, 4th, 5th, 6th and 9th abdominal segments bear ventrally a pair of unjointed stumpy appendages each. These are called prolegs or pseudolegs. Each leg is retractile and more or less cylindrical. The eighth segment carries a short dorsal *anal horn*. A series of respiratory spiracles or ostia are present on either lateral side of the abdomen.

The larva is a voracious eater and strongly gregarious. In the beginning, chopped young mulberry leaves are given as food but with the advancement of age, entire and matured leaves are provided as food. The caterpillar moves in a characteristic looping manner.

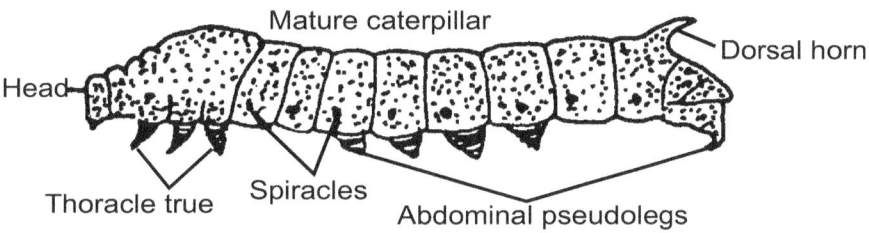

Fig. 4.6 (b) : Silk moth (*Bombyx mori*) Larva

The larval life lasts for 3-4 weeks (30-40 days). During this period, the larva moults four times. After each moult, the larva grows rapidly. A full grown larva is about 8.00 cm long and becomes transparent and golden brown in appearance. A pair of long sac like silk-glands now develop into the lateral side of the body inside. These are modified salivary glands. The little caterpillar, immediately after hatching begins to consume 30,000 times its own weight of mulberry leaves and grows rapidly.

Pupae : The full grown larva now stops feeding and becomes restless and if given a suitable place, such as dried bushy plants or Bamboo mountage (Chandrika), they soon begin to spin their cocoons. This takes about 3 days of constant motions of the head from side to side at the rate of about 65 per minutes. The cocoon is formed from a secretion from two large silk glands which are transformed labial glands (= salivary glands). These extend along the inside of the body and open through a common duct of the spinneret on the lower lip [Fig. 4.7 (a)]. As the clear viscous fluid is exposed to the air, it hardens into the fine silk fibre. Each silk gland extrudes a fine filament of pulpy material called *brin* or *fibroin* and two such brins are stuck together by *sericin* or *silkgum* in the spinneret to form a single continuous fibre known as the *seric bane* about 500 m long and 0.02 mm wide. Temperature and humidity influence the speed of spinning and quality of silk. The cocoons are oval and vary in colour, according to strain or race; from white to a beautiful golden yellow. Silk spinning activity of silkworms is a physiological function by which larvae probably get rid of excess of protein acquired from the mulberry leaves during the period of their growth. The cocoon also provides protection for the developing pupa.

The pupal stage is generally called the resting, inactive stage of the silkworm when it is incapable of feeding and appears quiescent. This stage is a transitional phase during which definite changes take place i.e. internal organs undergo a complete change and assume the new form of the adult moth. The mature silkworm larva passes through a short transitory stage of pre-pupa before becoming a pupa. During this prepupal stage, the dissolution of the larval organs takes place and this is followed by the formation of adult organs during the pupal stage. Soon after pupation the pupa is white in colour and soft but gradually turns brown to dark brown and the pupal skin becomes harder. The prominent morphological parts visible on pupa are a pair of large compound eyes, a pair of large antennae, fore and hind wings and the legs. Ten abdominal segments can be seen on the ventral side, but only nine seen from dorsal side. Seven pairs of spiracles are also seen on abdomen.

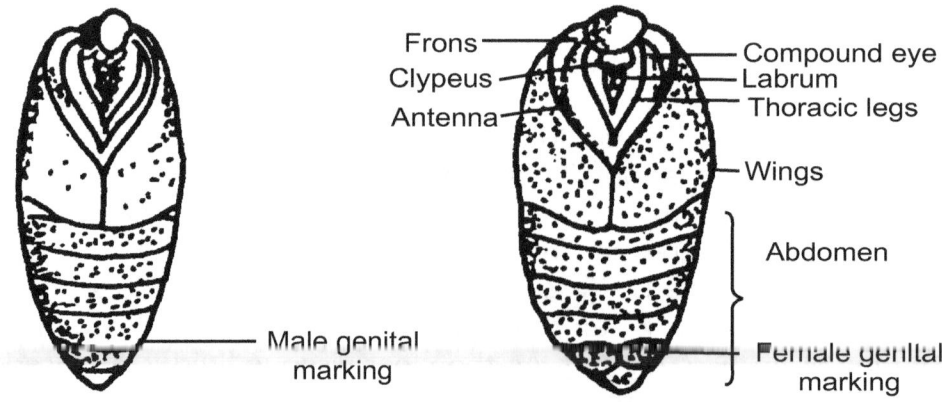

Fig. 4.7 : Male and female pupae *Bombyx mori*

Adult : Within the cocoon the pupa shrinks in length and in about 10-15 days a full-fledged moth emerges through an opening in the end of the cocoon. The cocoons from which the moth emerges are called pierced cocoons. They are of low value because they cannot be reeled, but they are carded and made into thread. The ashy-white moth has a fat body and wing expanse of about 5 cm. It takes no food and rarely attempts to fly but has high capacity for reproduction. The external features are described in external morphology of moth earlier.

4.5 Cultivation of Mulberry (Extra topic for Reference)

Cultivation and harvesting of mulberry plants is called *Moriculture*.

1. Selection of Mulberry Variety :

There are over 20 species of mulberry (Family-*Moracea*) of which four are more common. They are : *Morus alba, M. indica, M. serrata* and *M. Latifolia*. These plants grow both in tropical and temperate climates. An annual rainfall of 600 - 2600 mm is sufficient for its growth. The local species *M. indica* offers certain good features i.e. quick growing, hardiness, remaining fresh throughout the year, but its yield is rather low. Therefore, Central Silk Board have developed high yielding varieties such as Kanva-2, S-30, S-54 (suited for Karnataka, A. P., and Tamil Nadu states) and S-162, S-519, S-623 suited for Punjab, J and K, U. P. and W. Bengal states. These strains give 30-70% more leaves per hectare than the local strain.

Mulberry is a hardy perennial tree species grown in temperate, tropical and sub-tropical regions of the world. The leaves of mulberry form the specific food for the silkworm, *Bombyx mori*. L. Among the food plants mulberry alone contributes about 90% of raw silk productions of the world, the other 10% is from non-mulberry (Tassar, Eri and Muga) food plants. It has been shown that about 75% of the protein directly derived from mulberry leaf is the primary source for the silkworm for bio-synthesis of its silk.

2. Propagation :

Mulberry is propagated either through seeds or vegetatively. The vegetative method is most common. In India, the most common method of propagating mulberry is through cuttings in multivoltine regions like Karnataka and West Bengal. Exotic varieties are propagated through root grafts. In univoltine areas like Kashmir, the mulberry is propagated through seedlings.

3. Climate :

Mulberry can be grown under various climatic conditions ranging from temperate to tropical. A perusal of the geographical position of the mulberry growing countries of the world indicates that all of them except Brazil are located north of equator. Mulberry can be grown in all types of soil and climatic conditions.

(a) Atmospheric Temperature : It is found that mulberry requires temperature ranging from 24°C to 28°C for better growth and leaf yield. Mulberry plants do not grow well if the temperature is below 13°C and above 38°C because the growth and sprouting of buds cannot be obtained. In temperate regions, the plants remain dormant during the winter season. Thus, in temperate regions mulberry leaves are available for rearing purposes only during May to October. In the tropics, growth of mulberry is continuous throughout the year.

(b) Rainfall : Mulberry can be grown in places with rainfall ranging from 600 mm to 2500 mm. When the rainfall is low the growth is limited due to moisture shortage and result in low leaf yield. On an average 50 mm once in 10 days is considered ideal for mulberry.

(c) Atmospheric Humidity : The ideal humidity for mulberry leaf yielding is ranging in between 65 to 80 per cent. The quality of leaf produced during the rainy season is better than the leaf produced during other season because during the rainy season, the soil contains high moisture and high atmospheric humidity.

(d) Sunshine : This is also one of the important climatic factors which regulates the growth of mulberry. In the temperate countries, mulberry grows with a sunshine range of 5.0 to 10.2 hours a day while in the tropics, it grows well with a sunshine range of 9.0 to 13.0 hours a day.

(e) Elevation : In Japan, mulberry cultivation is practiced at altitudes from 22 m to 1735 m above MSL, while in the U.S.S.R. it is practiced 400 to 2000 m. Under tropical conditions and in India, mulberry is cultivated at altitudes between 300 to 800 m above MSL. However upto 700 m, MSL is ideal for good growth of mulberry.

4. Soils :

Mulberry can be grown in all types of soil which maintain the mulberry plants for sustained maximum productivity of quality leaves. It has to supply the following constantly :

(a) The essential major and minor plant nutrients.

(b) Oxygen for root respiration.

(c) Mechanical support or anchorage.

(d) As a storehouse for water.

Since, mulberry is a deep rooted, perennial, long-standing, hardy and monoculture crop. The soil should be deep, fertile, well drained, clay loam to loam in texture, friable, porous and with good moisture holding capacity. But it thrives exceedingly well in red loamy soil with pH ranging from 6.5 to 7.0. It can tolerate slightly alkaline and acidic conditions in the soil. However, the alkalinity can be corrected by applying gypsum/ sulphur and the acidity by adding lime to the respective soils. The soil quality has an influence not only on the leaf yield but also on their quality which are reflected on the growth of silkworms resulting in high cocoon yield with better quality. In lands, where mulberry is grown as a rainfed crop the organic content of the soil is naturally poor and the water holding capacity is less. The rain water therefore percolates very fast and goes underground so that very little amount of moisture is left on the strata where roots spread. This hazard can be overcome by adding organic matters like farmyard manure and compost. It is also by growing a mulch crop such as a leguminous species and subsequent mulching of the same into the soil. It works in two ways first by providing the humus required and secondly, by fixation of atmospheric nitrogen through the bacterial root nodules.

5. Planting :

(a) Location and Topography : Mulberry plantation should be established near the rearing house it is convenient for quick transport and immediate use of leaves for feeding because after harvesting mulberry leaves loss considerable moisture and wither during transport, specially in summer, will lead to wastage of leaves and economic loss to the farmers.

(b) Preparation of the Land : When once the land is selected for mulberry cultivation, the field has to be levelled and the fertility level improved. Levelling of the land depends upon its topography such as flat, incline and terrace type of fields. While levelling, the level of the underground water must be taken into consideration. In case, the water table is nearer the surface, proper drainage must be provided. If it is a hilly area, smaller terrace gardens with contour bunds have to be formed and proper drainage has to be provided for the water to move out. After levelling deep ploughing is necessary to remove the weeds and the soil has to be made into a fine tilth before the pits are prepared for planting.

Wherever mulberry has to be planted the land should be free from weeds as they are unwanted plants in the field of any crop. They compete with the crop for sunlight, water and nutrients. Some of the weeds known to release root exudates which render the soil unfit for the growth of the crop, as they are mainly phenolics and have adverse allelopathic effect. Some weeds also act as secondary hosts for many plant diseases and insect pests which destroy the crop. Hence, it is very important that mulberry cultivation should be taken up only in a land which is free from weeds like species of *cynodon* and *cyperus*. Periodic weeding is a must for better growth of mulberry.

(c) Planting Season : Early spring and late autumn seasons are best suitable for mulberry plantations. Planting in winter and summer seasons should be avoided. Planting should not be delayed in spring, if delayed the sprouted buds fall off and the plants do not grow well.

In India, planting season varies in different parts. In Karnataka, mulberry is planted during July-August with the onset of South-Western monsoon. Subsequent rains help for proper establishment of the crop. In West-Bengal, cuttings are planted during November (Late autumn). Planting during rainy season will result in rotting of the cuttings.

(d) Direction of Planting : In temperate regions, the direction of the rows of planting is important. Depending upon the light intensity (sunshine hours) and wind direction, mulberry seedlings are to be planted in rows either in North-South or East-West direction; making the rows parallel to the direction of wind. In tropics, where the sunlight is not a limiting factor, mulberry rows can be planted in any direction. In sloppy lands, the rows should be parallel to the contour lines.

(e) Planting Distance : The planting distance depends upon, the agroclimatic conditions (sunshine, temperature, precipitation etc.), soil fertility level, intensity of cultivation practices adopted including the training and harvesting methods and also the variety of mulberry planted. Regarding the plant spacing considerations like number of branches, and branching habits of the variety methods of training and fertilizer practices and moisture status in the soil should be kept in view.

Spacing for Mulberry cultivation in India :

		Spacing between rows	Spacing between plants
1.	Pit system (rainfall mulberry)	0.9 to 0.75 m	0.9 to 0.45 m
2.	Row system (irrigated)	0.45 to 0.60 m (0.3 to 0.45 m)	0.45 to 0.60 m (0.15 m)

The general pattern under **rainfall** condition is known as *'Pit system'* of cultivation and under **irrigation** the row planting is known as *'Kolar system'*. In this system, ridges and furrows are made at distance of 0.30 to 0.45 m. On either side of ridges, mulberry is planted at a distance of 0.10 to 0.50 m.

In West Bengal, where rainfall is heavy, a close planting called "*strip system*" is followed. In this method, spacing of 0.6 m between the strips is made, in each strip, 2 to 3 rows are planted at a distance of 0.15 m.

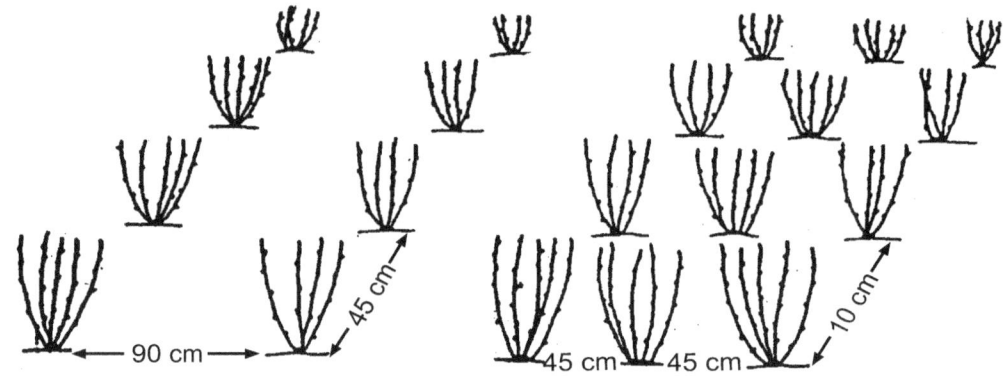

Fig. 4.8 : Planting distance

(f) Selection of Planting Material : Stem cuttings are obtained from 6-8 months old branches. Fully grown thick main stems and branches which are free from insects and diseases should be selected. These should be generally one and a half centimeter thick. The stem is cut into pieces with 3 to 5 buds of about 20 cm long. Cuttings should not be too woody or tender. The cuttings should be clean cut at an angle of 45° with a sharp tool without any split in the bark.

(g) Planting Method : Three methods of planting have been practiced in India.

1. Planting cuttings directly in the field.
2. Raising saplings in the nursery and planting in the fields.
3. Raising saplings in the plastic bags and transplanting.

If the cuttings are directly planted in the field there is bound to be atleast 20-30% gaps as the sprouting in any of the commercial varieties will be anywhere between 70-80%. Further, one cannot be sure of 100% sprouting when these gaps are planted again by fresh cuttings. This kind of planting will not give the farmer uniform leaves as the plants differ in their age which will result in poor cocoon yield. Hence, direct planting of cuttings is not recommended.

After preparation of land, pits of standard size of 40 cm width, 40 to 50 cm depth are made where interplanting distance is over 1.2 metre, trenches of 45 cm × 45 cm are opened in the planting row.

Farm yard manure or compost is applied in the pits or trenches, at the rate of 15 tonnes per hectare, over which leaf mould upto a thickness of about 10 cm is added, chemical fertilizers at the rate of 80 kg N, 100 kg P_2O_5 and 50 kg K_2O per hectare are also applied. After applying the fertilizers, the soil is filled to a depth of 5 to 10 cm and the saplings planted with the spacing as stated earlier.

6. Nursery :

Although mulberry can be propagated both by cuttings and saplings; planting of saplings is recommended as their survival and establishment is better. At least 3 to 5 months before the pits are ready, one should plan for the nursery. Nursery bed must be prepared before the cuttings are ready. The nursery bed should be 4-5 metres × 1.5-2 metres and about 30 cm above the ground level and it should be preferably in shade. The nursery bed has to be prepared with equal quantities of red soil, sand and manure. While planting cuttings in the nursery bed a distance of 15-20 cm from cutting to cutting and 10-15 cm from row to row has to be maintained. The cutting is pushed into the soil leaving only one bud exposed above the ground. If necessary, little fertilizers may be used after one month of planting to boost growth. It is important that the root system should not be damaged while uprooting the saplings. It is recommended that *only 3-4 month old saplings* are transplanted in pits and water should be given immediately after planting.

Raising of sapling in plastic bags is more beneficial than raising in nursery bed. The plastic bags of 20 cm and 25 cm size must be used and the mixture of red soil, sand and manure is filled. In each plastic bag, a cutting of 20 cm length is planted deep in the mixture. Bags kept under the shade and watered regularly. The great advantage of this method is that the root system is not affected during transplantation and plants will be well established after some time and plants could tolerate the drought situation in case of failure of irrigation/rains.

7. Manuring :

The importance of application of fertilizers and manures for both increased productivity and improved quality of mulberry leaves has been well recognised. It is fully realised that the native soil fertility is not sufficient alone; so application of manures and fertilizers is a must. The proper applications of manure are as follows :

1. Increases water retention capacity.
2. Improves the texture of soil helping in good rooting.
3. Increases microbial population.
4. Supplies micro-nutrients in addition to macro-nutrients.

The common organic manures are used for mulberry are farmyard manure and compost. Sometimes neem cake and ground nut cake are also used to a limited extent. Introduction of leguminous cover crops between the rows of main plantation not only protects the soil but also increases the fertility due to accumulation of nitrogen through symbiotic nitrogen fixation by bacteria.

Of the three major elements of fertilizers viz. Nitrogen, Phosphorus and Potassium, nitrogen is the most major important and vital for increased production of good quality leaves.

8. Interculture :

This is done to control weeds and simultaneously make the soil porous so as to allow water to soak deep in the soil and to ensure better aeration and enhance nitrification. All these can be achieved by man power with tools or by bullock drawn implements. First weeding is required 30 days after planting. This can be done by manual labour. To remove weeds ploughing of inter-space between the rows periodically to a depth of 15 cm is necessary. Under rainfed conditions, periodical ploughing is essential to remove weeds and conserve moisture and nutrients. Intercultivation should be done atleast 3-4 times a year.

9. Water Management / Irrigation

Water is the most important single input which controls agriculture productions. There are different methods of irrigation.

(a) Furrow method : In this method, the field is laid out into a series of ridges and furrows. The basal part of the furrows is made wet by the flowing water and ridge is moistened by the capillary movement of the water.

Advantages of this method are :

(i) It is suitable for wide spread as well as close spaced mulberry plantation.

(ii) Evaporation from the soil surface is relatively less.

(iii) The ridges carrying the plant root system are freely aerable helping root development.

(iv) Furrow serves as a drainage channel during heavy rains and thus water stagnation is avoided.

(b) Flat bed method : The field is divided into rectangular beds with bunds all around and channels on the sides. The bed size may vary from 3.5×2.0 m to 4.0×6 m.

The benefits are :

(i) It is suited for most soil types.

(ii) Relatively economic in use of water, their is low wastage of water due to run off.

(iii) The soil is not eroded.

(iv) Irrigation is quicker.

(c) Basin method : The basin method is suitable mostly for tree plantations. In this system, irrigation water from the supply source is laid into the basin around the trunk. The diameter of the basin may vary according to age size of tree from 1.0 to 1.5 m.

(d) Overhead or sprinkler : Method of irrigation can be practiced in undulating lands where low and high bushes are cultivated.

The advantages are :

(i) Most efficient in economizing water use.

(ii) There is uniform distribution of water on the foliage.

(iii) The percolation loss in porous and sandy soil is avoided.

(iv) Most suitable for emergency irrigation.

10. Pruning :

Pruning is a judicious removal of undesirable branches of mulberry plant with the following objectives :

1. To give the plant a proper shape and size.

2. To improve the leaf yield.
3. To improve the quality of leaves.
4. To adjust the leaf production to synchronize with the requirement for silkworm rearing.
5. To facilitate easy leaf harvest and intercultivation, also helps to divert the energy of the plant towards optimum leaf production.

Since, mulberry is a perennial plant, periodical pruning is necessary to maintain higher leaf yield. It is very important that the first leaf harvest should be done only 8 months after planting and the first pruning should be done after the first harvest of the leaves to allow proper establishment of the plant. This will facilitate the plant to develop a sturdy stem and an efficient root system.

The first pruning will be in May/June after the commencement of rains and it will be at 60 cm from the soil level. The second pruning will be in October/November after taking 2 or 3 successive leaf harvest and it will be at the same height as the first pruning for irrigated mulberry, but 90-100 cm (middle pruning) from the soil level for rainfed mulberry.

11. Quality of Leaves :

Leaf which is dark green, turgid, soft, thick with good moisture content and high percentage of protein is considered to be excellent. Such quality leaves will yield better silk. Chlorotic and drooping leaves are due to nutritional deficiency or excess of moisture or both.

4.6 Harvesting of Mulberry (Extra topic for Reference)

It is possible to harvest leaves 5-6 times in a year. Generally, the leaf yield is more in the first three harvests during rainy season and comparatively less during winter and summer. By adopting scientific recommendations regarding the initial establishment and yearly management of the mulberry garden, it is possible to harvest about **10,000 metric tonnes** of leaves from **rainfed garden** and **30,000** to **35,000 metric tonnes** from irrigated mulberry garden per hectare per year. It is important that the leaves should be harvested at the correct stage of maturity to suit the stage of worms, otherwise, quality of the cocoon will be poor.

Harvesting method or collecting method of mulberry leaves can be broadly classified into three types :
1. Branch or Shoot Cutting Method.
2. Leaf Plucking Method.
3. Bud Plucking Method.

1. Branch Cutting Method : In this method, the branches are cut close to the base. One of the types of this method is collecting all the branches before budding in spring. The new shoots formed in these are utilized. In another method, the collection is made during the rearing of mature silkworms in spring. In recent times, the practice of rearing on mulberry shoots throughout the year is becoming more and more popular.

2. Leaf Plucking Method : In this method, only the leaves are plucked from the stems and the branches. There are various types of plucking the leaves. For example, the leaves are plucked leaving behind a part of the leaf blade. In another method, the leaves are plucked close to the center of the stipule either by finger or using leaf plucker. In the third method, leaves are plucked by hand at random. Since, a large amount of leaves are required for rearing grown-up silkworms, the third method is often adopted.

Fig. 4.9 : Leaf plucking method

3. Bud Plucking Method : In this method, all the buds, that is, young leaves are plucked from the shoots and this method is adopted for rearing young silkworms in summer and autumn.

Branch cutting and shoot harvest method saves labour in picking leaves and distribution; bed changing and cleaning. It also minimizes the number of trays and shelves. The silk worms are fed on the floor itself placing them on cardboard or even paper. However, a large rearing space is required in this case. The leaves remain fresh for long as they are on branches.

Advantages of Shoot Harvest Method :
1. The leaves remain fresh on branches.
2. The labour is reduced to the extent of 50%.
3. For every kg of cocoon producing there is a saving of 2-3 kg of mulberry leaves.
4. Production of better quality and quantity cocoons is ensured.
5. Production of more organic manure.
6. Since, the worms are not often touched by hand and the excreta of the worms is collected at the bottom, there will be reduction in diseases.
7. There is no scope for bed changing and cleaning.
8. And there is good scope for better aeration and light in the rearing house.

Disadvantages :
1. Initial expenditure is high for the sericultures.
2. For silkworms rearing, 30% or more space is required.
3. Every time the silkworms are reared, there will be pruning. Hence, material for replanting will not be available.
4. According to some experts when the disease occurs, it will be difficult to remove the diseased worms.

Time of Leaf Harvest :

Leaves harvested in the afternoon contain comparatively less moisture and wither rapidly as compared to leaves harvested in early morning because of the fact that the process of photosynthesis and transpiration are active during the day time. Therefore, early morning is the most suitable time for leaf harvesting.

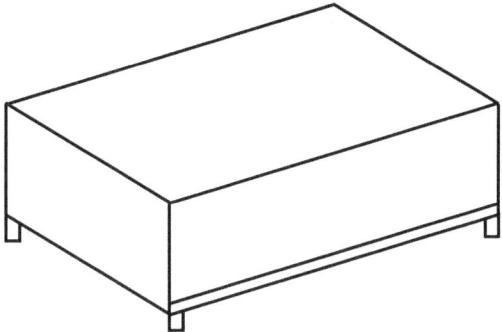

Fig. 4.10 : Wood leaf chamber for preservation of leaves

Preservation of leaves :

Fresh leaves are more palatable and nutritious for the silkworms. Therefore, leaves for young worms should be kept in baskets lined and covered with wet cloth. If the leaves of good quality are to be fed to the grown up worms, it should be stored in wooden frame container measuring of about 1.5 m × 3.0 m × 0.8 m size, lined and covered with wet gunny cloth. The leaves should be kept loosely and turned for aeration to prevent the rise of temperature within the heap of leaves. The cut shoots should be kept in erect position with cut ends upwards and covered by wet gunny cloth. There are ways to arrest the deterioration changes in the stored leaves, as their long storage results in lowering the qualitative values. The ideal condition to preserve the leaves is at temperature below 20°C with 90% relative humidity. Therefore, heaping up of leaves must be avoided as it leads to fermentation and the consequent degradation of chemicals within resulting in the reduction of nutritional value and palatability.

4.7 Silkworm Rearing

Sericulture, mulberry or non-mulberry, is an agro-industry comprising three main components viz. cultivation of food plants for the worms, rearing of silkworms, and reeling and spinning of silk. The first two are agricultural and the last one is industrial part. Mulberry sericulture is the major silk industry in India, so greater attention will be paid to it in this chapter.

India is one of the few countries having tropical and temperate sericulture where sericulture practices differ according to ecological conditions. In Kashmir, sericulture is practiced as a monocrop pattern with single cocoon harvest in a year. In tropical condition of Karnataka, multiple crops of 4-6 per year and in West Bengal a distinct four specific seasons are followed in a year. Following steps should undertake while rearing :

(a) *Insects* : *Bombyx mori*

(b) *Decision of Rearing time and season* : The rearing time is generally decided in accordance with the growth of mulberry leaves. The silkworms can be reared many times during the year; provided there is adequate quantity of good quality mulberry leaves in the garden. The rearing time should be decided taking into the following considerations :

1. Growth of mulberry plants.
2. Leaf quality and
3. Labour required for silkworm rearing.

Regarding the season and the number of silkworm rearings, the silkworms are reared in spring, summer, early autumn, late autumn and very late autumn. Usually, the rearing is possible from April or May to November.

4.7.1 Selection of Silkworm Variety

In Karnataka, bivoltine and multivoltine silkworm varieties as well as their hybrids are continuously used for the cocoon production. The hybrids are used for the commercial production of silk, while the pure varieties for the production of hybrid varieties. The multivoltine varieties are generally resistant and better acclamatized to the adverse environmental conditions when compared with bivoltines. The silkworm varieties are to be selected depending on the climatic conditions of the area, leaf quality, type of rearing house and rearing equipments.

For the silkworm rearing, following steps are involved as requisites and techniques.

4.7.2 Rearing House

Silkworms are very sensitive to weather conditions like humidity and temperature, therefore, they require a house or room in which they are to be reared should meet certain specification; so a sound knowledge of the requisites of a good site is very much essential. The site should be located in a place which can avoid dampness, stagnation of air, fast air flow and exposure to bright sunlight etc. Further, it should ensure an equable temperature, humidity and good ventilation. The ideal direction of the rearing house is north and south with door facing north and windows towards south for good ventilation. Further in the rearing house, the width of the room should be small in proportion to its length, to maintain equalities of temperature inside the room. The roof should have sufficiently high ceiling upto 10 or 50", so that wide fluctuations of temperature outside the room do not affect the conditions inside very much. The roof should be non-conducting material; thatched roof is ideal for the rearing house. However, the rearing house must be rat proof and pest proof, having a wide verandah of 5-6" around the rearing place.

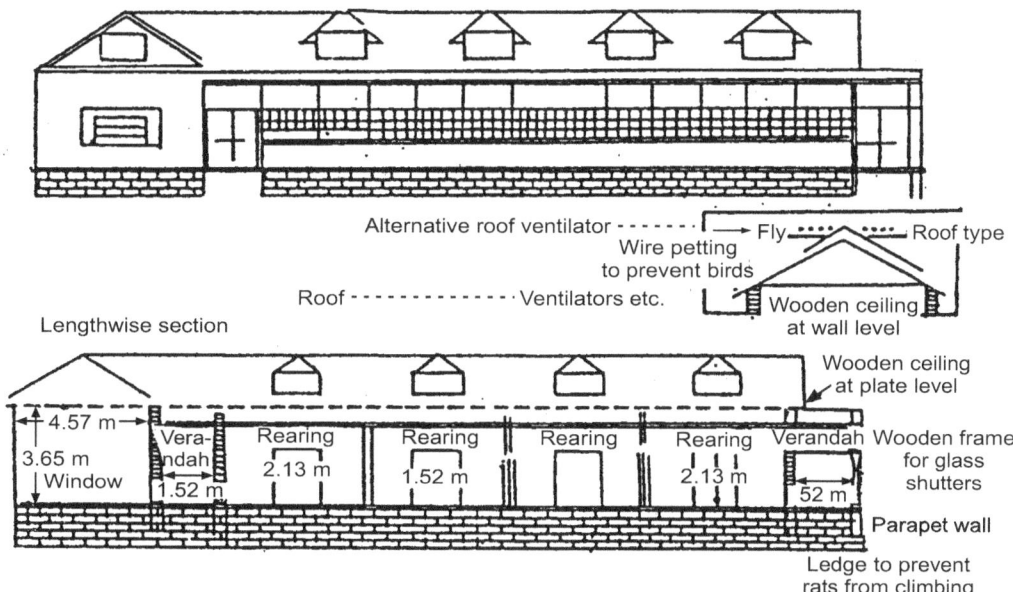

Fig. 4.11 : Model Rearing House

Recently, there has been a tendency to use improvised rearing sheds with roof and side walls made of plastic sheets or tarpaulins which prevent direct draughts of cold air from outside entering the sheds. This type of shed is usually used for shoot on floor rearings.

In India, mostly in south shelf rearing is practiced, so there are no separate rearing houses, but the rearing is done in the dwelling houses themselves. Similarly, in Jammu and Kashmir, floor rearing is practiced in the rearer's own houses.

A model rearing house design of convenient size for self rearing is shown in Fig. 4.11.

4.7.2.1 Disinfection of Rearing Room and Equipments

Disinfection is carried out after completing the rearing and before the next brushing. The disinfection is done for the rearing room and the rearing equipments. If diseased or dead silkworms are found, their excreta and bodies may have bacteria, viruses, fungi or pathogens and if these contaminate the rearing room, equipments and clothes, they will cause diseases in the larvae in the next rearing. Therefore, disinfection should be carried out more meticulously.

For disinfection, usually *formalin* or high grade bleaching powder is used. For disinfecting the rearing room of 10 tatami (1-Tatami = Mat) = 6" × 3" = 18 sq. ft; 167.2 sq. m area and 2.7 m height), 2% formalin is sprayed in the room. For bleaching powder, the product containing more than 60% effective chlorine is diluted to 200 times with water and 18 litres of this solution is sprayed. It is thus necessary to measure the size of the rearing room. The rearing equipments are usually disinfected along with the room itself. The quantity of disinfectant is then increased by 25 to 50%. The rearing equipments should be kept separately and not stacked so that the disinfectant can be applied on all of them.

4.7.3 Rearing Techniques

(a) Procurement of Quality Seeds : The use of quality seeds (silkworm eggs) is important step in successful sericulture. Good quality seeds can be obtained from grainages (grainages are the centres for the production of disease - free laying seeds (Dfls) of pure and hybrid races in large scale and subject them to examined for pebrine or any other disease the egg will hatch out in a day or two.

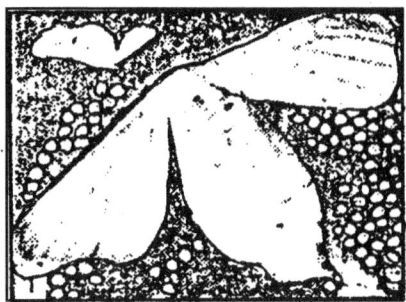
(a) Female Laying on Card Sheet

(b) Silkworm Eggs

Fig. 4.12

(b) Brushing : The silkworm rearing commences with the brushing i.e. transferring the newly hatched larvae from the egg sheet card to the rearing bed and gently provided with the mulberry leaves. This operation is called *brushing*. Chopped mulberry leaves are sprinkled over the newly hatched larvae [Fig. 4.13] which have developed sufficient appetite. If the larvae left on the egg card, they are transferred with the help of feather. The time of brushing should be around 10 A.M. or 11 A.M.

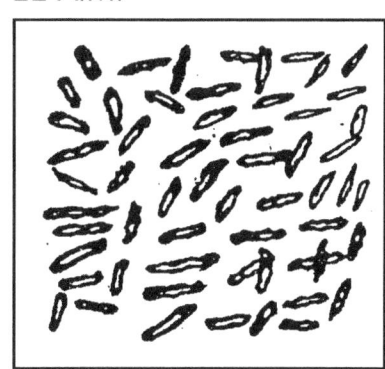

Fig. 4.13 : Young Larvae Hatching Out

(c) Quality of Food : Growth of silkworms depends on the right selection of mulberry leaves obtained from the high yielding mulberry varieties. The younger (I and II) instar larvae are to be given tender succulent leaves with a high moisture and the older instars, mature but soft leaves with lesser moisture content.

(d) Shape and Size of Leaves : Mulberry leaves are fed to the larvae in a chopped condition. Chopped leaves have certain advantages over the entire leaves.

1. Chopped leaves can be spread evenly, the quantity of feed can be regulated and the results assessed.
2. They prevent silkworm beds from getting damp in wet weather.
3. They do not curl up when the weather is dry.

The main disadvantage of chopping is that, it takes labour and expense. Shape of the chopped leaves is also important :

1. Square pieces are best when the air is dry because they prevent rapid withering.
2. Long thin strips or oblong pieces are suitable when season is wet.
3. Triangular pieces takes less labour and so can be given to older instars who consume large quantities of leaves. For chopping, leaves should be spreaded on chopping board and chopping should be carried out by a broad blade sharp-edged knife.

(e) Preparation of Feed Bed for Different Rearing Methods /Techniques : Feed bed is a layer of chopped leaves spread on a tray or over a larger area. In the case of younger (I and II instar) larvae, a good quality paraffin paper sheet (or newspaper) is spread in a rearing tray. Finally, chopped mulberry leaves are evenly scattered on the paper and the larvae carefully brushed onto the leaves. A second sheet of paraffin paper is placed loosely over the bed and in between the two sheets and on all sides water-soaked foam rubber-strips (or wet newspaper folds) are placed to maintain the humidity. To prevent muscardine (a fungus) disease, particularly at humid places, a thin layer of *ceresan lime* (slaked lime + ceresan) or dithane M-45 is spread over the bed as a prophylactic measure. In place of trays, wooden boxes (10-15 cm deep and of required sizes) with or without lids can be used. The boxes could be stacked one above the other but separated by thin wooden strips for ventilation. The older (III to V) instars can be reared by three-methods, namely, shelf rearing, floor rearing and shoot rearing.

(i) Shelf Rearing Method : Rearing of silkworms in round bamboo rearing trays arranged one over the other in tiers on rearing stands is called *shelf rearing*. A stand can accommodate 10-11 trays and therefore, this method provides economy of space but requires more labour for handling so many trays. Larvae are fed on chopped leaves in this method.

Fig. 4.14 : Shelf Rearing of Advanced Stage Larvae

(ii) Floor rearing method : This is another method of rearing silkworms on fixed rearing seats or benches; 5-7 × 1-1.5 m size constructed in 2-3 tiers of wooden or bamboo strips, are used for rearing the silkworms. Leaves in this method are also given in chopped state. This method is financially more economical than the first one because it does not involve labour in handling trays. This method is more used in Japan.

(iii) Shoot rearing method : Shoot rearing is very similar to floor rearing. Silkworms are reared on big branches in one or two tiers. The big shoots harvested from the fields are fed straight a way to the worms. The rearing seats are usually 1 m wide and of any length long. Shoot rearing is usually on a single tier, 20 cm above the ground or outdoor shoot rearing is possible only when the atmospheric conditions are favourable, at temperature approximately 25°C. To change the bed in this method, ropes parallel to each other are stretched on the old bed and new shoots are placed on these ropes. When all the larvae have climbed on the new branches, the ropes are rolled into loose bundles, the old bed and litter cleaned and the ropes and the branches spread again, making a new bed. This method is suitable for the IV and V instars, and saves both on labour (50-60%) and leaves (10-25%), so most economical of the three methods.

Fig. 4.15 : Shoot Rearing of Advanced Stage Larvae

(f) Number of Feeds : About the number of feeds to be given to different instars, it was earlier believed that all stages should be fed 10-12 times a day. However, recent findings show that 4-feeds a day are sufficient for each instar. The feeds are normally given at 9 a.m., 3, 5 and 9 p.m.

(g) Bed Cleaning : Periodical removal of unconsumed dry leaves along with worm excreta exuvia etc. and from the rearing bed termed as bed cleaning. It is necessary not only from the hygienic point of view but also from the point of proper growth of the larvae. This has to be done periodically i.e.

(i) Once during I instar (prior to first moult).
(ii) Twice during II instar (2 feedings after 1st moult and prior to second moult).
(iii) Thrice during III instar (2 feedings after second moult during the middle of the instar and prior to third moult).
(iv) Daily during IV and V instar.

Four methods are usually adopted for bed cleaning viz.

(i) Conventional method.
(ii) Husk method.
(iii) Net method.
(iv) The combined husk and net method.

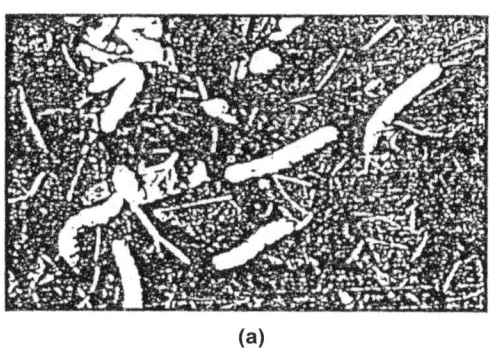
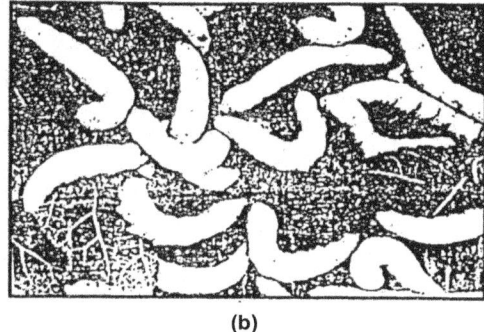

(a) (b)

Fig. 4.16 : IV and V instar Silkworms to Show Spacing

(i) Conventional Method : The worms in I to III instars are simply swept together with a feather and transferred from the old to the new bed and the worms in IV and V instars are transferred manually. This method is practiced by farmers.

(ii) The Husk Method : In this method, a thin and even layer of paddy husk is sprinkled over the bed to be changed and on the husk is scattered the chopped leaves. The worms quickly crawl through the husk to get at the feed where from they can be removed to the new tray. For the I and II instars, the husk may be broken (not powdered) by pounding. For the III instar, whole husk and for the IV and V instars, even chopped straw can be used. For the first two instars, husk could be substituted by the round holed mosquito net cloth. It helps to identify tiny larvae on white background.

(iii) Net Method : In this method, a cotton or nylon net of suitable size is spread over the old bed and fresh leaves are scattered on it. The larvae as usual migrate to the net in search of fresh leaves and can be collected and transferred to a new bed.

(iv) The Combined Husk and Net Method : In this, a thin layer of paddy husk is first sprinkled over the old bed and a net of suitable mesh is superimposed on it. Two successive feedings follow whereafter the net with the worms on it is transferred to another tray. This method combines the cleanness of husk method with the ease of transference of the net method. It also requires less skill and care in manipulation though it is slightly more expensive. Following Table 4.2 concludes the informations from feeding to bed cleaning.

Table 4.2 : Rearing, feeding and bed cleaning for different larval instars of *B. mori*

Instar	Rearing method	Leaf size (cm)	Feed No./day	Bed cleaning No./day
I	Tray and box rearing methods	0.5 – 2.0	4	1
II	Tray and box rearing methods	2 – 4	4	2
III	Shelf, floor and shoot rearing methods	4 – 6	4	3
IV and V	Shelf, floor and shoot rearing methods	entire leaf	4-5	1

(h) Spacing : Spacing means avoiding over-crowding of caterpillars by increasing the size of the feeding trays (areas) with the growth of the worms. For good results, rearing space may be doubled or tripled for I to III larval stages, 2-3 times more than this for the IV and 2 times more than this for the V instar.

It is well-known that silkworms grow very fast; nearly 10,000 times increase in weight and 7000 times increase in size during the short span of 24-30 days and leads to crowding. It increases accumulation of gases, heat and fermentation of faecal matter, particularly during the early stages when the temperature and humidity in the rearing beds are high. Such unhygienic conditions may lead to infection, death and loss of crop.

Moulting : Moulting is a very critical event in the life of caterpillars. When about to moult, the larvae attain their maximum size for the particular instar. At this stage carried out bed cleaning and leaves should be chopped to small size for pre-moult feeding.

When the larvae settle down for moulting, they stop feeding. It is advisable to sprinkle some lime powder after the last feed which prevents early ecdysing the larvae from commencing feeding and thus maintaining the uniform growth in all. During moulting, the worms are most susceptible to muscardine infection which could be prevented by dusting them with ceresan and lime powder.

(i) Mounting and Harvesting : Transferring mature (i.e. V instar) larvae to mountages (cocoonages or chandrikes) is called mounting. Towards the final larval instar, the silkworm stops feeding and gets ready to build the cocoon prior to transforming itself into the pupa inside the cocoon. The feeding during the final instar may last from 5 to 7 days in the case of multivoltine and bivoltine races in the tropical areas and 7 to 9 days in the case of bivoltine and univoltine races in sub-tropical areas. With the cessation of feeding and as the stomach contents empty, the fully mature larvae become translucent and yellowish in appearance, their body shrinks; which is a clear indication that the worm is fully ripe and is ready to be mounted onto mountages or cocooning frames or chandrikes. Such ripening larvae normally crawl towards the periphery of the rearing trays in search of suitable supports for (building) spinning their cocoons. This is the right time to pick them up and put them on mountages.

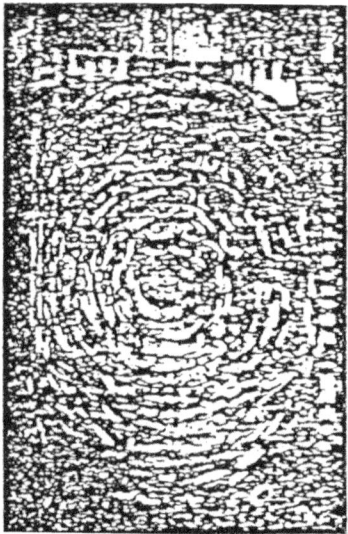

Fig. 4.17 : Mounting of Silkworms on Chandrika

Such silkworms attach themselves to the spirals of the mountages and start spinning cocoons. If unripe worms are put on the mountages, they will move and defecate spoiling the cocoons of the ripe worms or will fall off to be a loss to the rearer. Therefore, it is necessary that only right age larvae are put on the mountages and a correct density be maintained to avoid crowding (i.e. In the Indian type of mountages, or chandrikes, the mounting should be at the rate of about 50 worms per 0.1 m^2). Overcrowding may lead to the formation of double cocoons and also to the cocoons getting spoiled due to staining from the urine and excreta of the silkworms. Mounting done under optimum density gives more uniform and good quality cocoons.

To save labour and time in picking up ripe worms, three methods can be applied viz. (i) Free Mounting Method, (ii) Branch Mounting Method, (iii) Net Mounting Method.

- **(i) Free Mounting Method :** In this method, instead of collecting the mature worms from the beds, the mountages/chandrikes are placed in the beds themselves and the worms crawl upon to them.

- **(ii) The Branch Mounting Method :** In this, the branches of mulberry with green leaves are kept over the rearing bed and when the worms crawl onto them, they are shaken off on a net and transferred to the mountages.

- **(iii) The Net Mounting Method :** In this, a net is spreaded over the bed after feeding. The non-feeding immature (V instar) silkworms come up and crawl onto the net which is then shaken on a mat and the larvae transferred to the mountages.

- **(j) Environmental Conditions and Care during Cocoon Spinning :** Environmental conditions during mounting is important as it determines the quality of the cocoon's spun. Normally, it requires ventilation and dried atmosphere. Ideal conditions for good spinning are temperature of room not exceeding 26°C and relative humidity between 60-70%. Too high temperature induces the larvae to spin their cocoons in hurry and quality of cocoon is affected (i.e. irregular shaped cocoons of poor quality and thicker fibres). Much lower temperature causes delay in spinning, adversely affects the colour and texture of the silk, thread becomes thin, and cocoons flacid (uncompact) resulting in reeling trouble and wastage. So abnormal temperatures affect the health of the worms and make the cocoons unfit for seed purposes. Likewise, high humidity spoils the lustre of the filaments. Similarly, ventilation of the room should be such that humidity is reduced but the worms are not exposed to violent draught of wind or to direct sun.

(k) Harvesting of Cocoons : After the cocoons are completely formed, they are removed from the mountage and the surrounding's floss is removed is called *harvesting*. The cocoons are harvested only after ensuring that the spinning is complete and the mature larvae contained in the cocoons have metamorphosed into pupae on the 4th or 5th day of spinning.

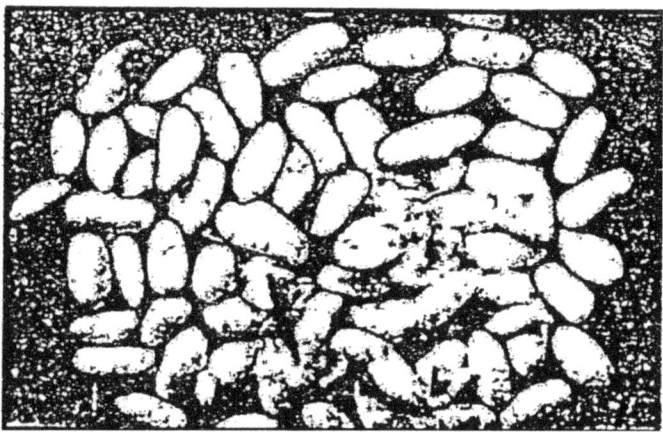

Fig. 4.18 (a) : Harvested Cocoons

The pupa when formed has a thin cuticular skin which is soft to the touch and ruptures easily if disturbed, injured; therefore, early harvesting of cocoons should be strictly avoided. In course of development, the pupal skin becomes hard and turns dark brown, at this stage the cocoons can be harvested. The proper time for harvesting cocoons is on the

7th or 8th day of spinning in the case of bivoltine and univoltine races, and on the 5th day in the case of multivoltine races. Harvesting must not be delayed beyond the period mentioned above because any parasitic insects (uziflies) infecting the silkworm larvae emerge from the pupa and damage the cocoons (i.e. uzifly often cuts a hole in them and comes out). Cocoons are normally harvested by hand.

(*l*) **Sorting of Cocoons :** Among the harvested cocoons there are normal cocoons, slightly defective cocoons, highly defective cocoons, double cocoons and unhealthy cocoons. It is necessary to reject the defective cocoons. This is known as sorting of cocoons. Sorting of cocoons is carried out mainly for double, thin-shelled, dead, dirty, loose shelled, very thin and transparent, thin middle shell, frame adherent and irregular cocoons. All these are carefully separated and rejected, only good cocoons that are normal are picked up for future checking.

The colour of the cocoon in the commonly reared silkworm strains is mostly white. Besides this colour there are cocoons of different colours such as golden yellow, flesh yellow, crimson, bamboo leaf colour and green. The colour pigment of cocoon is chiefly present in sericin. The cocoons of domestic silkworms are of various shapes : barrel shaped, oval, round or spindle shaped. The cocoons varies in its size according to the strains.

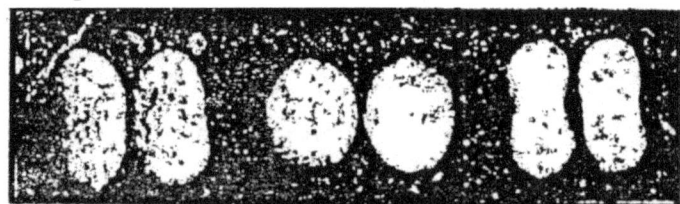

Fig. 4.18 (b) : Various Types of Normal Cocoons

(m) **Composition and Uses of Silk :** Silk filaments as ejected from the spinneret of the silkworm are composed of two strands (brins). Each brin consists of two distinguishable area -

a central core of fibrous protein - fibroin (75%), and surrounding envelope of gelatinous protein - sericin (25%).

Silk is valued for light, durable and lustrous fabrics. It is exceedingly hygroscopic, very hygienic and a poor conductor of heat and electricity. Hence, it is used as insulator in the coils of telephones and of wireless receivers. Silk is, ofcourse used extensively in the manufacture of woven and knitted garments. Fabrics for garments in various weaves, plain, twill, satin, crepe, georgette and velvets, knitted goods such as vests, gloves, socks, stocking, dyed, printed, embroidered figured and ornamented fabrics for saris, jackets, shawls, wrappers, handkerchiefs are made out of this material. It is also employed in the making of parachute components, fishing lines and elastic webs. Silkworm gut is used in surgical operations.

4.7.4 Important Diseases and Pests
(Extra topic for Reference)

Diseases : The silkworm, *Bombyx mori* that has been under domestication since time immemorial is prone to the attack of a number of diseases. Among the diseases *pebrine, grasserie, flacherie* and *muscardine* are important. They are all serious capable of destroying the entire stock (crop). Today, although no specific information on the loss due to various diseases is available, it is estimated that 30 to 40% of the total crop is lost due to diseases. Japan has reduced its loss to 10% in recent years.

4.7.4.1 Protozoan Disease

Pebrine : The Microsporidiosis of the silkworm is popularly known as *'Pebrine'* all over the world. It is a French name, in Hindi it is called *'Kata'*. De Quartrifages (1860) gave the name pebrine to this disease because of the characteristic infection and appearance of dark pepper like black spots on the body of the infected larvae. It is first reported in France in 1845.

Pathogen : Pebrine is caused by a protozoan *Nosema bombycis* nageli belonging to the order *Microsporidia*. The infection occurs either via the mother moth or orally. The microspores found in the body of diseased silkworms are oval and refractile. Their longitudinal and transverse diameters are 2-3 µ and 1.5-2.0 µ respectively. Transovarian transmission of the parasite has been observed.

Symptoms : Infected larvae show black spots resembling pepper sprinkled all over the integument. The larva becomes milky white, unequal size, sluggishness, slow and irregular growth are the main symptoms. Infected pupae are heavier and the cocoons are flimsy. The moths that emerge from infected pupae are deformed by having small wing and distorted antennae. Further, the eggs are laid very irregularly. The silk is of inferior quality both in strength and uniformity.

Control :
1. Use the disease free female moths and eggs.
2. The rearing house, equipments, eggs and workers thoroughly sterilized with 2% formalin.
3. Destruction of infected seeds and laying females.

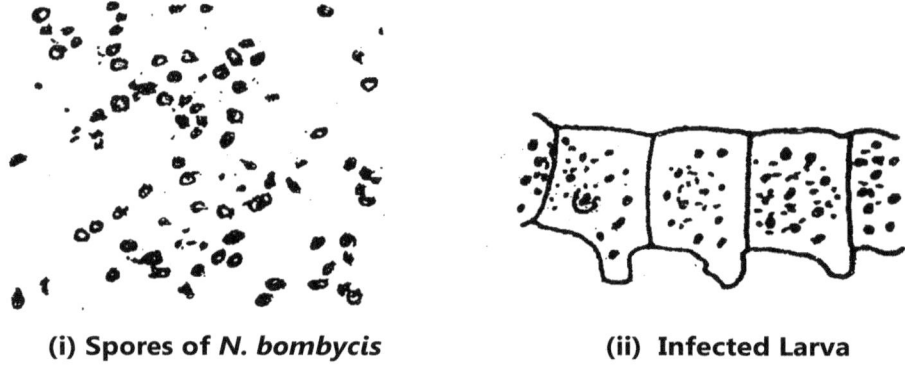

(i) Spores of *N. bombycis*   (ii) Infected Larva

Fig. 4.19 (a)

4.7.4.2 Fungal Disease

Muscardine : The disease caused by fungal pathogens in insects is called muscardine disease. Depending upon the etiology and colour of the spore, different kinds of muscardine of silk worms are identified. They are white muscardine, green muscardine, yellow muscardine, red, purplish red, orange muscardine, aspergillosis, pencillosis etc.

The first three are of greater importance. However aspergillosis is also important in recent times.

Following Table 4.3 shows the different kinds of muscardines of silkworms.

Table 4.3 : Fungal diseases

	Muscardine type	Casual organism
1.	White muscardine	*Beauveria bassiana (Bals)*
2.	Black muscardine	*B. brongniartti (Sacc)*
3.	Black muscardine	*Metarrhizium anisopliae*
4.	Green muscardine	*Spicaria prasina (Maublank Sawada)*
5.	Yellow muscardine	*Paecilomyces forinosus* = *Isaria farinosus (Dicks)*
6.	Red muscardine	*Sporosporella uvella (Krass)*
7.	Yellow red muscardine	*Paecilomyces fumosorosea*
8.	Purplish red muscardine	*Spicaria rubida*
9.	Orange muscardine	*Sterigmatocystis japonica*
10.	Aspergillosis/Brown muscardine	*Aspergillus flavus L., A. tamarii Kita*
11.	Pencillosis	*Penicillium citrinum* *P. granulatum*

(a) White Muscardine :

This disease is known by different names viz. Calcino, Sunnakaddi, Chitti and Chenakatu. It is first identified by **Bassi** in 1835.

Pathogen : *Beauveria bassiana* is causative organism. Its conidium is colourless, spherical or oval in shape, the size is 2.5-3.5-4.5 × 2.3-3.3-4.0 µ. Collectively they appear white in colour. The conidia germinate in about 6-8 hours at 26-28°C. The mycelia are colourless and branched.

Symptoms : In the early stage of the disease, the larvae loses appetite and becomes inactive. On progress, moist specks / oily stain appears on different parts of body. The larvae do experience diarrhoea and vomiting and consequently the body becomes limp losing its elasticity, around spiracles brown colour appears which later develops into black patch in 2-5 days of infection. After death, the body is soft initially and later becomes stiff and hard. This disease is very serious to aged silkworms.

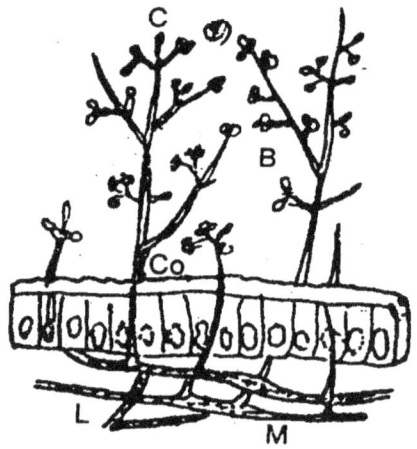

Fig. 4.19 (b) : Growth of the pathogen of white muscardine (Mitani) insertions; C formation of spores; Co basidia; B basidia stem; M mycelium; L crystal; H epidermal cells of the silkworm

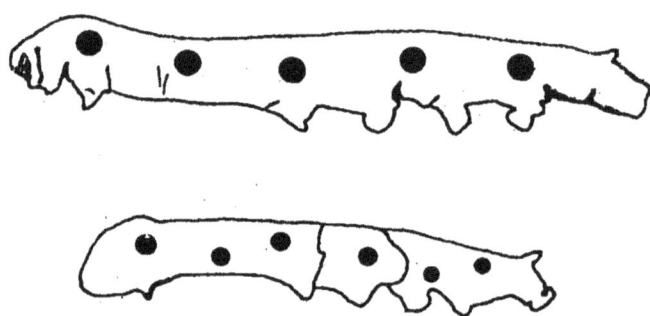

Fig. 4.20 : White Muscardine Affected Silkworms showing Spots like Oily Specks

(b) Green Muscardine :

Pathogen : *Spicaria prasina* is causative organism; conidia are round or oval, light green in colour and measure 3.5-4.0-5.2 × 2.0-2.5-3.2 µ. Under favourable conditions (22-23°C) they expand, from an end. The germ tube penetrates into the body, ramifies and reaches the body fluid and organizes the hyphal body.

Symptoms : As the disease develops, the worms loss appetite and become inactive. Symptomatic specks of either round, oval or of irregular shape with prominent periphery, clearly indicating the circumference, appear, which on coalescence form large specks. They appear dry and a little concave.

After death, the worms become stiff-hard and 2-3 days later the entire body becomes covered with mycelia and in 10-15 days later the mycelia bear fresh green conidia. This fungus also infects insects of various orders like *Coeleoptera*, *Lepidoptera* and *Hemiptera*.

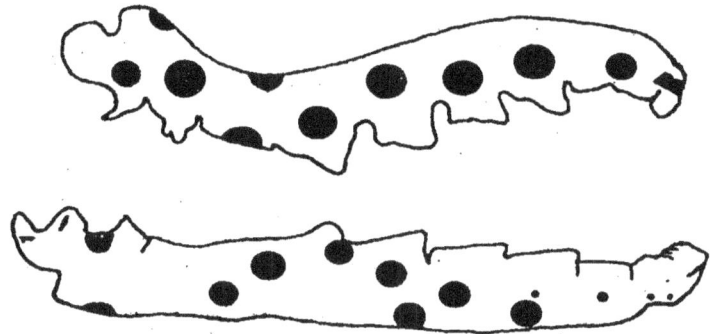

Fig. 4.21 : Green Muscardine

(c) Yellow Muscardine :

Pathogen : *Paecilomyces farinosa* (= *Isaria farinosa*). The conidia are oval but rarely spherical or bell shaped collectively appear yellow and measuring 2.0-2.9-3.7 × 1.5-2.5-3.5 µ in size. Under favourable conditions each gives out 1-2 germ tubes which form the 'appressorium' and later invade into host body.

Symptoms : In addition to becoming inactive, large specks appear around the spiracle and small specks appear over the body; with vomiting and diarrhoea. The body becomes hard and covered with yellow mycelia.

(d) Aspergillosis/Brown Muscardine :

This disease is caused by more than 10 species of the genus *Aspergillus*. Most of these fungi are distributed in the environment. They are saprophytic and become pathogenic only when conditions are favourable.

Pathogen : The important species are *Aspergillus flavus* Link, *A. tamarii kite* and *A. oryzae*. The conidiophores arise from mycelia and their tip is spheroidal or oval. The process of infection is almost similar to that of other muscardine fungi but the infection is localized and it does not extent to the body fluid.

Symptoms : The disease is very serious on chawki (I and II instar) worms. The infection is localised. Infected young worms become compact to lustrous and die soon. Mycelia emerge out from the spot of invasion and cause death. After death spore changes its colour with the age. Generally in the young worms, the body will not rot but in late age worms, the area which is not covered by mycelial mat will rot due to secondary infections. If the infection is by *A. tamarii*, initially it will be white and turn to greenish yellow, green, brown and finally to dark brown with large head like structures.

4.7.4.3 Bacterial and Viral Disease

Silkworm Flacherie : The term refers to flaccid condition of silkworm larvae suffering from dysentery. Flacherie is a 'sub-chronic' disease resulting primarily due to physiological disorders and secondarily by the infection of a bacterium.

(a) Viral Flacherie :

The viral flacherie is due to polyhedral and non-polyhedral viruses. Polyhedral viruses include cytoplasmic polyhedrosis virus, densonucleosis virus and kenchu virus diseases of silkworm.

(i) Infectious flacherie virus : It is caused by a virus of infectious flacherie I type.

Causal agent : Aizowa et. al. (1964) isolated spherical particles from diseased silkworms with a diameter of 30-32 nm and Kawase (1974) designated this as IFV.

Symptoms : Vomiting of digestive fluid, larval body looks transparent and sometimes body shrinkage is also observed. The infection is mainly through oral ingestion. Young worms are more susceptible to infection. The disease spreads through contaminated leaves.

Fig. 4.22 : Flacherie affected Silkworm showing Blackened Body

(ii) Cytoplasmic Polyhedrosis : This disease is caused by a virus which infects the cytoplasm of the cell.

Pathogen and Infection : Polyhedra of the virus are found in the cytoplasm of cells. The size of polyhedra particle is 0.5 to 1.5 µ. It looks hexagonal under the microscope. The spread of disease occurs through faeces.

Symptoms : The infected worms show stunted growth leading to a prolonged larval life. On progress, the midgut becomes opaque and pale yellow, later it discharges whitish faeces and spoils the bed. Polyhedra are completely filled in cytoplasm of cylindrical and goblet cells are released into the alimentary canal as the cell is broken down. Consequently, polyhedra pass along with faeces, thus the spread occurs. Incubation period is about one week.

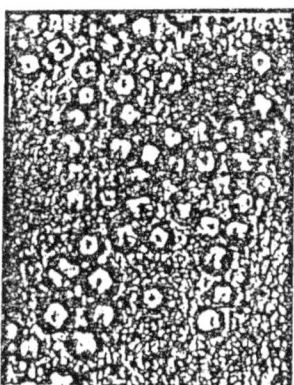

Fig. 4.23 : Hexagonal Polyhedra Bodies of Cytoplasmic Polyhedrosis of Silkworm

(iii) Kenchu disease of silkworm : This disease is referred as Kempu sappe, Kempunacchu and Nachu (Shyamala, 1978) and it appears to occur very frequently in Karnataka.

Pathogen : This is spherical or tetragonal, small, non-occluded virus of about 0.27 nm in diameter. Even single oral ingestion is enough to produce disease in all the stages of the insect.

Symptoms : Immediately after feeding, the worms appear normal but after 1-2 hours, they show dullness, paleness and in some cases a disproportionately large head. The affected worms survive for several days but in a retarded state, dead larvae develop brownish patches. Sometimes mating of pupae is noticed when III, IV and V instar larvae are infected and they construct small and flimsy cocoons.

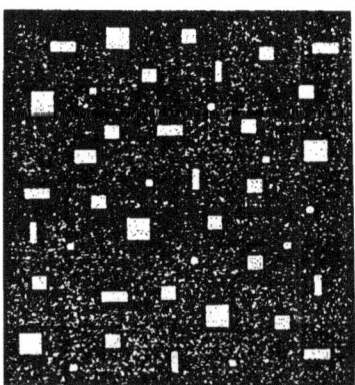

Fig. 4.24 : Tetragonal Polyhedral Bodies found in Cytoplasmic Polyhedrosis of Silkworm

(b) Bacterial Flacherie :

This disease of worms caused by bacteria. It includes sotto, septicemia and Rangi (court) disease of silkworms. The bacterial diseases take a heavy toll of silkworm crop under high humidity. In Karnataka, the annual damage caused by this disease is 20-40%.

Pathogen and Infection : From the affected worms, many species of bacteria have been isolated. They are :

1. *Aerobacter cloacae*
2. *Achromobacter superficialis*
3. *Achromobacter delmarvae*
4. *Staphylococcus albus*
5. *Escherichia freundii*
6. *Pseudomonas ovatis*
7. *Pseudomonas boreopolis.*

The spread and infection of disease is mainly by consumption of contaminated leaves. The dead larvae release pathogen to the surrounding and many are survived in the environment (air borne) within the rearing house.

Symptoms : In general, many species are involved in causing diseases which exhibit similar symptoms. The worm loses appetite and becomes sluggish. In the advanced stage, the larval body becomes very soft, discoloured and turns dark brown. Pulsation rate may increase rapidly and the worms wriggle due to pain. Later it vomits brownish fluid and passes very soft excreta which sticks to the rearing bed. Shadding of skin may not be proper during moulting.

(i) Sotto disease : The disease is caused by *Bacillus thuringiensis* Var. *Sotto*. Worms are killed by the toxin produced by the pathogen. Toxin is a rhombic crystal and is released out of the cell as the bacteria collapse. Pathogenicity is lost 3 hours when in contact with formalin (3%) and within 5 minutes if boiled.

Symptoms : In the beginning, the worm loses appetite, becomes inactive, shows combination of flacherie symptoms and finally die. In the advanced stage, the silkworm loses appetite suddenly, writhes, affected with convulsions and dies in a short period. The victim turns gradually to brown, blackish brown or black and begins to rot.

(ii) Septicemia : The disease is caused when bacilli similar to those of sotto bacillus, or to *colitis germs or B. prodigiosus* etc., infected the worms.

Symptoms : The septicemia condition of the body results due to multiplication of a certain *Bacillus* in the body fluid. The worm loses appetite and becomes inactive. At times it vomits fluids, the abdominal legs loose gripping power and finally dies. After the death rot begins quickly. The invasion is mainly through wound on the skin and in some cases through the alimentary canal.

4.7.4.4 Viral Disease

(a) Nuclear Polyhedrosis Virus (NPV) :

In Karnataka, it is called as *haluhula or haluthonde*, in Italy as *Giallume* and in France as *grasserie* or *Jaundice*.

Causal Agent and Infection : The infection is mainly through mouth. After ingestion of the virus, the protein coat is dissolved in the gut releasing the viral rods. These rods themselves attack midgut cells and the infectious sub-units are set free which multiply in different cells and also enter the nucleus (NPV) of the susceptible cells and multiply. Small spherical bodies appear and on maturity form rods. Bundles of such rods are surrounded by proteins and they crystallize to form the polyhedra.

Symptoms : About a week after infection inter-segmental membranes are swollen and the larvae appear to be under stress. Haemolymph becomes turbid, skin loses its tension, becomes fragile and ruptures easily, releasing the milky haemolymph. The dead larvae are soft and flabby. Young ones loose co-ordination in movement and crawl about in circles and also fail to moult and die soon.

The skin of diseased pupae is fragile and disintegrates easily on handling and occasionally black marking appears on the body at the time of death. The disease mainly affects IV and V instar larvae. The environmental factors and quality of leaves also influence the incidence of the disease.

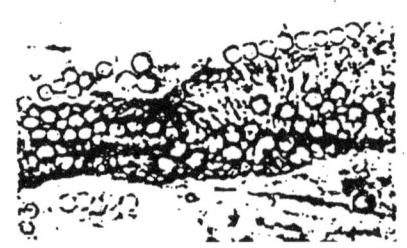 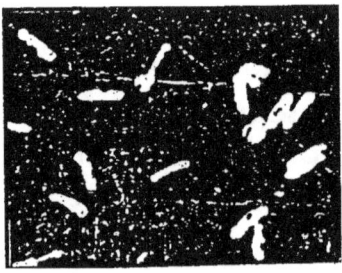

(a) Grasserie Polyhedral Bodies formed on the Tracheal Wall of Silkworm

(b) Grasserie Virus (BERCOLD)

(c) A Grasserie Infected Larva (Jaundiced) with Swollen Body and Nodded Segments

Fig. 4.25

Prevention and Control of Diseases :

For the success of the crop, healthy rearing is essential. To fight the diseases, several means have to be integrated to achieve the target; depending upon the etiology of the disease.

1. Before starting the silkworm rearing, the rearing house and the equipments need to be thoroughly washed with water and dried under sun. After this the entire rearing house along with equipments can be disinfected under airtight conditions with 2-4% formalin (800 ml for 10 m^2 area) or disinfected with 2% bleaching powder solution.
2. Surface disinfection of silkworm eggs should be carried out with 2% formalin to destroy pathogens.
3. Elimination of pebrine disease can be done by mass or individual mother moth examination. Thermotherapy of eggs or cocoons is equally effective.
4. As the fungi profusely proliferate in humid condition in the rearing environment/bed, it is better to keep the bed dry specially during moult and rainy season by dusting lime over the bed. In addition, sprinkling of formalin chaff every day before feeding helps in reducing the incidence of the disease.
5. While rearing, surface disinfection of the body of the silkworm larvae can be done by using, some of the effective disinfectants like Dithane M-45 with lime, chemicals like aliband, sunace, kinuban, patsol, chemichlon, shinsha dust, benzoic acid, benzoalknonium chloride etc. can also be used.
6. Administration of arsenic sulphide (0.01%), orally through leaves, is to check the bacterial diseases in general.
7. Oral administration of *nalidixic* acid is very effective in controlling NPV or B-propiolactone with guanylic acid (5 GMP) and guanosine is also effective against NPV of silkworm. Recently, application of a chemical *Imanine* is found to be very effective in controlling NPV.

In general, hygienic management, such as providing sufficient spacing, feeding with quality leaves for the particular stages (instars), creating good micro-environment with proper ventilation, helps in reducing the incidence of diseases. Following suggested preventive measures before and during rearing keep the pathogen away.

Following Table 4.4 gives lookout of diseases, pathogens, their symptoms and control measures; against particular diseases.

Table 4.4 : Diseases of Silkworm (B. mori)

Diseases	Pathogens	Mode of Infection	Stage of Infection	Symptoms	Control
1. Pebrine (protozoan)	Nosema bombycis	Ingestion of spores. Through infected eggs (seeds).	Eggs to adult (All stages).	**Egg** : Poor sticking, mostly unfertilized and dead. **Larva** : Black spotted winked body, poor appetite, sluggish. **Pupa** : Swollen, darkened body. **Adults** : Swollen abdomen, unstretched wings, poor egg laying capacity.	1. Use disease free females and eggs. 2. Sterilization of eggs, equipments, room and workers with 2% formaline. 3. Destruction of infected seeds and females.
2. Muscardine (Fungus)	Beauveria bassiana (white muscardine), Spicaria farinose (green muscardine) Isacria farinose. (Yellow muscardine)	Germinating spores and conidia penetrate through skin of larvae.	Larva, Pupa and Adult.	Hyphae come out from intersegmental membranes of larvae, limpness, vomiting, diarrhoea.	Proper rearing and sterilization.
3. Flacheriae (Bacterial)	Bacillus thuringiensis	Ingestion of spores	Mostly larvae	Looses appetite, slow growth, vomiting, body rott and becomes black or green.	Selection of resistant race, proper incubation of eggs and rearing conditions.
4. Grasserie (Virus)	Borrelia virus	Ingestion of polyhedra	Mostly larvae	Swelling of segments, easy rupture of skin, vomiting, slimsy cocoons.	Choice of resistant race and avoid injury while handling.

(b) Silkworm Pests :

Silkworms are attacked by number of pests and parasites. Among them dermestid beetles and uzi flies are more important.

1. Dermestid Beetles : The beetles belong to family-Dermesidae of order-Coeleoptera. This group of insects contains many genera which are destructive. Some of them are important from a sericulture point of view; namely *Dermestes cadverinus, D. valpinus, D. vorax, D. frishchi, D. versicolor* etc.

The adults of *D. cadverinus* are oval, elongated, dark brown with club shaped antennae, and is about 1 cm in length. The larvae are red-brown, spindle shaped with hairy skin.

The larvae and adults are attracted by the smell of stifled cocoons and the dried pupae inside. They bore into the cocoons and eat the dried pupae and sometimes the eggs and the damaged cocoon become unfit for reeling. Rarely, the young larvae attack living worms.

Control Measures for all Dermestid Beetles : To avoid damage, the rearing house and the cocoon store rooms must be cleaned frequently. Storing of rejected cocoons and perished eggs for long periods is to be avoided. Before and after emergence of moths, the egg production premises must be cleaned. Occasionally, the rooms could be fumigated with CH_3Br (Methyl bromide).

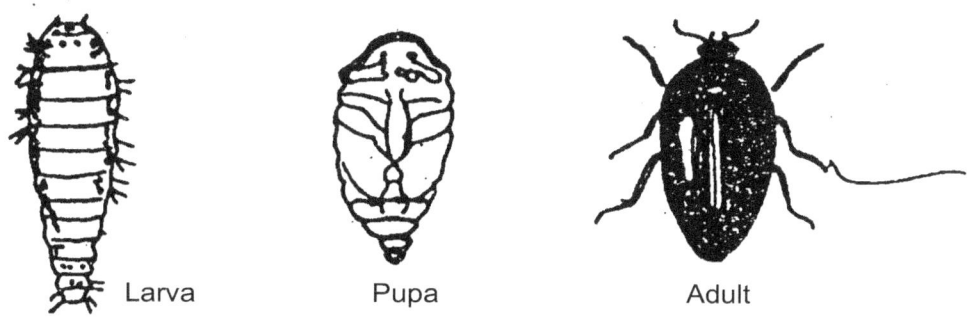

Fig. 4.26 : *Dermestes cadverinus*

2. Usi or Uzi-flies : These flies are most important parasites of silkworm, *B. mori*. These flies belong to the family *Tachinidae* of Diptera order. It is distributed in silk producing countries viz. China,

India, Japan, Korea, Thailand, Sri-Lanka and Burma. The tassar, muga, and eri are also parasitised by this fly.

In India, *Louis* reported this fly on mulberry silkworms in Bengal in 1880 and estimated that the loss to be 20,000 to 30,000 per annum. In Karnataka, this pest was first reported on silkworm crops during May, 1980 in Bylanarasapura village of Hosokote Taluka due to illegal transport of cocoons from West Bengal.

Fig. 4.27 : Female Uzi-fly of Silkworms (Araki)

The uzi-fly is larger than a housefly and is blackish grey in colour with four prominent longitudinal lines on the thoracic region and broad bands on the abdomen. The male fly is larger than female. In nature, these flies copulate in air and live on nectar of flowers and honey dew excreted by aphids and scale insects. The female enters the rearing site with a buzzing sound. Once she reaches the rearing tray, she wanders over the silk worms depositing oval, macrotype, creamy white eggs one at a time directly on the body of the silkworm (300 eggs in its life span). The act of egg laying is rapid and the fly glues tiny eggs to the intersegmental regions of worm body. The egg hatches in 1-3 days and the tiny *maggot* enters the body of worm by making a perforation. The parasitised silk worms show black scar on the integument at the point of penetration by this maggot. Maggots grow and 3 instars inside the host body. It feeds on fat bodies and lives 4-6 days inside the body of worms. The full grown maggot cuts the integument of the host after coming out crawls in search of cracks and crevices, soil or darker region where it forms puparium (last for 8-10 days) and emerges as imago fly.

Infestation by this fly in III, IV and early V instar results in the death of the silkworms before spinning the cocoons. If the parasitisation occurs after the middle of V instar, the parasitised worms mature two days earlier and construct poor quality cocoons. These cocoons become stained and are unfit for seed purpose due to the death of the worm inside the cocoon, thus making cocoons unfit for reeling.

Control : Fly proof doors, windows and ventilators should be used in the silkworm rearing house. All the crevices of the rooms should be closed to prevent maggots pupating in the soil.

3. Ants : This group of insects belongs to the family, Formicidae of order, Hymenoptera. This insect pest attacks silkworms in the rearing trays, which damage them (worms).

Control : Legs of rearing stands should be dipped in ant wells (filled with water + any good insecticide). When the ant attack is at the time of spinning, ash or kerosene can be poured on the floor around the legs of the chandrikes or bamboo mountage to keep the ants off.

4. Lizards, Birds, Rats and Squirrels : All these animals feed on silkworms. Mammals also predate on the pupae by biting open the cocoons.

Control : Rearing rooms should be kept free of Lizards with the help of insecticides. Birds could be scared away from the vicinity and for rat and squirrel trapping could be carried out in rearing houses.

(c) Position of Sericulture in India :

India has the unique distinction in the world as it produces all the four major varieties of silk viz. *Mulberry, Tassar, Eri* and *Muga*. However, India occupies fifth position in the world for silk production. The first four in order of production of silk are Japan, China, South Korea and U.S.S.R., Brazil, Italy come behind India.

In India, of the 6,29,143 villages, sericulture is being practiced in about 59,528 villages (9.5%) and this provides work (employs) to about 60 lakhs people; mostly tribals. Indian sericulture has shown a dynamic growth during last few years. Its silk production during the last 14 years has gone up from 3475 MT in 1978 to 14,140 metric tonnes in 1992-93.

The major silk producing states are Karnataka, A. P., Tamilnadu, W. Bengal and Jammu & Kashmir for mulberry silk. Sericulture is an export oriented industry exporting silk to over 50 countries of the world (European, U. S. A etc.) and bringing in foreign exchange worth about ₹ 250 crores.

India produces 5% mulberry silk, 10% tassar silk and 100% muga silk.

Table 4.5 : Production of raw silk (metric tonnes) by India during 1992-93

Mulberry	Tassar	Eri	Muga	Total
13,007	361	700	72	14,140

(d) Sericulture Research and Training Centres :

In India, there are four research centres working under the central silk board under the Ministry of Trade and Commerce.

1. Central Sericulture Research Station, Behrumpura, West Bengal (Mulberry).
2. Central Sericulture Research and Training Institute Mysore (Tassar).
3. Central Sericulture Research and Training Institute, Mysore (Tassar).
4. Central Tassar Research Station, Ranchi (Bihar).

These centres have extension centres in different parts of the country trying to reach to almost every silk producing region to give advise, guidance and undertake short and long term training courses.

4.8 Post Harvesting Process of Cocoons and Preparation of Cocoons for Marketing

After the cocoons are harvested, the silk is prepared by a number of successive processes. The process of unwinding the single long silk thread is called **reeling.** Before reeling, there are number of steps which include stifling, drying, storing, cooking and boiling, deflossing and riddling. After reeling, there is re-reeling, twisting, finishing etc. Before reeling, the cocoons should be sorted.

Cocoons should be firm and not yield to slight pressure, they should be smooth and small in size.

1. Stifling : It is the process of cocoon drying to kill the pupae inside before they emerge as adult. If stifling is delayed, the moth emerges by cutting the cocoon shell and the cocoon becomes unreelable as the silk thread breaks at many places. Such cocoons are called pierced cocoons. There are three methods of stifling.

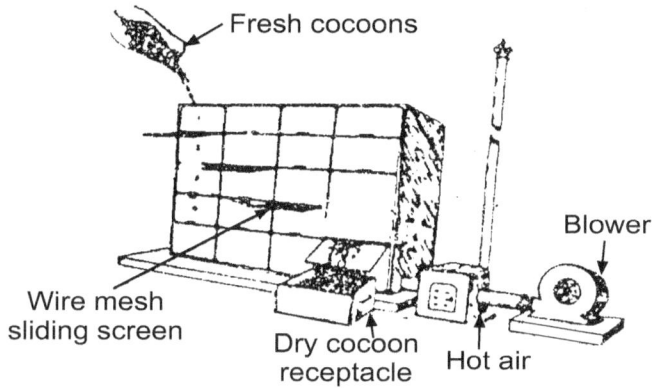

Fig. 4.28 : Stifling – Cocoon Drying Chamber

(a) **Sun Drying :** In this method, the cocoons are exposed to direct sun light till the pupa is killed and dried. For this process the freshly harvested cocoons are exposed to bright sunlight for a long time.

(b) **Steam Stifling :** In this type, the fresh cocoons are exposed to direct action of very hot wet steam for the required period. The cocoons may be stifled in a basket if the quantity is small or in barrels or large chambers if the quantity is large. They can be stored for one month.

(c) **Hot Air Stifling :** In this method, fresh cocoons are dried by means of hot air which can be stored for longer periods. By adopting this method, stifling and drying of the cocoons can be done simultaneously by hot air-conditioning.

There are other methods also which are used to kill the pupae, which include the use of infra red rays, cold air, radio wages, poisonous gases etc.

2. Sorting of Cocoons : Among the harvested cocoons there are normal cocoons, slightly defective cocoons, highly defective cocoons, double cocoons and unhealthy cocoons. It is necessary to reject the defective cocoons. This is known as sorting of cocoons. Sorting of cocoons is carried out mainly for double, thin-shelled, dead, dirty, loose shelled, very thin and transparent, thin middle shell, frame adherent and irregular cocoons. All these are carefully separated and rejected, only good cocoons that are normal are picked up for future checking.

The colour of the cocoon in the commonly reared silkworm strains is mostly white. Besides this colour there are cocoons of different colours such as golden yellow, flesh yellow, crimson, bamboo leaf colour and green. The colour pigment of cocoon is chiefly present in sericin. The cocoons of domestic silkworms are of various shapes : barrel shaped, oval, round or spindle shaped. The cocoons varies in its size according to the strains.

3. Storage of Cocoons : The storage of cocoons is also important. They must be protected from the fungus or *Dermestes* beetle, rats, ants and other insects. Preventive measures against the pests must be used as well as the storage rooms should be periodically disinfected.

4. Sorting of Cocoons : The cocoons are sorted again before reeling and double, crushed, stained, malformed, fluffy, flimsy and pierced cocoons are rejected. The workers doing this job are called 'sorters.' To detect internal defects in the cocoon, the cocoons are illuminated with electric bulbs or fluorescent light.

5. Deflossing : It is a process of removing the unreelable mass of silk called floss found on the cocoons. The process is done prior to reeling as the floss obstructs the easy flow of cocoons in the automatic mechanical processes and ultimately slows down the operations. The deflossing is done either by hand or machine operated brushes.

6. Cocoon Riddling : In this process, the cocoons are separated with sieve like devices into large medium and small sizes.

7. Cocoon Cooking or Boiling : By cooking the cocoons, the gummy sericin layer is dissolved and the thread is loosened for easy reeling. The cocoons are boiled or cooked in hot water to soften and swell the sericin before dissolving it. Boiling is done either by the open pan system or three pan system.

4.9 Reeling Equipments

Silk reeling in India is yet to be modernized. So far this sector was neglected. Even now marketing facilities for cocoons and establishment of reeling units are not adequate, which are deterrent to development of sericulture industry, particularly in new areas like Andhra Pradesh, Tamil Nadu, Uttar Pradesh etc. So the rearers from these states have to depend upon outsiders to buy their cocoons.

In India, as on today there are the following reeling devices :

(I)   Charkhas   22,500
(II) Cottage basin   7,000
(III) Filature basin   5,000
(IV) Automatic reeling   2,500 (ends)

(a) Charkha : Here cocoon cooking and reeling take place at high temperature and high speed respectively. With the result inferior and defective cocoons could be reeled more economically without considering the quality of raw silk. A majority of cocoons is inferior in, quality consisting of high percentage of defective cocoons, so charkha reeling is still dominating in the country. Secondly, demand for charkha silk is more, since the cost of charkha silk is lower and this silk is more suitable for handlooms for both warp and weft. Also charkha silk is widely used for weft in powerloom. So long as silk weaving is not modernized and quality consciousness is not brought about, demand for charkha silk continues to be more and hence charkha reeling does continue. However, there is a scope for improving crude charkha in its working condition and improving the quality of raw silk to a certain extent.

It has been possible to improve the crude version of charkha by extensive research studies. Improved version of charkha has been developed recently in the central Silk Technological Research Institute, Bengaluru.

(b) Cottage Basin : The principle in this reeling device is almost similar to the one in filature basin. The only difference between the cottage basin and the filature basin is that the cottage basin is of 6 ends reeling against 10 ends in filature basin and some of the mechanical parts such as jetteboute to increase the efficiency of cocoon casting are not present in the cottage basin. Moreover, cottage basin is normally hand driven, so that it can be used in rural areas where no electricity is available. It is also possible to improve the working of cottage basin so that the quality of silk reeled on this would be superior. The economical cottage basin unit would be of 12 basins.

(c) Filature Basin : Almost all the old filature establishment units are too big and the new units are too small under the government management. This device is considered to be the most modern type of reeling in the country. The quality of silk reeled on this device is supposed to be superior as compared to that reeled on the other two devices. However, it is not possible to produce international grade of raw silk even on this so called modern reeling device because of the various factors detailed as follows :

(1) The raw material i.e., cocoon is not upto the required quality to produce an international A grade silk; (2) the alignment of filature basin is not perfect. Basins manufactured by different firms are different in construction since the design of the basin is not standradised. (3) The preparatory processes in reeling such as cocoon stifling and cocoon cooking have not been so improved as to produce silk reeled on this filature basin comparable to higher grade.

Further, working conditions in reeling sector under government management are still non-industrialised. However, research studies have proved that it is possible to produce high grade silk from the existing improved varieties of cocoons such as bivoltine and improved multi X bivoltine hybrid cocoons reeled on well designed filature basins associated with improved cocoon drying and cocoon cooking process. It has also been found that instead of a very big filature unit in one place standard nits of the capacity of 50 basins each spread over all the sericultural areas would be highly efficient.

(d) Automatic Silk Reeling : Besides the above three devices there are about 2,500 ends automatic reeling devices imported from Japan mostly under Karnataka Silk Industries Corporation. However, research findings have shown that under Indian working conditions

and existing quality of multivoltine cocoons it is not advisable to invest heavily for establishing on automatic reeling machine in the country at present. But automatic reeling technique is quite suitable for bivoltine cocoons.

Types of Cocoons :

There are two main varieties of cocoons produced in the country namely Multivoltine and Bivoltine. But major portion is of multivoltine cocoons. Even in multivoltine cocoons there are two types of hybrids : ordinary multivoltine hybrid cocoons which are produced in rain fed areas and improved multivoltine hybrid cocoons which are produced in irrigated areas. Bivoltine cocoons are produced mainly in irrigated areas.

The bivoltine cocoons are the best in respect of cocoon weight; shell percentage, filament length, renditta, degumming loss and drainage. Improved multivoltine hybrid cocoons stand next and the ordinary multivoltine hybrid cocoons rate last.

Because of these varying cocoon characters, reeling techniques should be different for each of the above types of cocoons. Various processes involved in reeling technique are :

1. Cocoon stifling
2. Cocoon storage
3. Cocoon cooking
4. Reeling
5. Type of reeling device
6. Re-reeling
7. Packing.

4.9.1 Reeling of Multivoltine Cocoons

(a) Ordinary Multivoltine Hybrids : Normally Pure Mysore x C. Nichi, Pure Mysore x HS6 and Nistari etc., are considered to be ordinary multivoltine hybrids which are produced in rain fed areas. These cocoons are very flimsy, with the result shell portion is lower than the dried pupa, hence silk yield (renditta) is very poor. Even out of the available silk content reelability is very poor. Hardly about 50%

of the silk content is reeled into yarn and remaining 50% will be waste. So the technique of reeling normally followed for this type of cocoon will be charkha reeling. Charkha system of reeling is an Italian version of floating system of reeling i.e., it is associated with :

(a) Reeling of cooked cocoons which float in the reeling basin.
(b) High speed reeling.
(c) High basin temperature reeling
(d) Less number of reeling ends.

This version of reeling will improve the reelability of inferior and defective cocoons without considering the quality of silk. Charkha which is a simple device consists of a large cooking cum reeling pawn where boiling water is maintained. The cocoons are cooked in it and filaments collected in a bunch after brushing, are passed through a hole on an ordinary thread guide device (Tharapatti). Afterwards the thread is crossed with another co-thread for forming a Chambon type of croissure in order to agglutinate the filaments and remove the water from the body of the thread. Then it is passed through a distributor before it is wound on to a large wooden reel. Four threads are maintained in this device. One person rotates the reel by hand and another person sitting near the cooking pan manipulates the cocoon cooking and reeling.

The cocoons are steam stifled by ordinary basket system. Steam stifling for such cocoons is quite alright, since these inferior cocoons as mentioned earlier are very flimsy i.e., structure of shell is loose and flossy in nature containing more sericin which is easy to soften (there is a correlation between sericin content and the solubility of sericin i.e., easy cooking). So the steam stifling besides killing the pupa will soften the sericin easily and the cocoons are immediately reeled on charkha. If the cocoons are in semi-softened condition they are easy to cook and reel on charkha. It is not advisable to store such inferior cocoons for a long time particularly after steam - stifling. Sometimes fresh cocoons without stifling are also reeled on charkha, particularly defective cocoons such as urinated, melted and other defective cocoons. If reeled in fresh condition they would yield better as compared to that of stifled ones. This system of Charkha reeling is quite good and does not need re-reeling, since charkha reel (swift) itself is of larger periphery i.e., about 150 cm. So, directly the skeins are twisted into hanks for marketing purpose. The silk produced on charkha form ordinary multivoltine hybrid cocoons is no doubt inferior in quality i.e., raw silk is coarse and it suffers from many defects since no improved devices such as button/slub catcher and standard croissure system in reeling are used.

Therefore, charkha reeling technique is quite suitable for such of the ordinary multivoltine hybrid cocoons in the country. However, the present charkha used in the country is very crude in its alignment and also working conditions are hygienically very poor.

Improved Charka :

(i) ***Cooking basin :*** Appropriate cooking pan with a separation for cooking and reeling has been fixed. Partition will enable the basin temperature to be maintained at boiling point for cooking and at lower temperature for reeling basin. So the reeler feels easy to work and reels the cocoons simultaneously maintaining required number of cocoons in each end throughout the reeling time. Modified smokeless oven is incorporated.

(ii) ***Slub catcher :*** Simple slub catcher in place of crude Tharapatti has been incorporated, so that the major defects such as waste slubs etc., will be avoided. Efficient casting and piecing of thread takes place.

(iii) ***Croissure :*** Tavellette type of croissure has been provided. So all the four threads are independent in working resulting in compact and circular thread formation and effective removal of water from the thread.

(iv) ***Passage of thread :*** Passage of thread has been maintained as long as nearly 3 metres. So driage of thread is better. In addition, improved heating device has been incorporated. Charcoal/wood fire is kept in the perforated metal plate which is covered, so that hot surface of the metal cover would cause driage of silk thread on the swift.

(v) **Driving :** Chain type driving system has been incorporated resulting in easy rotation of reel.

(vi) **Swift :** Improved collapsable swift of 1 in periphery has been used.

(vii) **Traverse :** Traverse system has been improved so as to obtain better coiling in the bank.

So the above improvements in the Charkha have resulted in better working conditions and producing quality raw silk without affecting production. Experiments were conducted in reeling of multivoltine hybrid cocoons produced from three places namely Ramanagaram, Vijayapura and Kollegal. In each variety of cocoons three replications were maintained and mass reeling was done on Improved Charkha for 7 hours.

From the table we notice that although cocoons from Kollegal were inferior with high percentage of defective cocoons, the reeling performance on improved charkha was better.

This version of Charkha improves the quality of raw silk considerably without affecting production and yield as compared to crude charkha. So, it will be recommended in course of time, that this improved charkha should be used in all parts of the state (for both ordinary and even improved multivoltine hybrid cocoons). Cost of Charkha is about ₹ 1000/-.

(b) Improved multivoltine Hybrids : They are normally pure Mysore x N137 and Pure Mysore x NB18. Shell structure is again loose and is flossy in nature. However, silk content, as compared to the ordinary hybrids, is higher.

The reeling technique suitable for improved multivoltine cocoons is cottage basin or multiend filature basin reelings.

Cottage Basin : Cottage basin is an improved version over charkha and is indigenously designed. Here, cocoon cooking is done separately in boiling water basin and reeling is done in a hot water basin attached to the reeling bench. Thread is first passed through a button to clean the stubs and waste etc. Then it is independently passed through a tavellete type of croissure which is more efficient than that in Charkha. After the croissure the thread is passed through a traverse guide and finally on to a small reel. So the quality of silk is superior to Charkha silk. Superior quality cocoons like bivoltine can also be reeled on this device. But cottage basin is generally hand driven and alignment of the basin is not sufficiently perfect. With the result production of superior quality silk confirming to international standards is not possible.

Multiend Filature Basin : This reeling device is a further improved version over the cottage basin and is power driven. Boilers are invariably installed and steam is used for cooking and reeling purpose and also for cocoon stifling in special steam chambers. Recently, however, hot air drying methods are being introduced for bivoltine cocoons in some of the filature units in the country for improvising working efficiency and quality of reeled silk. Normally cocoon cooking is done according to the single pan system as in the case of the cottage basin. Three pan cooking system evolved by our institute wherein the cocoons are subjected to varying temperatures associated with hot air stifling has been found to be suitable for bivoltine cocoons on the multiend basin.

The quality of the silk reeled on this device is superior to that of cottage basin.

Cocoon stifling (for improved multivoltine hybrids) :

Steam stifling is quite suitable for improved multivoltine hybrid cocoons. But the method of steaming should be slightly improved over charkha system i.e., these cocoons should be steam stifled in thin layers using steam chambers. Small chambers can be fabricated locally with about half a dozen shelves inside the chamber with the capacity of accommodating about 10 kg cocoons at a time. If steam is available it can be directly used to stifle the cocoons in the chamber or else by boiling the water in a vessel, over which a chamber can be placed with perforated bottom. The entire portion is covered so that the steam vapour does not pass outside the chamber. This system of stifling avoids crushing of cocoons during steaming so that cocoons shell is maintained in normal shape without collapsing and cooking will be better. Cocoons can be preserved for quite sometime, say about 15 days without any deterioration in the quality of cocoons. The important points to be taken care of are that the cocoons should be stored in thin layer and preserved in wooden racks and the store room should be well ventilated so that aeration is free through the cocoons to avoid fungus attack. If possible cocoon store room should have humidity below 65%. All the defective cocoons should be sorted out before storing.

Cooking : For improved multivoltine cocoons open pan system of cooking is quite alright i.e., cocoons are treated in boiling water in an open pan for about 3 to 5 minutes and they are hand brushed in the same basin and after getting true ends the cooked cocoons will be transferred to reeling basin where the temperature is lower (about 40-50°C. Reeler will adjust the true ends after discarding improper cooked cocoons which are put back into the cooking basin.

Reeling : Reeler will maintain requisite number of cocoons per end in the cottage basin or multiend reeling basin as the case may be. Reeling will be done on smaller reels at low speed.

Normally, periphery of the reel is about 70 cm to 90 cm. Sometimes heating arrangement is provided near the reels. This is possible in multiend reeling basin where invariably steam is generated by boiler for stifling, cooking and reeling etc. So steam pipes can be provided by the rear side of the reel so that the thread on the reel is immediately dried effectively avoiding gum spots etc. So the quality of raw silk is improved considerably on this system on reeling compared to either on cottage basin or multiend reeling basin with improved multivoltine hybrid cocoons. After reeling, raw silk is re-reeled on to standard sized reel (swift) from the small reels, this is called re-reeling. The object of re-reeling is :

(i) To prepare standard sized hanks (150 cm periphery hand).

(ii) It improves the quality of raw silk by avoiding gum spots and also minimising the loose ends, stubs and waste particles etc. Before re-reeling, it is advisable to soak the small reels in plain or dilute alkaline solution so that re-reeling will be smooth without breaks. During re-reeling, grant reeling i.e., diamond formation in the hanks is possible with the result coiling system is improved so that effective driage takes place. Secondly, unwinding in the further preparatory operations before weaving will be easier with lower breakdowns. Effective heating of silk is also possible during re-reeling, by providing steam pipes below the swift. Hanks are prepared by giving adequate twist by means of a hank making machine. The standard weight of the hank is 60-70 g. A number of hanks, say about 30, will be bundled and pressed into 'Book' for marketing. So the improved multivoltine cocoons, if reeled with this technique i.e., steam stifling, cooking in open pan and reeling on cottage or multiend reeling basin associated with re-reeling will give better reeling results and also the quality of silk is improved. This silk is superior to that of charkha. Winding, size deviation, evenness, and tenacity etc., are improved considerably. Further, this silk has very good demand for warp fetching higher rate of price as compared to charkha silk (Economical cottage and multiend reeling units are worked out and projects have been published by the author).

Experiments were conducted with both Bivoltine and improved Multivoltine hybrid cocoons following an automatic reeling technique (associated with hot air drying and pressurized cooking) and also multiend filature reeling technique (associated with steam stifling and open air cooking).

4.9.2 Reeling of Bivoltine Cocoons

Bivoltine cocoons are superior to the above two categories of multivoltine hybrid cocoons. Cocoon shell is very compact, shell content is more and cocoons are less flossy in nature. The present bivoltine hybrid cocoons are NB4D2 x KA and NB7 x NB18. Reeling techniques for bivoltine cocoons are given as follows.

Cocoon stifling : Steam stifling is not suitable for bivoltine cocoons since steam stifling is instantaneous pupa killing device with certain pressure. On account of compact shelled cocoon, permeation of air or water/steam is difficult. So it requires delayed drying process which is possible with the help of hot air stifling or drying system. If cocoons are steamed, there is the likelihood of the cocoons getting collapsed. Once the cocoons are collapsed they don't recover their original shape on account of poor permeability of air, water or steam etc. Collapsed cocoons will give problem during cooking.

Cooking : Bivoltine cocoons should not be cooked in open pan system. Bivoltine cocoon shell is very compact and it is not possible to soften all the cocoon layers uniformly on account of poor permeability of water through shell in open pan cooking. Within the short time of boiling, only outer layer is softened whereas inner layer is still hard. If cooking is prolonged until inner layer is softened then the outer layer is more cooked than necessary resulting in more waste and poor yield. So cooking system for bivoltine cocoons should be changed either to three pan system or pressurized system.

Pan Cooking System : Cocoons will be taken in wire mesh cage and cooked in the first pan at lower temperature 65 + 5°C for about one minute and then in the second pan at boiling point for about a 1½ minutes and finally at about 65 + 5°C for one minute. The cooked cocoons are hand brushed at boiling point.

The cocoons cooked with three pan system can be reeled on multiend reeling machine or even on automatic reeling machine. With this system of cooking it is possible to allow hot water into the shell to some extent (about 22 to 30%) so that the inner layer will be softened resulting in uniform degree of cooking. This will help unwinding the filament smoothly in reeling. However, three pan cooking does not provide for sunken system of reeling. Sunken system of reeling is possible only with pressurized system of reeling. Sunken system of reeling is associated with

1. Reeling of cooked cocoons which sink under water in reeling bath.
2. Low basin temperature.
3. Low speed reeling.
4. Large number of reeling ends.

This version of reeling is normally followed in an automatic reeling system which is very popular in Japan. This version of reeling is suitable for compact shelled cocoons like bivoltine cocoons in achieving better reeling performances and producing quality raw silk.

Three pan cooking system for bivoltine cocoons may be economically practised in smaller unit of multiend reeling basins (10-20 basins) whereas in bigger units of multiend reeling basins or automatic reeling basins pressurized system of cooking can be practised. Experiments were conducted with hot air dried bivoltine cocoons reeling on an automatic reeling machine (associated with pressurized cooking) and on multiend filature basins (associated with three pan cooking).

4.9.3 Pressurized Cooking System

(a) Cylindrical cocoon boiling machine :

Cocoon boiling machine is simple in construction and easy to operate. At a time about 6-7 kg of green bivoltine cocoons can be cooked. Total cooking time is about 22 minutes. So about 100 kg of cocoons can be cooked per day of 8 hours working by one person and he can feed to about 100 end unit. There are 12 perforated thin steel baskets each holding 300 to 350 cocoons and after loading these baskets with cocoons, they will be immersed in hot water at about 75°C for 30 seconds, raised above water level for side steaming at 85°C for 4 to 5 minutes, immersed in 75°C hot water for 30 seconds, raised above water level for main steaming at boiling point for about 10 minutes. The steam valve is stopped for 30 seconds. Then finally they are immersed in boiling water for 30 seconds and cold water is sprayed to bring the temperature to 75°C for about 5 minutes.

(b) Conveyor system of cooking :

The principle involved in conveyor system of cooking is the same as compared to the above cylindrical type. The only difference is that the conveyor system is power driven and cocoons are moving during cooking. The main principle involved in both these pressurized cooking systems is to cook the cocoons to achieve sunken system of reeling particularly on automatic reeling machine. There is a continuous chain on which baskets are mounted. Cocoons are fed to the top basket which will move slowly into various cooking chambers.

Generally the sequence of cooking is as follows :

Pretreatment (Soaking in hot water 1-2 min.) Finishing part (Hot water 1-2 min. 65-55°C) Transporting part (Hot water 1.5 min. 30-40°C) Transporting part (Hot water 1.5 min. 30-40°C)	Permeation – I (High temp. part) (Hot water 1-2 min. 70-80°C) Adjustment part (Hot water 98-95 85-70°C, 3 min.) Transport to reeling section (Hot water 98-95 85-70°C 3 min.) Transport to reeling section	Permeation – II (Low temp. part) (Warm water 2-3 min. 60-75°C) Steam cooking part (90-95-98-99°C pressure of water head 5-10 mm. 3 min.) (90-95-98-99°C pressure of water head 5-10 mm. 3 min.)

Automatic Reeling :

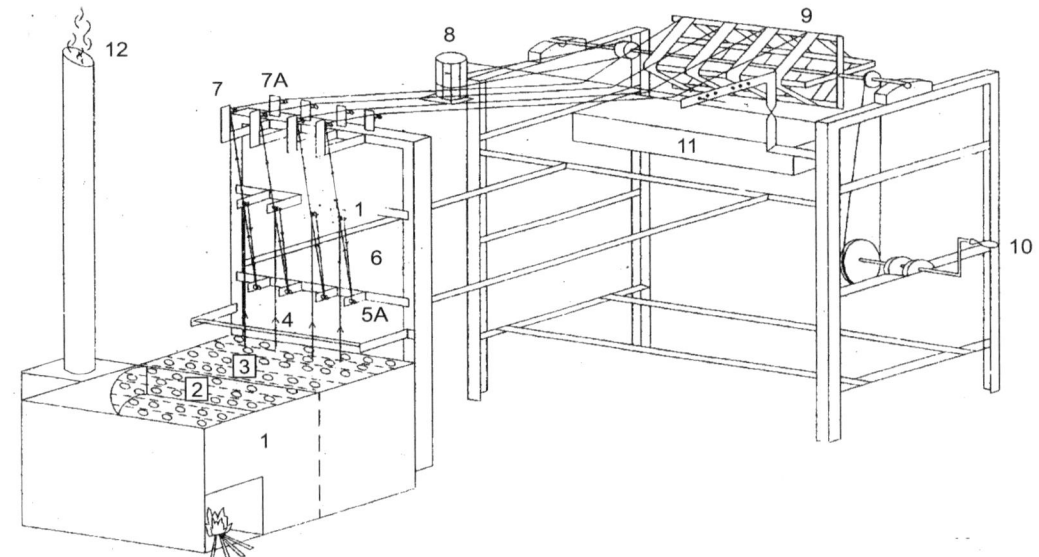

1. Oven
2. Cooking Basin
3. Reeling Basin
4. Slub Catcher
5. & 5A. Croissure Pulleys
6. Croissure
7. & 7A. Thread Guides
8. Traverse System
9. Reel
10. Driving Handle
11. Heating Device
12. Chimney

Fig. 4.29 : Improved Charkha

Collective filaments are initially drawn through Jette-boute; slub catcher or button on to the top croissure pulley guide, pulley-denier indicator device - lower croissure, pulley-corissure-guide pulley-tension pulley brake lever and finally on to the reel through ring attached to the traverse bar.

4.10 Raw Silk Yarn

Raw silk yarn is made up of a number of individual filaments which are simultaneously reeled (unwound from the cocoon together). Normally, filaments from 8 to 10, 10 to 12 or even 14 to 16 cocoons are reeled together to make a commercial raw silk yarn depending upon the size of raw silk required in the weaving industry. This type of silk is more common and is known as reeled silk or raw silk which is available in the following sizes : 13/15 denier, 20/22 denier, 28/32 denier and 40/44 denier, etc. While preparing raw silk yarn in reeling process, quite a bit of silk waste is extracted and this waste is also converted into spun yarn which is rather coarse and slightly uneven as compared to raw silk or reeled silk.

Silk fibre is the finest and also quite strong amongst the natural fibres. Besides its fineness it has a very good lustre and that is why silk fibre is known as Queen of Textiles. Tenacity of silk is from 3 to 4 gm per denier (tenacity is the breaking strength of fibre expressed in gm per denier). Elongation of silk fibre is from 16 to 22%. Examining separately the bave from the external middle and interior layers of the cocoon, it is found that the tenacity increases from the exterior to interior of the cocoon shell. The elongation varies inversely. Silk fibre has good resistance to heat. Silk fibre is not affected by heat upto the extent of 140°C. If silk fibre is exposed to sun light it gradually changes colour. Since, it has peculiar characteristics when it is wet, after washing it creases which is not easily removed by ironing. So ironing is a problem for silk garments.

Degumming loss in silk filament of cocoon is not uniform throughout its length because sericin distribution is uneven along the filament. May be because of this uneven distribution the fineness of silk fibre also varies along the same filament i.e., filament is coarser in the external layer and gradually it becomes finer throughout the internal layers of the shell.

As stated earlier sericin is easily dissolved in alkaline hot water. It dissolves completely in boiling soap solution and sericin has all the common protein reaction. It is precipitated in solution by tanin and by acetate of lead. Fibroin does not dissolve in boiling distilled water nor in boiling soap solution. Sericin and fibroin are proteins consisting of alfa amino - acids in a chain molecules with peptide linkage of the group $-NH_2$ of amino-acid and the group $-COOH$ of another. The amino-acids are definitely identified by total hydrolysis of fibroin.

4.11 Microscopic Examinations of Silk Fibre

Under the microscope the raw bave is seen to consist of two strands of fibroin included in a layer of sericin. These two strands or brins even under their covering of sericin can be seen clearly as two transparent cylinders. Fairly regular in thickness the layer of sericin appears as a delicate lighter band of rather irregular size parallel with the outer edges of the two brins of fibroin along the inner edge by which the two brins are attached. The layer of sericin shows as a dark line that has appearance of a small duct.

Thickness of filament in fact varies considerably either by reason of unequal distribution of sericin or displacement of the fibroin strands. Thickness of the degummed filament is from 12.7 to 16.4 microns.

Cross section of silk fibre under microscopic view is not cylindrical but triangular. It indicates that fibroin strand which is almost perfect is cylindrical form in the serrictery is submitted to pressure in its passage through the spinnerets which gradually becomes stronger as the serrictery discharges its content so that the final portion of filaments are no longer cylindrical but have almost the shape of a ribbon.

Specific weight of silk fibre is found to be about 1.34% which is almost equal to that of wool which is another proteinatious animal fibre.

4.11.1 Silk Reeling Technology

Since, the worm has already spun a long continuous silk fibre (filament), there is no further spinning to prepare a yarn as in the case of other natural fibres, except that of individual long filaments that are combined together after unwinding them from cocoons and winding the resultant yarn on to a convenient device. This process is called silk reeling. Silk reeling is simpler than spinning. Before reeling there are some preparatory processes for cocoons. They are described as follows :

(i) Cocoon Testing : The object of this operation is to asses the quality of cocoons so that both efficiency in reeling and quality of yarn can be determined. Cocoon testing is carried out very systematically in sericulturally advanced countries like Japan etc., But in India, it is yet to be followed. The important cocoon characteristics which are taken into consideration for assessing the quality of cocoons are (1) Cocoon weight, (2) Shell weight, (3) Shell percentage, (4) Filament length, (5) Filament size, (6) Reelability, (7) Raw silk percentage, (8) Filament neatness and (9) Sericin content.

4.11.2 Stifling or Drying of Cocoons

The object of this process is to kill the silkworm in order to avoid moth emergence so that the continuous filament is preserved in the cocoon shell. Secondly, this operation enables the cocoon to get dried so that the cocoons can be stored for along period before reeling them. The commercial methods of cocoon stifling/drying in India are (1) sun drying, (2) steam stifling and (3) hot air drying. Besides these commercial methods there are other methods like infrared treatment, cold storage, ultraviolet rays and fumigation with some gases. However, these are not practically viable in the commercial processing. Sun drying and steam stifling are very common in India whereas hot air drying is popular in sericulturally advanced countries like Japan. Sun drying is cheaper but it is defective. Steam stifling is alright for multivoltine cocoons whereas bivoltine cocoons if treated by this method can not be stored for a long period, besides, reliability of bivoltine cocoons suffers by steam stifling.

Hot air stifling method is suitable for good quality cocoons such as Bivoltine and also, from this method, complete driage of cocoon is possible enabling to store the cocoons for a long time.

There are two types of hot air stifling :
1. *Italian type* : Here the cocoons are first subjected to low temperature and then gradually subjected to high temperature.
2. *Japanese type* : Here the cocoons are first subjected to high temperature and then gradually subjected to low temperature.

Generally the cocoons are first treated to 100-110°C and then gradually treated to lower temperature of 50°C within about 5 hours, and cocoons are fully dried to the extent of 40% or 100 kg fresh cocoons will be reduced to 40 kg.

4.11.3 Storage of Cocoons

Dead pupa is inside the cocoons and it has proteinous substance. Unless the cocoons are dried and preserved properly certain dermestides will attack the pupa and damage the cocoons. The common one is *Dennestes lardarius*. Cocoons are affected due to the following reasons during storage :

(1) Mould attack due to moisture content and damp surroundings.
(2) Dermestides.
(3) Insects : To avoid these, stained cocoons may be stored and cocoon storage may be away from by-products.

4.11.4 Sorting of Cocoons

(For size variation, defective cocoons, colour variation). Sorting of cocoons according to size is done on a special equipment known as Raddling in advanced countries. Uniform size and cocoon building have impact on cooking property.

Defective Cocoons are :

(a) Double, (b) Pierced, (c) Inside stained (melted) or dead cocoons, (d) Outside stained (urinated), (e) Thin and (f) Flimsy, (g)

Pointed or constricted, (h) Mould, (i) Immature. These can be used for spinning. Sorting is done by hand in India.

4.11.5 Reeling Technique

(a) Cocoon Cooking or Boiling or Maceration :

The object of cocoon cooking is to soften the sticky substance sericin so that the cocoon shell is loosened enabling the filament to be unwound smoothly. There are different systems of cooking as follows :

(1) Open pan system (single basin) used in India.

(2) Three pan system used to a small extent in India.

(3) Conveyor or central cocoon boiling machine used in Japan.

The first and second systems are used in research institutes in India for floating system of reeling or top (Three pans can be used for sunken system if modified) reeling. The third system is used for sunken system of reeling.

Floating system of reeling is associated with (1) reeling of cooked cocoons which float in the reeling basin, (2) high speed reeling, (3) high basin temperature reeling and (4) large number of reeling ends.

The sunken system of reeling is associated with (1) reeling cooked cocoons which sink under water in reeling basin, (2) low speed reeling, (3) low basin - temperature and (4) large number of reeling ends.

The sunken system of cooking has been derived from three pan system but now the system used in Japan is continuous or conveyor system cooking or central cocoon boiled machine.

(b) Brushing :

The object of brushing is to remove entangled mass of filament. They are of two types :

(1) Practical in (India)

(2) Mechanical brushing (used in Advanced countries like Japan, Italy etc.)

4.11.6 Reeling (Devices)

(i) Country charkha, Improved CSTRI Charkha - hand driven.

(ii) Cottage basin - hand driven or power driven.

(iii) Filature reeling basin - power driven with more mechanisms such as

Jette-boute

| Direct reeling filature machine (1920) old type also called hand reeling machine in Japan (Reeling is comparatively at high speed in high temperature water). No re-reeling is necessary. | Modern multiend reeling machine (1926). Reeling on small reels at slow speed and in low temperature water (re-reeling on standard size reeling is followed). |

The above three devices are common in India

		Production of Silk
Number of charkhas	22,500	50%
Number of cottage basins	7,000	40%
Number of filatures	5,000	10%

Reeling operations on filature basin

Japan		India
43.5%	Feeding ends to jette-boute (casting of cocoons).	29%
16.6%	Cleaning of pupa and dropped cocoons.	27%
7.2%	Preparation of cooked cocoons for feeding.	9.6%
16.4%	Gathering clear ends in the basin and final adjustment through jette-boute etc.	16.0%
6.3%	Mending and restarting on thread breakages.	17.4%
4.1%	Miscellaneous	1%

Objects of Croissue :

(a) Removal of water (water in the silk thread at that point is almost
equal to the weight of silk, i.e., 100%, to the extent of 65-70%).

(b) Thread becomes more cohesive as the filaments are attached more firmly by croissue.

(c) Thread becomes cleaner as many defects are eliminated, weak and defective portions can be discarded when they break under croissue tension.

"Tavella"

Italian type used in cottage basin & filature basin

(Sufficient uniform tension so yarn quality improves.)

"Chambon"

French type used in Charkha

(Less tension as compared to Tavella type so less advantageous.)

Also production is affected more when break occurs.

Length of croissue is as much as 20 cm.

Efficacy of croissure depends on the following :

(a) Croissue angle.

(b) Number of spirals i.e., length of croissue - greater the number higher the efficacy.

(c) Velocity of reeling - higher the velocity, higher the efficacy.

Tenacity and elongation dyanamometrical properties of the silk are not appreciably affected by the length of the croissure.

Mechanical reeling - first taken up by the American Engineer E.W. Serrel towards the end of the last century.

(iv) Semi-automatic reeling machine 'ODA' type (brushing and collecting of ends is done mechanically.)

(v) Automatic reeling machine (every thing is automatic) (Both are common in Japan).

(1954) Constant number of cocoon type. (1959) Constant number of denier type which is popular now-a-days 4-5 small units are also working in India.

Automatic reeling machines in Japan account for about 95%.

Sunken system of reeling is in practice in the automatic reeling machineries. One operator handles about 80 to 100 ends.

4.11.7 Re-reeling for Making Standard Sized Hanks

Hand weight – 70 g.

Length (for 20/220) = 30,000 M

Grant reel = Traverse

In our machine bevels are as follows :

One - 16/25 0.64

275 m/min.

Grant reeling : The diamond formation of skein is known as grant reeling. The guide through which the thread passes into the reel shall pass to and fro along the reel in such a manner that a definite ratio exists between the revolution of reel and the guide of the traverse, so that the thread forms clearly defined diamond in the skein. 13/24 bevel combination will produce 13 diamonds.

4.11.8 Skeining

International standard skein

Hank	58" - 59" Circumference
Diamonds	13 - 18
Width of skein	- 65 - 70 g upto 12D
Weight of skein	- 65 - 70 g upto 12D - 70 - 15 g upto 24D
	- 80 - 90 g upto 32D
	- 90 - 100 g above 32D

Twisting of hanks by skeining machine and tube.

4.11.9 Book Making and Baling

Twisted skeins are packed into bundles of 2 kg and they are known as books. Books are packed into bales. International silk bale weigh 60 kg whereas Indian bale is 20 kg Bales are sent to market.

Renditta - A ratio between cocoon weight and silk weight. It is the quantity of cocoons to produce a unit quantity of silk. Normally in India it is expressed on the basis of fresh cocoon weight.

For example - 10 kg of fresh cocoons are required to produce one kg of raw silk. So the renditta is 10.

4.12 Sericulture as Labour Intensive Agro-industry

Sericulture is a multidisciplinary programme which involves cultivation of food plants like mulberry, silkworm rearing and silk reeling, weaving and marketing. It is well known that sericulture is a labour intensive agro-industry, well suited for economically backward sections of the under developed and developing countries which have an agriculture base and problems of providing, employment not only to the agriculture poor but also to the landless labourers.

Sericulture, of late, has come to stay as a highly remunerative argo-industry with less investment and rich dividends. The following reasons are identified for intensively practising sericulture in it developing, country like India.

Mulberry plant is a drought resistant tree/shrub which could be grown in varieties of soils both under irrigated and rainfed conditions. Sericulture involves low investment. Once the plantation is established it will continue to yield for 15 to 20 years with minimum expenditure for maintenance. Therefore, maximum turnout can be obtained with minimum investment. It is highly suitable, as it is within the reach of small and marginal farmers. Sericulture involves a number of processes right from mulberry cultivation through silkworm rearing, reeling, throwing, weaving and marketing, and engaging a large number of people including the household members like women, children and old people. Sericulture is a labour-intensive rural industry creating employment to atleast for 12-13 people per hectare of mulberry. All the sericultural activities are village based and hence prevents migration of people from rural to urban areas in search of jobs. Silk being an expensive commodity used mostly by the affluent society, transfer of money from rich to poor is ensured. There is high export possibility creating trade surplus. Sericulture is a good source for earnings foreign exchange.

Presently, India is earning about 750 crores from export of silk fabrics and garments. Mulberry ensures higher income per unit area than that from a number of agricultural crops. Sericulture gives income 5-6 times a year.

Sericulture technology is very simple. It can be followed even by illiterate farmers. Most of the sericulture activities do not involve hard labour, as they can be attended conveniently by women and even old people. Sericulture mostly requires use of simple appliances which are easily available in rural areas. In drought conditions, when most of the agricultural crops do not revive even after a few showers, mulberry being a perennial crop will sprout and yield leaves for rearing silk worms. Sericulture could be a more advantageous agro-industry for improving the economy of the deprived sections of the society like schedule castes and schedule tribes. Non-mulberry sericulture is largely practised by the tribals. Sericulture provides self-employment opportunities to the educated unemployed youth in its varied sectors.

4.13 World Silk Scenario

A cursory look at world raw silk production atleast in the past few years could enable one to understand the trends in different countries.

Comparison of periodic raw silk production in Metric Tonnes

Country	1938	1978	1987	1990	1992
China	4,855	12,000	35,000	46,4000	54,500
India	690	3,475	8,455	11,487	13,000
Japan	43,150	15,960	7,864	5,720	5,085
USSR	1,900	3,200	4,000	4,094	4,000
South Korea	1,875	4,235	1,650	1,200	1,200
Brazil	35	1,250	1,780	1,693	2,373
Thailand	–	–	–	–	1,700
Other Countries	4,045	2,200	2,874	2,285	2,210
Total	56,500	49,360	62,503	72,879	84,068

The above table indicates the following :

1. The raw silk production in China and India has increased several times.
2. Japan was a leading country in raw silk production until 1978. At present is producing less than that of India and occupies only the third place in world raw silk production.
3. USSR has doubled its production and stands better than South Korea.
4. Silk production in South Korea is reduced considerably after 1978.

While comparing the raw silk production of India with that of China, one remembers that the production gap between China and India is very big and India's production is about ¼ of China. Sericulture in China is mostly of temperate kind and it produces 70% of bivoltine silk, whereas that of India is mostly tropical and it produces 90% of multivoltine x Bivoltine silk.

4.14 Indian Silk

India has the unique distinction in the world as it produces all the four major varieties of silk viz. mulberry, Tassar, Eri and Muga.

In India, of the 6,29,143 villages, sericulture is being practised in about 59,528 villages which will be 9.5%. During the year 1990-91 the area under mulberry was 3,13,109 hectares. (Statistical Biennial 1992). Indian sericulture has shown a dynamic growth during last few years. Its silk production during the last 14 years has gone up from 3475 metric tonnes in 1978 to 14,140 metric tonnes in 1992-93 recording a total growth of little over 400%. Similarly, India's export has gone up front 33 crores in 1978 to about 750 crores in 1992-93.

Comparison of the four kinds of silk in India from 1988 to 1992 is as follows :

Year	Mulberry	Non-mulberry			Total
		Tasar	Eri	Muga	
1988-90	9,683	358	565	45	10,651
1989-90	10,905	465	589	57	12,016
1990-91	11,487	484	624	70	12,665
1991-92	10,657	426	707	73	11,863
1992-93	13,007	361	700	72	14,140

The major silk producing states in India are Karnataka, Andhra Pradesh, Tamil Nadu, West Bengal and Jammu and Kashmir for mulberry silk. Bihar, Orissa and Madhya Pradesh are known for Tassar silk and Assam for Eri and Muga silks. Even Manipur and Meghalaya are producing Eri silk (1992 statistical biennial). Karnataka stands first in silk production and then comes Andhra Pradesh and Tamilnadu. In Karnataka only Mysore, Kolar, Bangaluru, Mandga, and Tumkur are the traditional sericulture belts. But today sericulture is being practiced in all the districts of the state.

Factors that contributed to an increase in silk productivity in India are :

1. A great awareness among the farmers about the advantages of practicing sericulture as it gives better profit than those of most of the agricultural crops.
2. There is a progressive change by replacing the traditional mulberry by substituting improved high yielding M_5 (Kanva), S_{54} and other varieties.
3. A wide network of chawki rearing centres under the expert supervision of qualified technical staff has been established to bring down the mortality rate and to ensure yield of high quality cocoon.
4. A well organised system has been established in the supply of disease - free layings (eggs) to the farmers.
5. A large number of extension and technical service centres have been established all over the country to educate the farmers to improve mulberry cultivation and silkworm rearing.

Inspite of many advantages of practising sericulture, it is necessary to know whether the expansion of mulberry cultivation encroaches upon the production of food crops as viewed by some sections. In India, out of 144 million hectares of cultivable, land, mulberry is grown only in about 10.2 million hectares (1985 statistics) which is about 0.14%, giving employment to about six million people and it has gone up to 0.241 million hectares in 86-87 accounting for 0.17% of the cultivable land in the country. In Karnataka about 0.139 million hectares are under mulberry cultivation providing employment to two million people. Therefore, the total mulberry area in Karnataka accounts for 0.99% of the total cultivable area. In Japan, at one time, mulberry occupied about 4% of total net sown area which is only one - seventh of Japan's geographical area, cultivated.

Sericulture as a Means of Income Levelling

Sericulture plays a vital role in transferring wealth from richer sections to poorer sections of the society. Silk is consumed mostly by the affluent and the money so spent by them on purchase of silk is distributed among the sericulturists like mulberry cultivators and cocoon producers, reelers, twisters, weavers and traders.

Summary of the percentage of distribution of money from sale of soft-silk fabric of weight 40, 50 and 60 gm/m is given as follows :

Category of persons	Soft silk fabric of		
	40 gm/metre	50 gm/metre (% share)	60 gm/metre
Cocoon	51.5	54.6	56.8
Producer	6.2	6.6	6.8
Reeler	8.2	8.8	9.1
Twister	14.5	12.3	10.7
Weaver	19.6	17.7	16.6
Trader			
Total	100.00	100.00	100.00

Although systematic studies have not been undertaken regarding world demand for silk, increase in silk price and increased production over the last fifteen years show that the overall world demand for silk will remain far above the actual supplies. Even though man made fibres such as nylon, rayon and terylene will continue to play their role in the world consumption of textiles, silk cannot be and will not be displayed from its premier position as it is considered, even today as the undisputed "Empress of textiles".

4.15 Sericulture in Andhra Pradesh

Sericulture is an agro-based labour intensive industry which provides gainful employment to the rural and unemployed youth and helps to uplift the socioeconomic status of small and marginal farmers. The economic advantages of sericulture industry lies in its high employment potential with low investment. One hectare of mulberry creates employment to (12) persons throughout the year. 60% of them are women thereby supporting a greater role for women in development. It requires low gestation period and continues to yield for 15-16 years with little expenditure on maintenance. It gives higher returns, unlike other agricultural crops.

Andhra Pradesh occupies first position in productivity and second position in the country next to Karnataka in production of silk. Andhra Pradesh produces all the four popular varieties of silkworm cocoons namely Mulberry, Tassar, Eri and Muga. Andhra Pradesh has got very strong and traditional weaving base with more than a lakh number of handlooms mostly concentrated in weaving pockets like Dharmavaram, Pochampally, Gadval, Patur, Peddapuram, Narayanpet, etc., In the last decade number of cotton weavers have taken to silk weaving in centers like Rayadurg and Proddatur because of better income in silk weaving.

As a rural agro based industry, Sericulture has now expanded to almost all districts in the state.

4.16 Sericulture at a Glance

Sr. No.	Item	Units	2005-06
1.	Employment generation	Lakh persons	4.88
2.	Area under mulberry cultivation	Cumulative in acres	97,646
3.	CB cocoon production	In MTs	46,785
	Bivoltine cocoon production	In MTs	1,239
	Total Cocoon Production	**In MTs**	**48,024**
4.	Cocoon production/100 Dfls	In kg	54.4
5.	Raw silk production	In MTs	5,336
6.	Sericulture farmers	In Nos.	76,971
7.	Tassar food plantation available for rearing	In acres	25,000
8.	Tassar Dfls brushed	Lakh nos.	8.82
9.	Tassar Cocoon production	Lakh nos.	113.53
10.	Tassar rearers	(In No.s).	3,000
11.	Area under Castor and Topioca	In lakh hectares	3.74
12.	Eri Dfls brushed	(In Nos).	1.759
13.	Eri cocoon production	MTs	33.500

4.17 Rearing Appliances (Extra Reference Topic)

Following rearing equipments are required for the proper rearing of silkworms, without which the rearing would be a partial success.

(a) Rearing stands : Rearing stands are made of wood or bamboo and are portable for transportation. A rearing stand may be constructed and have dimensions like 2.5 m high × 1.5 m long × 1 m wide and should have 10 shelves with a space of 20 cm between each shelf. The trays are arranged on the shelves and each stand can accommodate 10 rearing trays. Six stands are enough for each rearing room.

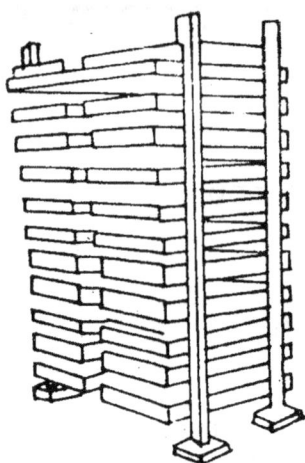

Fig. 4.30 : Rearing Stand with Ant Wells

(b) Ant wells : Ants are a serious menace to silkworms. To protect them, the legs of the rearing stand are kept in rectangular or circular enamel or concrete bowls containing water mixed with good insecticide. The Ant wells may be made of concrete or stone blocks 20 cm square and 7.5 cm high with a deep groove of 2.5 cm running all round the top.

(c) Rearing trays : These are used to rear silkworms and are usually made up of early stage locally available cheap material like bamboo so that they are light (in weight) and easy to handle. They are either circular (1.2-1.4 m diameter and 7.5 cm depth) or rectangular (0.7-0.9 m × 0.9-1.2 m). Sometimes, box type wooden trays are employed to rear early instars (I and II instar larvae).

(a) Rearing Stand with Rectangular Wooden Trays

(b) Rearing Stand with Circular Trays

Fig. 4.31

(d) Paraffin paper : Thick craft paper sheets coated with paraffin wax (M.P. 55°C) are required to cover the rearing trays to maintain the humidity in rearing beds and prevent withering of chopped leaves. It is used for rearing early stage silkworms.

(e) Foam rubber strips : Pieces (2.5 × 2.5 cm) of foam rubber soaked in water are kept all round silkworm rearing beds to maintain humidity during the first two instars. Newspaper folded strips moistened with water could be a convenient substitute.

(f) Chopsticks : Chopsticks are tapering bamboo rods meant to pick up younger stages of larvae to ensure their hygienic handling and preventing from injuries. These are made of bamboo, approximately 17.5-20 cm long and tapering to one end.

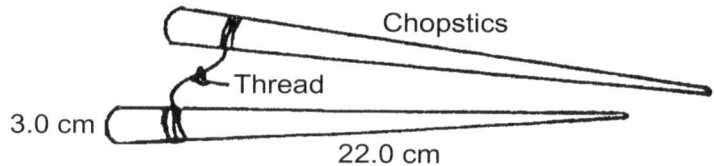

Fig. 4.32 : Chopsticks

(g) Feathers : Bird feathers, preferably white, are important items of silkworm rearing room. They are used for brushing the delicate newly hatched larvae (worms) onto the rearing bed to prevent injuries.

Fig. 4.33 : Feather

(h) Leaf chamber : Mulberry leaves harvested from the field are stored and preserved fresh for feeding the worms at set intervals during the day. The leaves can be stored in cool rooms or in the rooms covered with cloth or polythene sheets. They can be also stored in leaf chambers (1.5 m long, 0.9 m wide and 0.8 m deep) of wooden strips fixed some distance apart of some porous board. The chamber with leaves is covered all over with gunny bag cloth kept moist during the summer months and dry days.

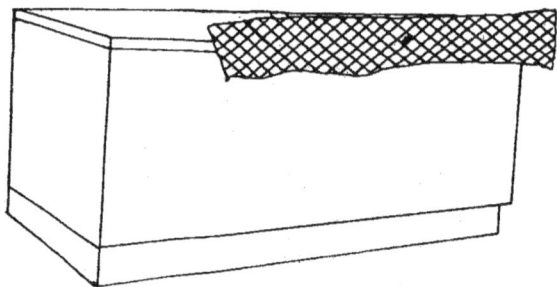

Fig. 4.34 : Leaf Chamber

(i) Chopping board : This is made of soft wood and is used for cutting the leaf to the suitable sizes required for feeding the worms in the different instars. The size of the board is 0.9 m × 0.9 m and 5 cm thick or of any convenient size.

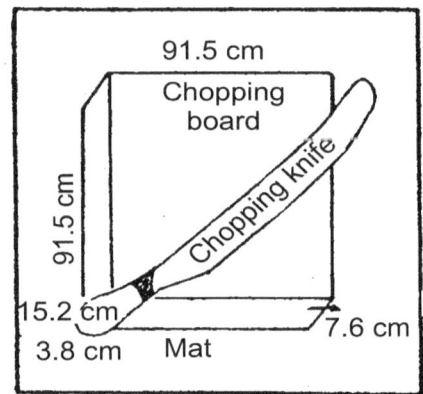

Fig. 4.35 : Chopping Board and Knife

(j) Chopping knives : Chopping knives are used for cutting the mulberry leaves. They are usually 0.3-0.5 m long with a broad knife blade and a wooden handle. Two sized knives, small and large for chopping small pieces for younger instars and large pieces for older instars are needed. Chopped leaves falling on the mat are better collected in an enamelled receptacle (please refer to Fig. 4.35).

(k) Mats : Mats usually 1.2 × 1.8 m are used for collecting the leaves. When chopping is done on the floor, they prevent the dust and dirt on the floor getting mixed in with the leaves.

(l) Cleaning nets : Nets made up of cotton or nylon of the mesh size suitable for different instars are used for changing and of beds so that the left over leaf pieces and litter are filtered out without the larvae being touched by hand. Mesh sizes suitable for I, II, III, IV and V instars are 2 mm², 10 mm² and 20 mm² respectively.

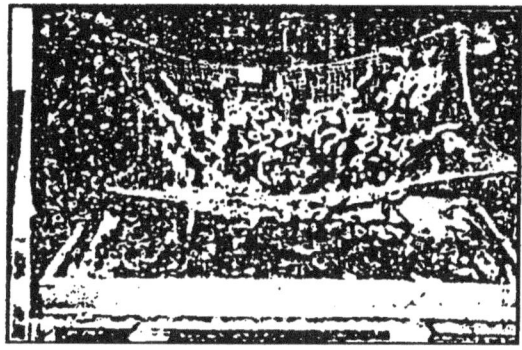

Fig. 4.36 : Cleaning Net

(m) Mountages : Mountages (cocoon-ages) are used as supports for the silkworms to spin cocoons. They are made up of rectangular bamboo mat tied on 4 bomboo sticks and bearing on its surface spirals of bamboo tapes (1.8 m long, 1.2 m wide and 5-6 m spiral tapes leaving a gap of 5-6 cm).

The ripe worms about to spin cocoons are transferred onto them. The larvae suspend themselves to the spirals and spin cocoons. The mountages are also called as *chandrikes* in India.

Fig. 4.37 : Bamboo Mountage (chandrika) with Cocoons

The advantages of chandrikes are :

1. They are cheap and easily made.
2. It can be easily stored/stacked.
3. Excreta of spinning worms dry up soon due to free passages and thus prevents cocoons from getting stained.
4. It can be easily shifted from place to place.
5. It can be easily disinfected.

(n) Feeding stands : These are small wooden stands 0.9 m high used for holding the trays during feeding and cleaning.

Fig. 4.38 : Feeding Stand

(o) Miscellaneous Appliances : These include a *hygrometer* to measure humidity, a *thermometer* to record temperature of the rearing room, a *charcoal stove* to heat the rooms in winter, *disinfection pads* of gunny soaked in 2% formalin to disinfect the feet of the workers entering the rearing room, a *sprayer* to disinfect the rooms themselves, and humidity (70-80%).

Moths usually emerge in early morning hours. The emerging moths are sexed (i.e. identified for the sex) and used as reproductive seeds (for breeding purpose) and industrial seeds (for supply of eggs). Males are kept in the trays of the females and as soon as copulation occur, the pair is transferred to black plastic celluler or vessel and allowed for three hours mating to secure maximum fertilized eggs. Male moths are then stored at 5°C to be used for a second mating while the female moths are kept in vessel for egg laying within 12 hours, 400-600 eggs are laid. (Each layer is examined for pebrine). Generally, females are forced to lay eggs on paper sheets or cards whose surface has been coated with a gummy substance. The egg sheets/cards are washed with 2% formalin for 1 hour to disinfect the eggs and again with water to remove traces of formalin. The sheets are dried in shade and transferred to incubators for hatching.

In commercial production, 50-100 moths are allowed to lay eggs on paper sheets. The egg sheets are soaked in water to loosen the eggs. The loose eggs are washed in salt solution to remove unfertilized eggs which float on the surface. The fertilized eggs thus separated are disinfected (2% formalin), shade dried and packed (loose) in egg boxes to be despatched to buyers.

The eggs produced in a grainage should be properly incubated under the conditions of optimum temperature (25°C), humidity (80%), air (0.3 m/sec.) and light (16 hrs). This will create uniformity in embryonic development and all the eggs will hatch out on $10^{th}/11^{th}$ day after oviposition. The eggs, one day prior to hatching, change their colour to blue, due to the pigmentation of the embryo. The blue stage gives clear indication a *stand* for wash-basin containing 2% formalin to disinfect the hands of the workers handling the worms and *leaf-baskets* to transport mulberry leaves from the gardens to the rearing house.

4.18 Economics of Sericulture

Sericulture is a multidisciplinary programme which involves : cultivation of food plants like mulberry, silkworm rearing, silk rearing, weaving and marketing. Sericulture is a labour intensive agro-industry, well suited for economically backward sections of the under-developed and develpoing countries which have an agriculture base; which creates employment to atleast for 12 to 13 people per hectare of mulberry.

Sericulture requires low investment. Once the plantation is established it will continue to yield for 15-20 years, with minimum expenditure for maintenance. Therefore, maximum turnout can be obtained with minimum investment.

There is high export possibility creating trade surplus. Sericulture is a good source for earning foreign exchange. Presently, India is earning about 750 crores from export of silk fabrics and garments.

The research achievements coupled with extension efforts have lead the industry to a impressive growth.

Sericulture today has become an important rural occupation with industrial sector structure, outbeating other major cash crops. The development of modern techniques opened up new avenues. Today many developing countries are availing this opportunity and have taken up this new venture. Although the research results have proved that it is possible to achieve 195 kg silk production per hectare per year. This will go a long way in upliftment of rural economics.

Economics of sericulture for **one acre.**

(I) Non-recurring Investment :

(A) Mulberry plantation expenditure

1.	Preparation of land	₹	1,500/-
2.	Mulberry sapling preparation	₹	500/-
3.	Cow dung manure	₹	1,250/-
4.	Synthetic fertilizers (NPK)	₹	2,150/-
5.	Water charges	₹	500/-
6.	Interculture	₹	150/-
7.	Weeding	₹	300/-
8.	Miscellaneous	₹	500/-

(B) Silkworm rearing equipment expenditure

1.	Rectangular rearing trays - 10 (₹ 50/tray)	₹	500/-
2.	Circular rearing type - 20 (₹ 20/tray)	₹	400/-
3.	Chopping board - 2 (₹ 50/board)	₹	100/-
4.	Chopping knives - 2 (₹ 10/knife)	₹	20/-
5.	Wooden stand-2 (₹ 100/stand)	₹	200/-
6.	Ant wells - 8 (₹ 20 each)	₹	160/-

Contd...

7.	Leaf chamber box - 1	₹	250/-
8.	Bed cleaning nets - 16 (₹ 10 each)	₹	160/-
9.	Foam pad - 1 kg	₹	200/-
10.	Chandrikes - 25	₹	2,000/-
11.	Sprayer - 1	₹	1,500-
12.	Hygrometer - 1	₹	100/-
	Total	₹	**5,590/-**

(C) **Rearing house expenditure ₹ 15,000/-**
(Construction)

(II) **Recurring Expenditure :**

Rearing expenditure

1.	Egg sheets (200 egg masses)	₹	250/-
2.	Rearing of silkworms (1-3 instars) and mounting of Vth instar larvae on chandrikes - labour charges	₹	1,350/-
3.	Paraffin paper, formaline, newspapers, etc.	₹	150/-
	Total	₹	**1,750**

(III) **Regular Income Yearwise :**

(a) **Income for 1st year :**
  (i) From 400 egg sheets will get 120 kg cocoon production
    Rate ₹ 137/- kg of cocoon   ₹ 16,440/-
  (ii) Income from mulberry cuttings
    at the end of first year   ₹ 2,800/-
                              Total ₹ 19,240/-

(b) **Income for 2nd year :**
  (i) From 800 egg masses will get 240 kg cocoon production
    Rate ₹ 137/- kg of cocoons   ₹ 32,880
  (ii) Income from mulberry cuttings
    at the end of 2nd year   ₹ 2,800
                              Total ₹ 35,680

(c) There is regular income from third year at the amount Rs. 35,680/-.

4.19 Brief Idea (Definition and Scope) of Branches of Applied Zoology

Science is an organised body of knowledge supported by observation and experimentation, derived from the study of natural phenomena of the entire material universe.

Pure or basic science is that part of science which deals with understanding and interpreting natural phenomena without considering their practical application in human welfare. Therefore, basic science is pursued for its own shake.

Applied science deals with application of scientific principles which benefit human beings in increasing comforts and protection. Technology is the study and utilisation of techniques for producing material necessities of the human race. Biology is the study of living organisms is a part of science like physics and chemistry. Biology developed all the three constituents of science basic, applied and technology.

Zoology deals with the study of animals. Vast number of animals are living on the planet earth. Since time immemorial, man has always been using these living animals as food, shelters, medicine and agricultural purposes. Large number of animals useful to mankind while others are harmful or dangerous to man and cause great economic losses. Each and every animal has its own importance and status in nature, however some animals like birds, fishes, prawns, oysters, useful insects like honey bee, silk worm and lac insect etc. are playing an important role in human welfare. There are variety of harmful insect and rodent pests which are competitors of human beings for food and natural resources. Some insects like honey bee; silkworm, lac insects are gaining too much importance in the small scale industries which suit the aim of our nation. These small scale industries provide employment to people and raise socioeconomic status of the nation.

These are all the applied or economic aspects of zoology which are included in syllabi of Indian as well as foreign universities.

In the subject zoology several animals are being studied to understand the life and activities of animals. They are studied purely from academic point of view. The study of animals is simply to gain knowledge of animal, its life and activities is called pure or basic zoology. It should, however, be remembered that the knowledge of pure branches is necessary for studying applied branches of the subject.

Applied Zoology : It is the branch of zoology in which useful and harmful animals are studied and the knowledge is applied to improve the health and welfare of mankind. It is also called 'Economic Zoology'. There are the following different branches of Applied Zoology.

(1) Sericulture : Sericulture is the art and science of rearing of silkworms in order to obtain silk. It involves :
  (a) Selection and cultivation of mulberry food plants for silk moth larvae.
  (b) Maintenance, improvement and rearing of silk moth stock.
  (c) Protection against pest and diseases.
  (d) Extraction and finishing of silkthread.
  (e) Marketing.

The sericulture is an important cottage industry, but is now basis of large industries in China, Japan, India and some European countries, where the silk worm, *Bombyx mori* is reared on mulberry leaves on a mass scale to get raw silk from the cocoons of the caterpillars of the moth. The eggs hatch into caterpillars which voraciously feed on the fresh mulberry leaves. Then the larva secrete sticky secretion from silk glands around itself forming hard cocoon of silk fibres. It is called pupa. The pupa is killed by drying it in sun or by boiling. The raw silk fibres are reeled out into silk threads. Depending on the types of silkworms four types of silk have been identified namely, Mulberry silk, Tassar silk, Eri silk and Muga silk.

(2) Apiculture : Apiculture or bee-keeping is the science or technique of rearing honey bees for honey and wax from their comb or bee hives. Selection of sites for quality honey and protection of bees and combs from pests and diseases are part of apiculture.

Bees are economically important social insects. They not only provide us with honey and wax, but they are also responsible for pollination of flowers of the majority of commercially important plants. The common Indian honey bees are *Apis dorsata, Apis florea* and *Apis, mellifera Apis indica*. All of them occur in nature as wild insects. However, because of their high economic importance, the honey bees, especially *Apis mellifera* are domesticated and cultured, viz., reared and bred in artificial hives. The honey bee is a colonial, social insect living in hives. Each member performs its assigned role. Artificial hives are used for honey. Various tools are required in apiculture.

(3) Poultry : Poultry farming deals with the rearing of fowls (chicken), ducks, turkeys and pheasants for their eggs and meat. Poultry and poultry products are a rich source of animal proteins and other nutrients such as fats, vitamins and minerals. Poultry birds are easy to raise, can be acclimatized to a wide range of climatic conditions, have short life span and are prolific breeders. Poultry farming requires less space, is easier to manage and maintain and brings fast returns within a span of six months. The poultry houses are kept comfortably, well ventilated and illuminated. Birds of different ages are kept in separate houses. The desi type or indigenous and improved type or exotic breeds are used. The exotic breeds are classified into American class, English class, Mediterranean class and Asiatic class. White Leghorn, Rhode Island Red, Plymouth Rock and New Hampshire are the examples of exotic type.

(4) Dairy Science : The use of mammalian milk has proved to be a boon for mankind since time immemorial. Milk is called complete food and has provided life for the man. Mammals like cow, buffalo and goat provide milk for human consumption in the form of butter, curd and ghee or for preparation of other edible food items, sweets etc. Thus, dairy science deals with collection of milk and conversion of milk into various milk products. It also deals with increase the milk yield. Indian cows are cross breed with European breeds like Holstein, Brown Swiss, Jersey, Red Dane. The Karanswiss and Sunandini are the breeds developed through cross breeding at National Dairy Research Institute, Karnal and in Kerala, respectively.

(5) Fishery Science : The cultivation and management of fishes, prawns and pearl oysters in a scientific way to make it commercially viable and at the same time making harvest of quality food animals and pearl possible, is known as fishery. The term fisheries refers to the capture and culture of aquatic animals for the use of human beings. Fishery management is nothing but skillful steps taken by man and complete exploitation of aquatic resources. Inland and marine fisheries are the two divisions of fishery.

Pisciculture is the production of fishes. Fishes are reared in small rivers, lakes and canals. Fish eggs are introduced into nurseries (hatcheries). The young ones hatched from the eggs are fed, tendered and nursed and harvested when full grown. Aquaculture techniques of induced breeding by the administration of pituitary hormones have helped in the production of fish in pure form. Hatcheries with circulating water have ensured almost 100 per cent hatching of fertilized eggs.

Calta catla, Labeo rohita, Clarius batracus, Cyprimus carpio are common important freshwater species. Bombay duck *(Herpadon)* Eel, *Hilsa, Pomphret, Salmon* and Sardine are some of the important marine species. Fishes provide proteins, vitamins, feed for cattle and poultry, and fertilizers.

(6) Pearl Culture : A large number of molluscs are found in river, sea and brackish water, which used by man for food, shell and pearl industries. Pearl is a white, highly shining globular body found in the shell of mollusca oyster. Pearl is secreted by the mantle of marine as well as fresh water bivalves called pearl oysters. Collection of oyster from sea or river bed, opening the shell (valves) and getting the pearl from them is collectively termed 'Pearl fishery'. These are the pearls formed naturally in the body of animal. Natural pearl formation is very slow process hence now the oysters are cultured for producing pearls in pearl industry. Introduction of large particles of desired shape and size made it possible to get pearls of different shape and size. This technique is called artificial pearl culture and Japan was the first to develop scientific pearl culture. *Pinctata fucata, P. uulgaris, P. margaritifera, P. anomioides* are some of the important species of oyster for pearl culture. Pearls are largely used in ornaments and in medicines.

(7) Lac Culture: Lac is known to Indian people since time immemorial. It is reported in our vedic literatures as well as in Mogal period. It is supposed to be the native insect of India and today also the Indian states produce more than 85% of total lac produced in the world. Its production, management, distribution and culture was well known to Indian citizens in vedic period but today it is done in more scientific and organised way.

Lac is produced by an insect *Tacchardia lacca* which is small in size and colonial in habit. Lac is a resin like product which the lac insect produces and itself it is surrounded in it as a protective measure of the insect which harms the tree also.

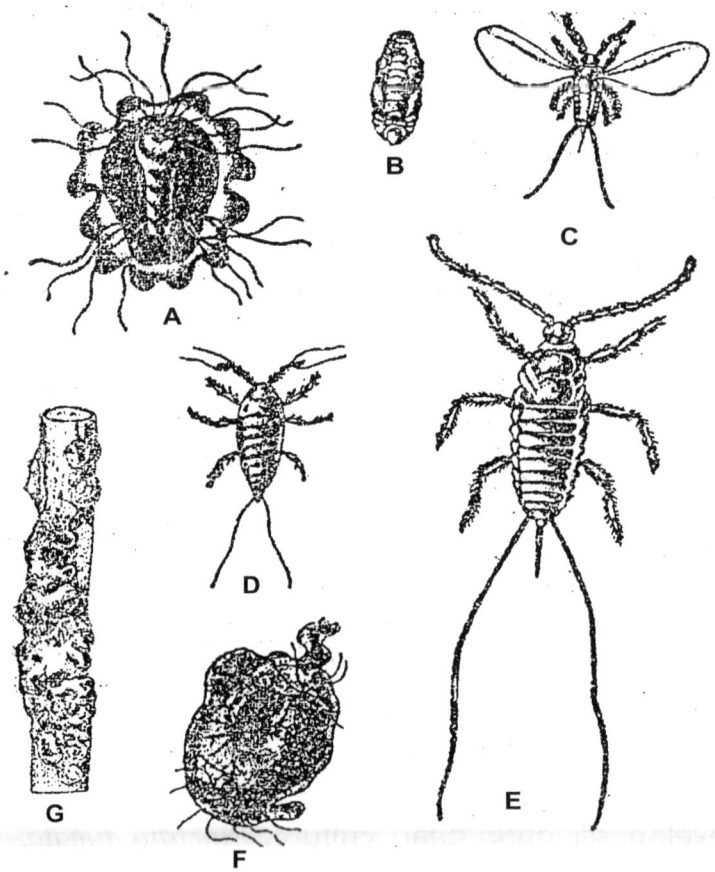

Fig. 4.39 : Lac insects

Lac is produced from the posterior part of the female insect only but males do not produce lac. The females are larger than males with oval or pear shaped body enveloped in a cell like covering. It is almost flattened reduced legs, antennae, wings and other body appendages but piercing and sucking type of mouth parts are highly evolved and well developed. The females are bigger with a small pore at the hind end of abdomen.

The males are small, cylindrical with a pair of weak wings, three pairs of legs, piercing and sucking types of mouth parts. The caudal style is present. The organs are fully developed and are not degenerated like the females.

The lac insects are generally found on the common trees like Ber, Pippal, Palas, Kusum, Babhool etc.

These insects are always associated with the new succulant branches of trees and suck the juice regularly. The twig harbouring these insects generally dries up and is defoliated. Climatic conditions and type of tree play a vital role in the production of lac and its quality.

Life cycle : The female after producing the required amount of lac stops feeding and its body shrinks considerably. It lays about 300-400 small, rounded eggs at a time and the female die leaving an encrustation full of eggs. The hatching of eggs is governed by the temperature and humidity.

The larvae come out in large number from encrustation. They are equipped with piercing and sucking type of mouth parts. They more on succulent shoot where they can feed easily. The larvae settle in a close association with each other. Therefore, twig is not seen.

They feed upon the sap and secrete pink coloured resin like substance from their dermal glands. This becomes hard when comes in contact with air and is known as lac. Lac deposition is done in all parts of the body except the mouth parts, spiracles and anal pores. This covering is called 'cell' which protects the larva and all the post embryonic stages are completed inside the cell. The larvae moult thrice inside the cell and become sexually mature. The male and female are almost alike but they become distinct. within two weeks.

The male is marked by its elongated cell. It contains two opening at anterior end. Female cell is rounded with irregular marine which with six holes through hair which like fibres may emerge.

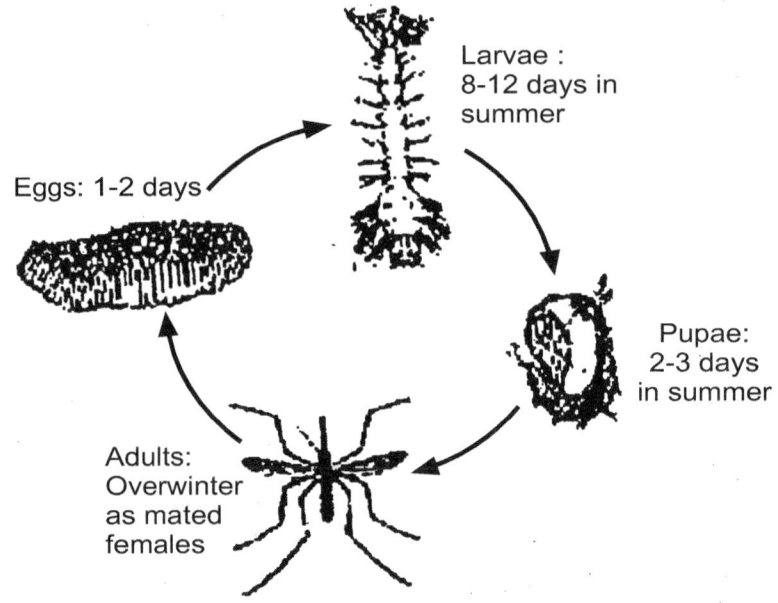

Fig. 4.40 : Life cycle of Lac insect

The male cell produces winged and wingless males which are active and come out of the cell, walk over lac crustation of the female and fertilize the female. Both males are capable of fertilizing the female but the winged males move faster than the wingless males. They possess well developed legs, wings and other appendages. Whereas the female larva after three moultings becomes sexually mature, but the appendages are reduced. The sexually mature female gets fertilized through the anal opening present in the cell. It grows very fast and produces more resin like substances, white, thin, fibrous, hair like processes come out of the thread and give a white appearance.

The females live longer than males but never come out of their cells. Depending upon the completion of life cycle stages and production of lac generally two crops are produced in a year. One is called Baishakhi and other Kartiki crop. The period of crop depends upon the climatic conditions, rainfall, temperature and humidity as well as the type of host plant available. Various type of plants have different period of defoliation and emergence of new leaves. So they directly govern the production of lac and maturation of post embryonic stages. Generally, eggs are laid in summer and winter seasons which get matured with stipulated period and produce in two seasons.

Adverse climatic factors like hot wind, high rainfall, drought, high temperature and humidity, and extreme cold, foggy weather are the enemies of lac insect which kill newly emerged males. Rats, squirrels, bats feed on lac insects and damage the deposited lac. Some moths and larvae also eat the eggs of lac insect.

The lac contains resin, dye and hard wax. A small amount of water and mineral is also found in it. The composition of lac is, Resin 60-85%, dye 2 - 10%, wax 6%, aluminous protein 5 - 8%, minerals 6 - 7% and water 3 - 4%.

Artificially lac production is obtained with more scientific way. Artificial inoculation of lac in the plant gives better and regular supply, as well as the amount of lac received is also much higher than that of natural inoculation.

Use of lac: Lac is used in a variety of ways, bangles, toys, wood work, sealing waxes, bad conductors, records, varnishes, polish, inks, filling the spaces, and silvering the mirror are the some of the uses of lac.

8) Goat Farming: Goats are multipurpose animals which can produce milk, meat, fiber, skin together. Compared to cow and other livestock farming, goat farming requires less space and additional facilities. Commercial goat farming in India is becoming very popular day by day. As goat farming is a proven highly profitable business idea so, the popularity of this business is increasing rapidly in India. Human populations are growing and creating a significant and increasing demand for additional animal protein foods. The goat can play an important role in meeting these demands. Huge market demand and proper spread ensures fast profitability and sustainability of this business for long term. In India, the goats are among the main meat producing animals. Most of the people prefer goat meat and has huge domestic demand. Along with meat production, goats are also very suitable for milk, fiber and skin production. They also produce high quality manure which helps to increase the crop production. Goat has a great and important contribution in the rural economy. Specifically in mountainous, semi-arid and arid regions of India. There are more than 25% goats among the total livestock in the country.

It is really very easy to maintain a goat farm compared to other farm animals. They are smaller in size but reach slaughter age faster. Goats can adopt themselves with almost all types of agro-climatic condition and diseases are less in goats when they are vaccinated periodically. Goat products like meat and milk has no religious taboo and highly accepted for consumption throughout the world. They has a less demand of housing and other management. Production costs like infrastructure, feeding and treatment are less. For goat farming one has a select a suitable location and proper breed. In India presently there are 22 Indian goat breeds available for goat farming. Some of them are Osmanababadi, Jamunpatri, Beetel, Sirohi, Sojat, Totapari, Malbari etc. The foreign breeds are Boer, Sannen and Danascus. Proper housing is required. Always special care and management is important in goat farming.

9) Pig farming or Piggary: Pig farming is the raising and breeding of domestic pigs. It is a branch of animal husbandry. Pigs are raised principally as food (e.g. pork, bacon, gammon) and sometimes for their skin.

Pigs are amenable to many different styles of farming. Intensive commercial units, commercial free range enterprises, extensive farming – being allowed to wonder around a village, town or city or tethered in a simple shelter or kept in a pen outside the owners house. Historically, pigs were kept in small numbers and were closely associated with the residence of the owner, or in the same village or town. They were valued as a source of meat, fat and for the ability to turn inedible food into meat and often fed household food waste if kept on a homestead. Pigs have been farmed to dispose of municipal garbage on a large scale. All these forms of pigform are in use today. In developed nations, commercial forms house thousands of pigs in climate controlled building. Pigs are a popular form of livestock, with more than one billion pigs killed each year worldwide, 100 million of them in the USA. The majority of pigs are used for human food but also supply skin, fat and other materials for use as clothing, ingredients for processed foods cosmetics and other medical use.

Almost all of the pig can be used as food. Preparations of pig parts into specialities include: sausage, bacon, gammon, ham, skin into pork scratching, feet into trotters, head into a meat jelly called head cheese (brawn) and consumption of the liver, chitterlings and blood (blood pudding or black pudding).

Pigs are farmed in many countries, but main countries are in Asia. China is net importer of pigs and largest exporters of pigs are the USA, European union and Canada.

4.20 Vermitechnology

Techniques and Importance of Vermiculture and Vermiwash

Vermiculture essentially means the scientific culturing / rearing of earthworms. Vermiculture, Vermitechnology, Vermiculture bio-technology, Earthworm farming all deal with the culture and application of earthworms for various purposes viz. (1) As in the production of vermicompost (rich bio-fertilizer), (2) Earthworm protein as animal feed for livestock, (3) Some species for the treatment of industrial wastes. (4) Earthworms play a significant role in the biotic components of soil processes, which include turning and mixing of soils. The Green Revolution showed great promise, especially during the period between the 1960's and 1970's, during which food production increased substantially in India. This increase in food production, was due to a number of reasons i.e. more land was brought under agriculture, high external and chemical input based and ignores the fact that biological communities in the soil are essential for continuous soil fertility.

Among the 1800 known species of earthworm more than half belong to Megascolecides, is largest and widely distributed. It contains 30 Indian genera of which *Pheretima* is the largest.

Habit and Habitat : Earthworm is the best known, soil-inhabiting animal; occurs in diverse habitats and traced in forest, grassland, gardens orchards, plant-nursery and greenhouse. Organic material like manure, litter, composite, humus, effluents and kitchen drainage are highly attractive for some species, while others are hydrophilous and few live under snow and high mountains, hence identification of the various earthworm species on the basis of their microhabitat is important to farmers, because such type of studies will provide guidelines for application of appropriate species which will suit to their agro-climatic condition and soil-texture. Ecological factors like pH, moisture content, salinity and temperature play an important role in the habitat of earthworm.

This soil aerator is an important bio-agent of the underground fauna, who is active day and night silently and secretely carrying on the tasking and laborious job of scavenger on the dead plant and animal remains.

Earthworm is a member of the soil biota (diverse assemblage of micro and macro organisms); and is master in mixing different soil components and production of surface and subsurface castings. Earthworm consumes the soil organic material and converts it into rich humus.

General Morphological Features of Earthworm : The morphology, anatomy, etc. for the earthworm - *Pheretima posthuma* is studied by you last year. Though general morphological pecularities have been described in general for the most genera.

Earthworms are terrestrial annelids, with external and internal metameric segmentation throughout the long, narrow and cylindrical body. They lack any appendages and suckers but have a few hook-like setae on all segments except the first and the last one.

Mouth opens on the first segments (Peristomium) which bears a hole overhanging the mouth.

The clitellum is a prominent circular band of glandular tissue and indicates maturity. It consist about 4 - 10 segments which lie anywhere between the 14th and 30th segment depending on species. All Earthworms have the short hook like setae embedded in the skin with which they hold gain on the substratum during burrowing and locomotion.

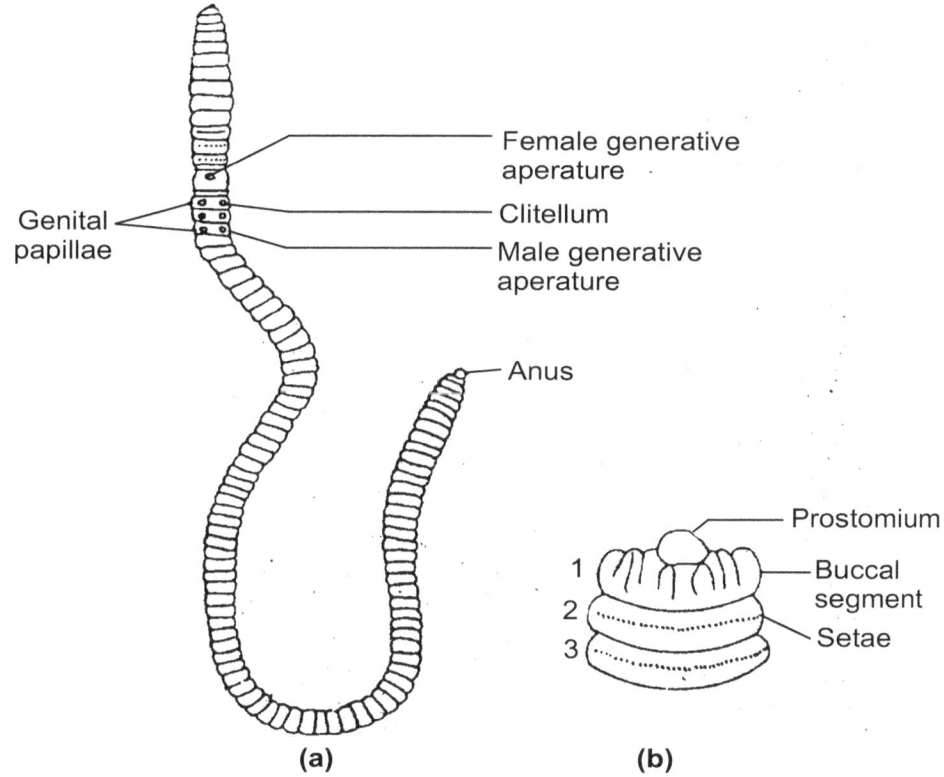

Fig. 4.41 : (a) Ventral view of an earthworm
(b) Dorsal view of prostomium and first three segments.

Earthworms are Hermaphrodite with few gonads in definite segmental locations. Male and female reproductive pores are located on the ventral region between the 13th and 38th segments.

Useful Species of Earthworms :

All over the world, including the tropical and temperate regions many species of earthworms are tested for mass cultivation. These worms occur in diverse habitats. i.e. organic materials like manure, compost, litter, humus, effluents and kitchen drainage etc.

Earthworms are omnivorous but they mostly derive nutrition from dead organic matter, which generally does not occur abundantly in the soil. As a result, they are adapted to swallow large quantities of soil for extracting sufficient nourishment from it. Earthworms vary in size and shape. In India, some peregrine species like - *Microscolex phosphoreus* (Duges), *Dichogaster saliens* (Beddard) and *Bimastos parvus* (Eisen) are less than 20 mm long. While some endemic geophagous forms, such as *Drawida nilamburenis* (Bourne) and *Drawida grandis* (Bourne) may reach upto one meter in length. *Megascolides australis* (McCoy) from Australia is about 4 meters in length. The world's largest known worm *Microchaetus microchaetus* (Rapp) found in South Africa has a length of over 7 meters.

An African species, *Eudrilus eugeniae* and an European worm, *Eisenia fetida* are being cultured in several parts of the world. These species have also been transported to India and *Eudrilus eugeniae* is being cultured in South India for producing biofertiliser. The Indigenous compost worm species like *Perionyx excavatus, Perionyx sansibaricus* and *Dichogaster bolaui* could be used for vermicomposting. These species are surface dwellers and deeply pigmented and morphology of their alimentary canal (reduced or absence of typhlosole) indicated epigeic (surface dweller) way of their life. Certain litter dwelling species of *Perionyx, Amynthus* and *Megascolex, Lumbricus* may also be used in the degradation of organic wastes.

In maharashtra species like *Pontoscolex, Corethrasus, Perionyx excavates, Perionyx sansibaricus, Pheretima elongate, Eudrigaster, Eudrilus eugeniae, Eugenia foetida, Pheretima posthuma* are widely being used. Since, these worms have to not only effect quick conversion, but also reproduce faster. The best choice for vermicomposting are two epigeic species, - *Eudrilus eugeniae* and *Eisenia foetida*.

The following account describes some of the important species of earthworm and it is applicable more or less to other species also which are useful in vermiculture.

(a) *Eudrilus eugeniae* : It is one of the widely used exotic species in vermiculture. This cosmopolitan *Eudrilid* is originally from Africa and popularly called as the "African Night Crawler". This species is widely cultured and distributed by earthworm growers all over the world and has been found to be the best for vermicomposting and the production of protein meal. It has excellent growth and high conversion ratios. This species occur in orchard and natural farming with the temperature ranging from 19 - 22°C and soil depth 15 - 22 cm, with variable moisture content. This *Eudrilid* species have 8 - setae per segment. Male pore is single on segment 17/18. They possess meganephridial nephridia.

In routine culture methods, optimum temperature for this species was found to be 20°–28°C. Hatching at 25°C, about 3 weeks cocoons were deposited. It can grow to a maximum weight of 2.5 g in 8 - 10 weeks.

(b) *Elsenia foetida* : This is a fast growing earthworm, with annual cocoon production almost 35 times as compared to that of *E. eugeniae*. The conversion ratios for this species are high and make it suitable for use in vermicomposting. The morphological features and other factors are more or less resemble with *E. eugeniae*.

(c) *Perionyx sansibaricus* (Family-Megascolecidae): It is one of the best known indigenous species for vermicomposting mostly occur in social forestry in the depth ranging from 3-8 cm, temperature 20-28°C but varied pH and at moisture content ranging from 20-40%.

This species have single pointed setae. Male pores are situated on 17th or 18th segment and female pores on 14th segment. The other species - *Perionyx excavatus* resembles with the *P. sansibaricus*. Both have been found to be good converters of organic waste and are better suited for the southern parts of the country where the summer temperature does not rise as high as in central and North India. This species is purely used for the purpose of vermicomposting.

(d) *Pontoscolex corethrurus* : It is an endogeic (deep soil dweller) shallow burrowing worm, around 2 cm in length. This is a geo-phytophagous species and usually not used for vermicomposting.

(e) *Eudichogaster species* : It is one of Indian species of Michaelson. These found in monoculture vegetation and mixed farming at depth ranges from 10-30 cm and moisture content from 17-30%, temperature - 19 - 24°C.

It belongs to the family Octochaetidae. The pre-intestinal region is long with intestinal origin in or behind segment fifteen. Excretory system meronepheric.

(f) *Polypheretima elongata* (Kingberg) : It is one of the most widely distributed species of the Megascolecid group. These species are found in monoculture farming at 20 cm depth, 25% moisture content and at the temperature 21°C.

It is characterised by the arrangement of numerous setae in a ring in each segment.

Of many species of earthworms, tested for mass cultivation all over the world, *Eisenia fetida, Eudrilus eugeniae* and *Perionyx excavatus* come in the order of preference for their ability to degrade the wastes. Their high biomass production may attain an increase of 40-90 times in a period of 3-6 months with adequate space and food.

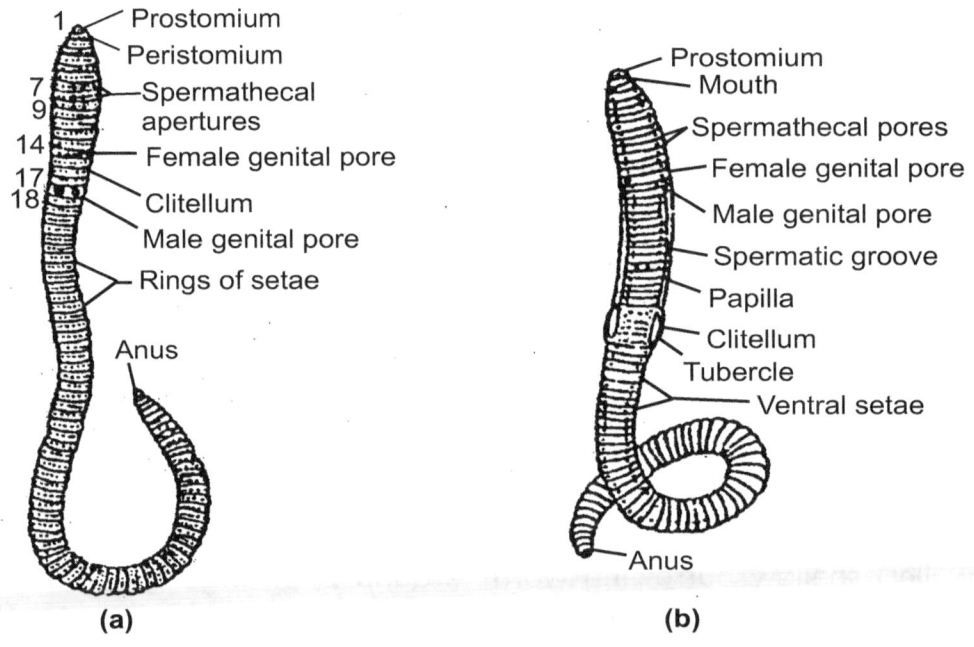

Fig. 4.42 : *(a) Megascolex, (b) Lumbricus*

Methods of Vermiculture :

Earthworms feed upon a variety of organic material and could be produced commerically for recycling biodegradable organic wastes, production of biofertilisers and animal protein for poultry and fish food. Vermiculture is feasible in suitable containers or specially designed boxes in small scale or shades in farm in large scale, since they are omnivorous, able to withstand environmental changes and resistant to many diseases. The technology is very simple and can easily be adapted in India, especially in rural areas. It is possible to culture worms both indoors and outdoors depending upon the local climatic conditions.

Following are some of the important guidelines for various culture methods.

(I) Culturing Techniques in Small Scale

(1) The culture boxes or containers should be made up of light weight materials like plastic, wood, tin etc. (for indoor). Which could easily be carried from one place to another.

(2) The culture boxes or containers should be non-porous to minimise loss of moisture from culture medium.

(3) The size of the boxes / containers may vary according to the need. Reynolds (1977) used a specially designed wooden box which is more convenient and useful. It measures 50 cm in length, 35 cm in width and 15-20 cm in depth. The bottom of the box is provided with a few holes of 50 mm in diameter.

(4) Plastic window screen is placed on the inside bottom with a burlop (or jute cloth) lining on top of the screened sides before the culture medium is added. This prevents the culture medium from sticking to the box and escape of worms through the holes but allows the excess of water to drain.

(5) Top of the box is covered with a burlop (or jute cloth) frame before inoculation of medium and earthworms.

The plastic tubs are more useful because these are more durable, lighter in weight and could easily be arranged one above the other in vertical rows on concrete shelves in limited space.

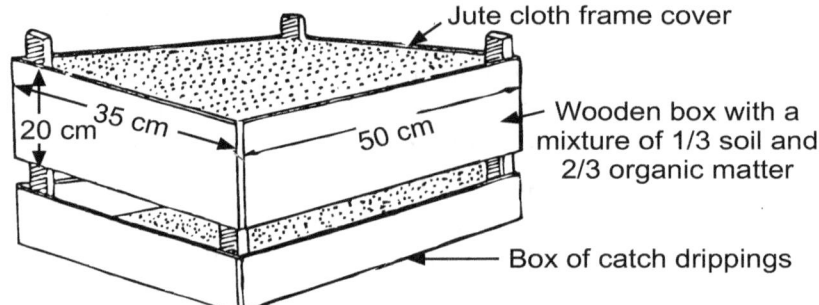

Fig. 4.43 : A design of vermiculture wooden box

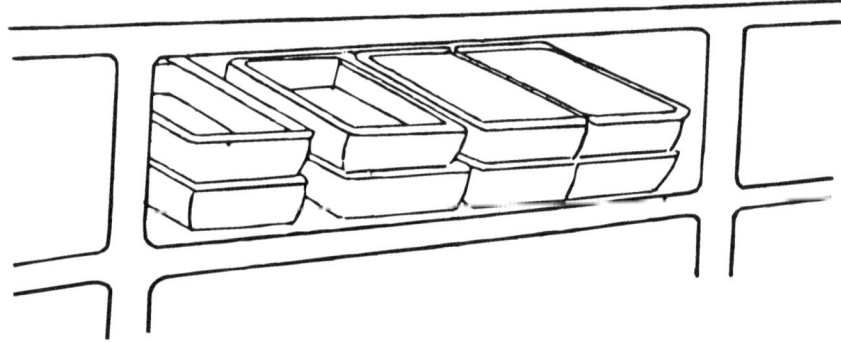

Fig. 4.44 : A diagrammatic representation of indoor vermiculture in vertical rows of plastic tubs

(6) A mixture of 1/3 soil and 2/3 organic matter is to be more useful in culture containers. Beds in plastic or wooden boxes are prepared by spreading a sand layer of 2-4 cm in height over which another layer of equal thickness of soil is added. Organic matter is placed on one side of the container.

(7) Water is added to the culture medium so as to hold 25-30% of moisture.

Indoor cultures are preferably kept in a cool building at a temperature between 10°C and 15°C for lumbricids (e.g. *Eisenia fetida*) and about 20°C for tropical species (e.g. *Eudrilus eugeniae* and *Perionyx excavates*).

(8) Sources of common organic materials are : decayed leaves, hay, straw, rice or wheat bran, vegetable wastes, cow dung, poultry droppings, biogas sludge etc.

The following precautions should be taken during vermiculture:

(1) The culture medium must have sufficient organic material to avoid its formation into a soggy mass.

(2) Moisture of the medium should be maintained at required levels by sprinkling water regularly. Overwatering affects the culture adversely.

(3) Presence of a low watt light will prevent the worms from crawling out of boxes.

(4) Outdoor cultures at places with low temperature in winters should be covered with suitable insulation materials like wheat straw, dry hay or weeds, manure, compost etc.

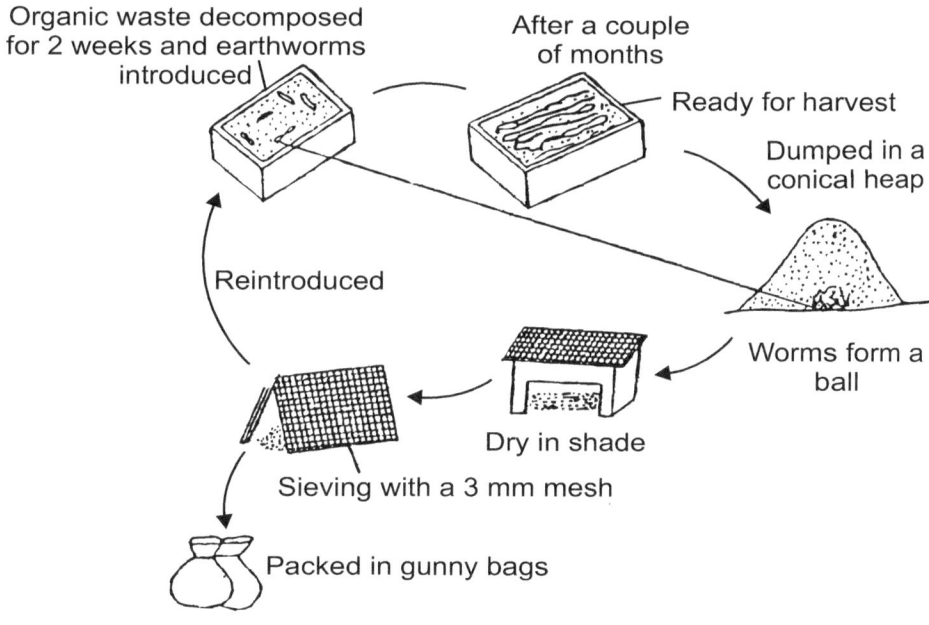

Fig. 4.45 : One vermicomposting production cycle

Large outdoor vermiculture beds may be established on waste lands. The culture bed is generally prepared with a bottom layer of 10 cm high gravel over which plastic window screen is placed with its edges raised up to 20 cm in height. A layer of 2-4 cm sand is laid over the window screen layer. A mixture of 1/3 soil and 2/3 organic matter is spread over the sand layer. The bed is slightly raised in the middle which allows drainage of excess of water on sides during the rains. The bottom layers of gravel and sand also help in maintaining the water content in the culture. The window screen prevents the escape of worms.

Bioconversion of Kitchen Waste in to Manure for Garden :

Kitchen waste is generated daily in large quantities. It is not a waste but a resource at the wrong place at the wrong time. Kitchen waste is mostly organic in nature and can be easily converted to compost by the action of various bacteria, fungi and earthworms, hence the term Bioconversion. Currently, municipal garbage is subjected to bioconversion on a large scale by "Excel Industries" at their treatment plant at Chincholi and Deonar. Green cross society has set up a "Vermiculture project" at Versova sewage pumping station for the treatment of vegetable waste collected from four Bungalows area. Agriculture college in Pune has popularized the bioconversion of garden leaf litter and farm waste into manure by composting in a pit. Excel Industries Ltd. has also developed a simple and economical technique to treat kitchen waste and garden leaf litter using mixed bacterial and fungal inoculum. By this process, within 21 days rich manure is ready for use in gardening.

(A) Vermiprocessing of Kitchen Waste (small scale)
At House Varanda / Garden

(i) **Preparation of Vermiculture Bed :** Take a plastic bucket (18-20 litres capacity) and make a drainage hole at the bottom.
- Put 3 inches of soil layer.
- Put 1 inch of the vermiculture layer.
- Again put 1 inch of soil.
- Sprinkle a layer of cowdung and cover it with grass cuttings or leaves of 3 inches thickness.
- Moisten the entire systems gently by sprinkling water, which has been stored in a tub for three days (storage removes chlorine from water).
- As grass and leaves dissolve, add more of the same and continue to maintain 3 inches of this mulch layer.

- Do not allow the system to become soggy due to excess water.
- The system will take 6 to 8 weeks for the earthworms to hatch and stabilise.

(ii) Treatment of Kitchen Waste using Vermiculture Bed :
- Spread the kitchen waste on the vermiculture bed.
- First, put waste vegetable greens on the vermiculture bed.
- Rock dust or black sand should be sprinkled every day with the food waste.
- Lime should be sprinkled with fruit peels and non-vegetable waste.
- Bad smell indicates overloading. Insect flies indicate acidity. Allow the vermiculture bed to be airy. If the vermiculture bed is functioning properly, it will not smell.
- Stir the top occassionally. The entire contents can be used as manure within 3 months of treatment.
- Set up a second vermiculture bed using a small portion of the above manure as vermiculture.

(B) Excel Technology for recyling Kitchen waste or Municipal Garbage (in large scale) :
- Ensure that the garbage collected from the colony is dumped at a common place and make a 4 × 4 × 4 feet heap; in a shady place.
- Before the scorching heat starts, sprinkle water in 1 : 10 ratio on it. (i.e. 10-buckets of garbage : 1 bucket water). If the garbage is already wet the ratio of water should be reduced.
- Spray microbial slurry in the evening everyday. (500 g Celrich in 10 litres water; Celrich is available at Excel Industries).
- On the next day morning more garbage can be added on top of the heap.
- From the 4th day onwards the temperature starts rising and goes upto 70°C, this gets rid of the harmful pathogens.
- The process of adding fresh garbage and sprinkling microbial slurry should be carried on for 1 week.

- On the 8th day, turn the garbage upside down using a shovel.
- Continue to add fresh garbage and slurry for another week to the same dump.
- After 14 days no more fresh garbage should be added to the heap.
- For the next coming week, water and slurry treatment should be done on alternate days.
- By the 22nd day, the garbage will have turned into rich manure.
- The manure so obtained can be used either in proportion with soil or directly in gardens for flowering plants, trees, lawns etc.

(II) Culturing technique at farm and production of vernicompost :

Vermicomposting is the process of converting organic waste into vermicompost through the action of epigeic (surface dweller) earthworm species. Before the worms can ingest the waste, partial decomposition is essential. The mesophilic and thermophilic stages generate the heat in the compost pile; which destroy the earthworms. Once these stages are passed, the pile cools down and worms can be introduced.

Vermicompost is the cast or excreta of epigeic earthworm species which may be cultured on animal dung and other organic wastes.

Technique :

(1) Containers : Any kind of container described earlier, will serve the purpose or container can be constructed in brick masonry and cement. Stone slabs can be used for the sides and bottom and all the joints are cemented. The constructed container should have a 1 cu.m volume. The dimensions are 1.6 m long, 1 m wide and 0.75 m high and contain around 6 to 7 thousand wornas. The height of the waste pile should not be more than 0.6 m.

(2) Shelter : All the operations should be done under shade to prevent direct sunlight and rain.

(3) Feed mixture : Any organic waste like sugarcane thrash, coir pith, leaf litter, kitchen waste etc., can be mixed with dung in the ratio of around 1 : 8 and put in the container. If dung is not available, a little vermicompost from the previous harvest or even a little soil can be added to the waste. The waste must be allowed to decompose for 2 to 3 weeks. After the material cools, the worms can be introduced.

Production of Vermicompost : The worms feeding actively assimilate only 5 to 10 per cent for their growth and the rest is excreted as loose granular rice shaped pellets. The castings are left on the surface.

Collection : The castings can be collected, once conversion is over, by observing pellets, the material can be dumped on the ground. Small conical heaps can be made and left for a few hours. The worms converge and form a ball at the base. The worms then taken out and introduced to the next feed lot. The casts are to be dried in the shade and then sieved through a 3 mm sieve to separate the cocoons and young ones which can be introduced to fresh culture beds.

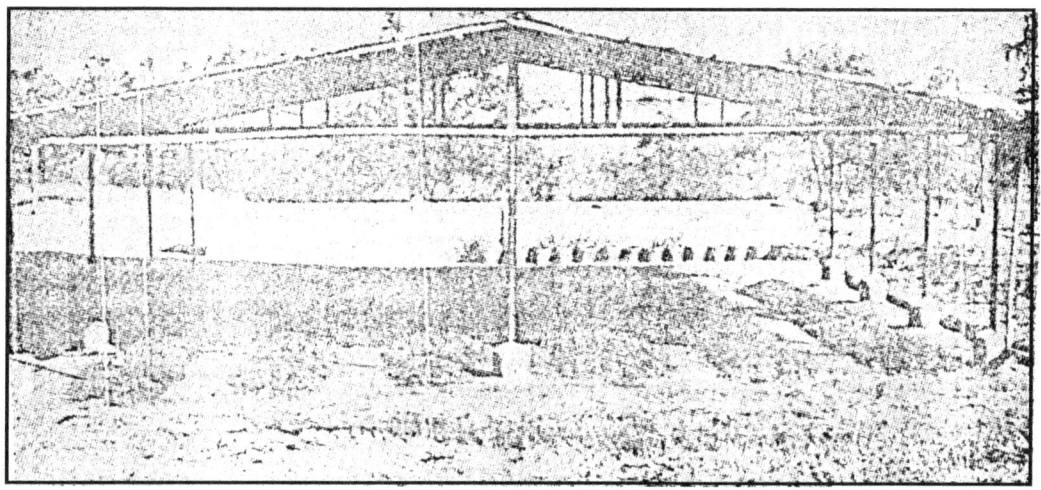

Fig. 4.47 (a)

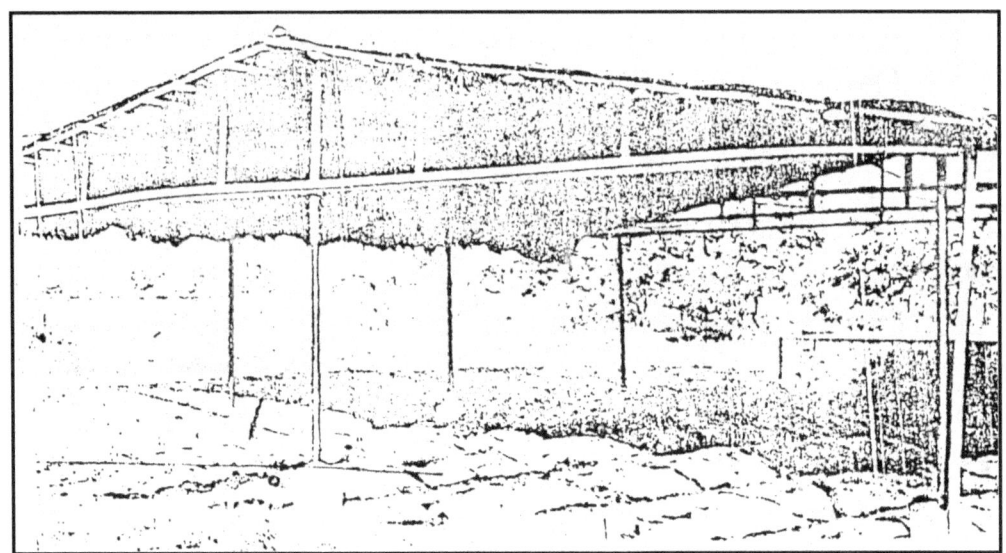

Fig. 4.47 (b)

Precautionary Measures :
 (1) Water logging should be avoid, which leads to anaerobiosis and increase acidity. The acidity is fatal to earthworms.
 (2) Temperature should be maintained in the range of 20-30°C.
 (3) Earthworms should be handled carefully and damaged worms removed immediately to prevent the spread of infection in other worms.
 (4) Predators like Ants should be kept away by providing a ditch of standing water around the unit. Rats and larger animals like cats and dogs have to be kept away by providing a metal mesh over the structure.
 (5) The minimum space required for a population of 2000 worms is around 1 sq.m with a 30 cm high bed.

Factors Influencing the Culturing of Earthworms :

Several factors control the culturing and maintenance of healthy earthworm populations, of which the following are most important:

(1) Food : The food and its quality control the establishment and continuity of earthworm populations. Higher nitrogen ratios helps in faster growth and greater production of cocoons. For feeding on fresh waste, decomposition by microbial activity is essential.

Predigested material like dung is favourite food for many litter species. The carbon Nitrogen ratio should be moderate.

(2) Moisture : Moisture should be maintained at around 50% so that the microbial activity is high and the food matter is easy to feed upon. Excess water leads to anaerobic conditions which creates acidic conditions This condition reduce productivity and cause migration.

(3) Temperature : This factor affects metabolism, growth and reproduction. So it should be maintained within 20–30°C. If soil is exposed to the sun, lose moistures quickly and are usually devoid of earthworms. Earthworms maintain lower body temperatures than the surrounding by their metabolic adjustments.

(4) Light : Earthworms are very sensitive to light. The photoreceptor cells detect light and the earthworms moves away to avoid strong light. The endogeic species emerge at the surface only at night.

(5) Hydrogen ion concentration (pH) : Earthworms are sensitive to changes in pH. They prefer conditions of neutral reaction. They cannot survive if the pH falls below 6 and either migrate or are killed.

(6) Predators : Earthworms are preyed upon by many species of ants, birds, toads, salamanders, snakes, moles, rats, cats, dogs etc. Moles catch earthworms, bite off 3 to 5 anterior segments to prevent locomotion and keep them in their burrows. A variety of invertebrates also feed on earthworms. These include flatworms, centipedes, staphylinid beetles etc.

Economic Importance :

To a common man earthworms are rather insignificant animals which generally come out on the soil surface during rains and serve as bait for angling but for farmers and agriculturist they are of utmost importance as they bring in the decomposition of organic matter in the soil.

The following are some of the most important factors in view of economic importance of vermiculture.

(1) Soil becomes loose and got a greater capacity to retain air and moisture due to high densities of earthworms. Soils with

earthworms drain water 4-10 times faster than soils without earthworms. Both these factors are important for growing crops.

(2) Burrowing habit of earthworms, leads tunneling in soil which aerate the soil and helps in increasing the air holding capacity of soil.

(3) Earthworms deposite their castings on the surface at night. In due course, they bring the sub-soil to the top and expose it to bacterial action. Bacteria helps in decomposition of cellulose.

(4) Earthworms also take the rich humus from soil surface to plant-roots and help in maintaining soil pH.

(5) Soil nitrogen is generally bound to organic complexes so it is not readily available to plants. This bound nitrogen is converted into available forms like ammonia, nitrates and nitrites as it passes through the digestive tract of earthworm thus earthworm castings are rich in nitrates, calcium, magnesium, phosphorus and potassium. This casting when added to the soil increases soil fertility and promotes plant growth thereby increasing crop production.

(6) Earthworm contains 50-70% of protein in dry weight basis and all essential amino acids. It is one of the important food materials for most of the animals.

(7) Earthworm tissues content high amount of proteins which after proper processing could benefit as food to the live stock and aquaculture. Earthworms have been used as human food by Maoris in New Zealand and the natives of New Guineas as they are richer in arginine tryptophan and tyrosine.

(8) In Indian Unani system of Medicine, the external application of preparations made from the dried worms is used in treating wounds, piles, chronic boils, sorethroat, etc. and when taken internally for curing respiratory aliments, jaundice; rheumatic pains etc.

(9) Earthworms also play key role in environmental management. The sewage and city organic waste can be converted into vermicompost which is act as a good biofertiliser for plants.

(10) One of the significant advantages of vermicompost is the quick nutrient absorption by plants unlike other organic manures. This is because of the digestion of the organic matter by earthworms.

Chemical composition of worm casts

Organic carbon (%)	9.15 to 17.88
Total nitrogen (%)	0.50 to 0.90
Available phosphorus (%)	0.10 to 0.26
Available potassium (%)	0.15 to 0.56
Available sodium (%)	0.05 to 0.30
Calcium and magnesium (MEQ / 100 g)	22.67 to 47.60
Copper (ppm)	2.00 to 9.50
Iron (ppm)	5.70 to 9.30
Zinc (ppm)	5.70 to 11.50
Available sulphur (ppm)	128.00 to 548.00

Significance of Gut in the formation of Vermicompost : The morphological features of earthworm favour burrowing habit and the gut functions as a *bioreactor* where organic matter is grounded to fine particles and then transformed into castings

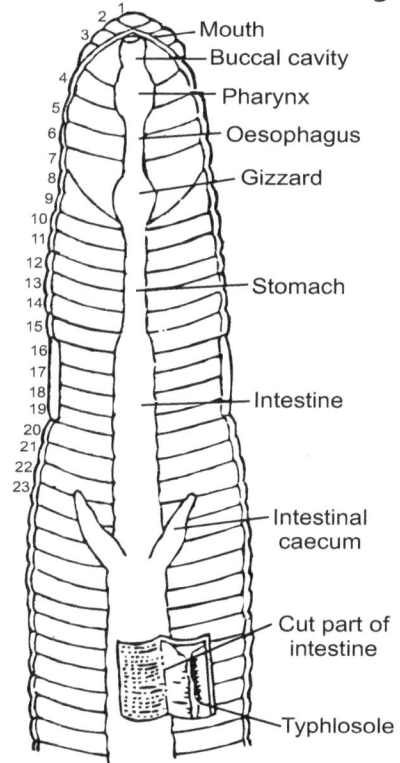

Fig. 4.48 : Gut of the Earthworm

Evan and Guild in 1947, distinguished two ecological categories of Earthworms as litter feeder and soil feeders. Litter feeder group possesses active gizzard and soil feeder group has a well developed active typhlosole. The gut content (enzymes and microflora) could be utilised as tools for determining functional establishment of worms. Earthworm gut is a straight tube extending from mouth to anus and is differentiated into functional regions. The gut content consists mucous, organic, mineral matter and organismal components and variety of enzymes.

When food is ingested it is subjected to acid mucous containing amylase and then the gizzard helps in fragmenting the food. Comparison of particle sizes in casts and in surrounding soil have led. Some research workers to conclude that earthworm can break particles into small sizes by griding in the gizzard.

In some species calciferous glands discharge amorphous calcium carbonate particles which influences the pH of intestinal fluid. But the digestive ability of earthworm is due to the presence of digestive enzymes like amylase, cellulase, protease, lipase, ehitinase and lichenase. Enzymes operate in a medium of pH ranging between 6.3 and 7.3 which encourages the growth of bacterial colonies. The decomposition of organic matter also depends on the physico-chemical conditions of the sub-soil as well as the nature of the organic matter.

Certain species of actinomycetes of gut content, involve in the chemical transformation of organic materials, formation of clay/humus complexes and production of cementing substances which improve the crumb structure of soil hence earthworms are widely used in the production of vermicompost.

Vermicompost as Biofertilizer :

Vermiculture, the technology of producing rich bio-fertilisers and animal protein by using earthworms, has well established itself commercially in many developed countries. It has been estimated that one million worms can convert about 120 tonnes of organic wastes into Bio-fertilisers in about one month's time. According to conservative estimates over 2,000 million tonnes of solid and liquid excreta of animals and human beings and another 200 million tonnes from crop straws are available as wastes annually in the country. Besides this there are vast quantities of domestic garbage and industrial wastes. Thus, production of biofertiliser through vermicomposting/ vermiculture has a bright future in India. Vermicomposting is the process of converting organic waste into vermicompost through the action of epigeic earthworm species. The earthworms consume the soil matter and convert it into humus within a short period of time and thereby increase the soil fertility within 24 hours. They can pass soil almost equivalent to their own weight through the 'alimentary canal excrete the soil as ' cast '. They have therefore rightly been called the nature's ploughman. Thus, the soil is being constantly and continuously turned over and over again by the worms i.e. organic matter is cycled and recycled, so that the humus formation is natural and a continuous process and enrichment of soil helps in agriculture and forestry. By planning and managing agricultural operations, supplemented with input from the earthworms, the farmers can get significant increase in crop yields. Countries like U.S.A., U.K. and Japan have realized this potential of earthworms and are therefore taking vermiculture quite seriously as an aid to farming.

As part of biotechnology, vermiculture has attracted attention, since it is an entirely natural process which maintains the environmental balance and leaves no adverse effects.

According to Bhole, the soil with worm casts, in comparison to soil without the worms, has 5 times more nitrogen, 7 times more phosphorus, 11 times more potassium, 2 times more magnesium and calcium each; along with other trace elements and soil nutrients are soluble in water and readily available to the root systems.

Increase in the organic wastes mainly due to growth of human population, agricultural and Industry is a global problem and a serious constrain in the maintenance of a clean and healthy environment; but due to benefit of vermiculture, the earthworms should be considered nature's most useful converters of these waste products. Experiments with worms have shown that the recycling the utilisable organic wastes arising out of household garbage, city refuge, sweage sludge and paper, food and wood industries.

Vermitechnology has the following applications :

(1) Use of epigeic earthworms in the production of vermicompost. This technology can be used for urbon and rural waste recycling for conversion of organic wastes to manure.

(2) Vermicompost as a manure in agriculture or as inoculum for improving and maintaining soil fertility.

(3) Earthworm protein as animal feed for livestock. (Protein meal can be prepared from many earthworm species and used as livestock. This meal content 60%, protein. 7-10% fat, 8 to 10% ash and 0.55% calcium, 1% phosphorus).

(4) Earthworm species for the treatment of industrial wastes.

(5) Earthworms play a significant role in the biotic components of soil processes, which include turning and mixing of soils.

(6) Earthworm (*isenia foetida, Eudrilus eugeniae*) species are used for treatment of different types of industrial effluents.

Points to Remember

- The rearing of silkworm for the production of raw silk is called sericulture.
- Sericulutre is regular industry in India.
- Asam, Bengal, Chennai, Mysore and Jammu and Kashmir are the well known silk producing centres.
- *Bombayx mori* the well known silk moth.
- There are six species produce silk.
- Eri, Tassar, muga are different moths produce silk.
- Life cycle of *Bombyx mori* include eggs, larva cocoon and adult stages.
- Mulberry has different species used as food for silkworm larvae.

- Leaves of mulbery plants are harvested 56 times in a year.
- There are many stages involved in silkworm rearing, like selection of silkworm variety, rearing house and disinfection of rearing room and equipments.
- Different rearing techniques are used for rearing.
- Silkworms are attacted by protozoan, fungal bacterial and viral diseases.
- Dermestid beetles, uzi flies, ants, lizards, birds, rats and squirrels are the pest of silkworm.
- Post harvesting of cocoons involves stifling, sorting of cocoons, storage of cocoons, deflossing cocoon riddling and cocoon cooking or boiling.
- Reeling equipments include charkhas, cottage basin, filature basin and automatic reeling.
- Two types of cocoons are produced in our country namely multivoltine and bivoltine.
- There are different steps in reeling techniques.
- Sericulture is labour intensive agroindustry.
- China is topper in raw silk production.
- India produces all four major varieties of silk namely mulbery, tassar, eri and muga.
- Andhra Pradesh is first position in productivity and second in silk production.
- There are different appliances used in rearing of silkworms, namely rearing stands, ant wells, rearing trays, paraffin paper, foam rubber strips, chopsticks, feathers, leaf chamber, chopping board, chopping knives, mats, cleaning nets and mountages.
- In applied zoology useful and harmful animals are studied and the knowledge is applied to improve health and welfare of mankind.
- Sericulture, poultry science, dairy science fishery science, pearl culture, lac culture, goat and pig farming are some important branches of applied zoology.
- Pig farming and goat farming are important business.
- Vermiculture deals with culture and application of earthworms for various purposes.

- Different species of earthworms are used for vermitechnology.
- There are different techniques used fro earthworm culture.
- Kitchen waste can be converted into manure by earthworms.
- Vermicompost is the best biofertilizer.

Exercise

1. Describe the external morphology and life cycle of *Bombyx mori*.
2. Write short note on male and female pupae.
3. Give an account of cultivation of mulberry. Add a note on harvesting.
4. What is pruning ? Discuss its objectives.
5. Write a short note on climate in moriculture.
6. What is planting ? Describe the methods and factors responsible for planting of mulberry.
7. What is harvesting ? Describe different methods for harvesting of mulberry leaves.
8. Write short note on preservation of leaves.
9. Give an account of rearing technique for silkworm (B. mori).
10. Describe the rearing house.
11. Explain disinfection of rearing room and equipments.
12. Describe protozoan, fungal, viral and bacterial diseases of silkworm.
13. Write short notes on :
    (a) Rearing house
    (b) Pebrine
    (c) Flacherie virus
    (d) Uzi fly
    (e) Shelf rearing
    (f) Shoot rearing
    (g) Floor rearing.
14. Explain the process of silk preparation from cocoons.
15. Explain reeling equipments.
16. Describe the reeling of multivoltine cocoons.
17. Describe improved charka.
18. Explain reeling techniques for bivoltine cocoons.

19. Write short notes on :
    (a) Raw silk yarn,
    (b) Drying of cocoons.
20. Explain sericulture as labour intensive agro-industry.
21. Write the factors that affected the productivity of silk in India.
22. Write short notes on :
    (a) World silk scenario
    (b) Indian silk
    (c) Sericulture as a means of income levelling
    (d) Sericulture in Andhra Pradesh.
23. Describe the economics of silkworm rearing.
24. Give an account of rearing appliances commonly used in sericulture.
25. Write short notes on :
    (a) Rearing appliances
    (b) Miscellaneous appliances.
26. What is applied zoology? Describe in brief different branches of applied zoology.
27. Define vermitechnology. Describe how earthworms are useful for manufacture of manure.
28. Write short notes on :
    i) Sericultre
    ii) Apiculture
    iii) pearl culture
    iv) Poultry
    v) Fishery science
    vi) Lac and culture
    vii) Goat farming
    viii) Piggary
    ix) Diary science
    x) Vermiculture

www.ingramcontent.com/pod-product-compliance
Lightning Source LLC
Chambersburg PA
CBHW080424230426
43662CB00015B/2210